*America in
Theological
Perspective*

edited by THOMAS M. McFADDEN

AMERICA IN THEOLOGICAL PERSPECTIVE

The Annual Publication
of the College Theology Society

A Crossroad Book
THE SEABURY PRESS • NEW YORK

The Seabury Press
815 Second Avenue
New York, N.Y. 10017

Printed in the United States of America

LIBRARY OF CONGRESS CATALOGING IN PUBLICATION DATA

College Theology Society.
America in theological perspective.
"A Crossroad book."
"All essays . . . were, with two exceptions, delivered at the 1975
convention of the College Theology Society at Boston College."
    1. United States—Religion—Congresses.
I. McFadden, Thomas M. II. Title.
BR515.C64 1976   200'.973   75–45201
ISBN 0–8164–0294–9

Contents

INTRODUCTION *Thomas M. McFadden*   vii

I. *THE AMERICAN CATHOLIC EXPERIENCE*   1

Square Peg in a Round Hole: 3
On Being Roman Catholic in America
James Hennesey, S.J.

Catholic Ethics with an American Accent   13
Daniel C. Maguire

Democracy as a Theological Problem   37
in Isaac Hecker's Apologetics
Joseph F. Gower

Catholic Identity in America   56
Elizabeth K. McKeown

II. *RELIGION AND AMERICAN CULTURE*   69

The Radical Reformation and the American Experience   71
Franklin H. Littell

Church/State Relations   87
in the American Revolutionary Era
Thomas O'Brien Hanley, S.J.

Civil Religion, Theology, and Politics in America   99
Marie Augusta Neal, S.N.D.

A Catholic Perspective on American Civil Religion   123
Mary L. Schneider

H. Richard Niebuhr   140
and Reshaping American Christianity
John J. Mawhinney, S.J.

American Culture and Modernism: Shailer Mathew's   163
Interpretation of American Christianity
Francis S. Fiorenza

III. *PROSPECTS FOR THE FUTURE*   187

American Technocracy and the Religious Spirit: 189
An Unholy Alliance?
   David M. Thomas

America: The Myth of the Hunter   206
   Leonard J. Biallas

Search for a Center   230
   Russell L. Jaberg

LIST OF CONTRIBUTORS   247

Introduction

The United States Bicentennial is providing the opportunity for a great deal of national introspection—some critical, a great deal narcissistic—from a variety of viewpoints. This volume operates from within a theological perspective in trying to understand the dynamisms that have gone into the formation of the complex reality that is the American nation. Several articles specify the discussion even further, considering the American Roman Catholic experience in particular.

The argument implied in all the articles is the crucial interrelationship that obtains between a nation's self-image and values, and its religious perceptions. Religion does not come "full-blown from the mind of Zeus." It is temporal and spacial, linked to a culture with whose world-view it stands in creative tension. There is no such thing as an a-cultural religion, independent from its surrounding milieu. Nor is there—or, at least, nor should there be—a culture independent from the articulation of the people's deepest sense of social justice, human solidarity, and cosmic coherence proceeding from the transcendent reference that is the ground of all justice and solidarity. Thus America has formed the Christianity that has been celebrated within its shores; the study of American Christianity will show us a different religion perspective from its European counterpart. And, as everyone agrees, no understanding of American history is possible without a clear awareness of the religious forces that have continually molded American expectations and social structures. This relationship has not always been for the good. America has had its share of religious as well as political chauvinism. But the relationship has been there; the historical past with all its implications for creating a future correlation between religion and culture is available to us.

The dominant religious influence in America has undoubtedly been Protestantism. Since this has been the case, Roman Catholicism has felt itself to be the proverbial "square peg in a round hole," as James Hennesey describes the situation in the opening essay. The first part of this book considers that "square peg" more extensively, and points out that the search for a Catholic identity in America has been based upon a number of concordances between American ideals and the Catholic perception of human existence.

Part II considers, within a wider parameter, the relation between religion and American culture. The essays by Franklin H. Littell and Thomas O'Brien Hanley deal with religion and early American history. The rest of the essays in this section deal, in one way or another, with American civil religion, and the danger of enshrining the nation, its history and its ideals, as the object of religious worship. These essays are critical in their insistence upon Christianity's need to stand apart from and, at times, in judgment upon civil religion.

History is a chronicle of change, and it seems proper that any examination of American cultural history address itself to the future as well as the past. Part III, therefore, speaks of the possible prospects for the future relationship between American culture and religion. The need to discover a new religious myth according to which we can understand ourselves, a new planetary center to take the place of an outworn humanism, a new discovery of the religious spirit that will oppose taking man's measure by technological measures alone—this is the hope for the leavening presence of religion upon the American scene.

All essays included here were, with two exceptions, delivered at the 1975 convention of the College Theology Society at Boston College. Clearly, therefore, the book is a reflection of the competence and professional capacities of the members of the College Theology Society, its members and invited speakers. Its appearance reflects the leadership of the Society's national officers: Rev. Matthew C. Kohmescher, S.M., of the University of Dayton, President; Sr. Maura Campbell, O.P., of Caldwell College, Vice-President; Rev. Richard L. Schebera, S.M.M., of St. Louis University, Secretary; and Dr. Thomas Ryan of St. Joseph's College (Philadelphia), Treasurer.

The editor would also like to acknowledge with gratitude his parents, in whom Christian faith and the highest ideals of the American Dream have been so humanly united.

Thomas M. McFadden
St. Joseph's College, Philadelphia

I.

The American Catholic Experience

JAMES HENNESEY, S. J.

square peg in a round hole: on being roman catholic in america

American Catholic history has not been a traditional best-seller in the classroom. Its practitioners have been relatively few and scattered variously in history and religious studies departments, but in a distinctly auxiliary role in both. There were Thomas T. McAvoy of Notre Dame and those whom he trained, and John Tracy Ellis of The Catholic University and those whom he trained. McAvoy focused on the theme of the Catholic community as American minority; Ellis and his students write largely about bishops, councils, and the history of institutions. There were others: studies came from Columbia and Harvard and Illinois and Yale and so on. Herbert Eugene Bolton and his students, as well as Franciscan historians, have worked on the Southwest. Ludwig Hertling even introduced the subject to the Gregorian University in Rome and some interesting theses were produced. Hertling's retirement furnished me the occasion for the absolute high point of a varied career—the opportunity to teach American Catholic history in Latin at the Gregorian University. It also provided me with some of the more interestingly motivated students I have had. One was a travel agent who somehow had convinced himself that a course in American Catholicism would win him a larger share of the transatlantic tourist market. Others hoped that it would further their chances for an American visa. But when all those little consolations are counted up, the fact remains that there has not exactly been a seller's market in the field.

Things are changing. Nearly one hundred serious students traveled to Notre Dame in October 1974 for a conference on American Catholic history, and they represented a startling cross-section of the American academic world. An *American Catholic Studies Newsletter* is in the works.[1] Boston College has hosted, and John Carroll University will host, conferences in the field. An ongoing Notre Dame seminar has proved hugely attractive to students and professors from a wide radius. Examples can be multiplied. Historians of American Catholicism have a new lease on life. What is it all about?

Perhaps some of my own experiences suggest an answer. Each year I offer the divinity students at Jesuit School of Theology in Chicago a tutorial in American Catholic history. There are three initial set readings, and then each student moves on to an individualized program. The set readings are Martin Marty's *Righteous Empire*, John Tracy Ellis's *American Catholicism*, and an earlier version of this essay.[2] We move from there to immigration history, Black and Latino Catholicism, American Indians and the church, various ethnic histories, social history. Only rarely do we consider classical institutional history, and themes like turn-of-the-century Americanism generally enter only indirectly. Student reactions are most instructive. I have two initial questions: Do you find in Marty and in Ellis anything of your own autobiography? And, what is the concept of "church" that comes through in the readings? Some resist identification with the *Righteous Empire*, some admit that its implications have been more part of their *Weltanschauung* than they had thought. Others are attracted by the triumphant Americanization of Catholic tradition, while there are those who resist identification with it. Most become sharply aware of the inadequacy of the melting-pot myth to explain who we are, and they are genuinely fascinated by the whole problem of our collective autobiography.

THE UNDENIABLE DIFFERENCES

Who then is this American Roman Catholic community? There are various ways of putting it. I picked the metaphor—like all metaphors, inadequate—of the square peg in a round hole. There is, and always has been, something different about the community which has shared the history of the Church of Rome and of the United States of America. The component parts of that difference have been variously explained. Writing his *Religion in America* in the 1840s, Robert Baird listed Roman Catholics among "non-Evangelical denominations . . . who either renounce, or fail faithfully to exhibit the fundamental and saving truths of the Gospel." He went on to note that "of all forms of error in the United States, Romanism is by far the most formidable, because of the number of its adherents, the organization, wealth, influence and worldly and unscrupulous policy of its hierarchy." He had specific problems, too. He was bothered by efforts to obtain public funds for Catholic schools "in which neither the sacred scriptures, nor any portions of them, are read, but avowedly sectarian instruction is given." He was also disturbed by concentration of church property under the control of the bishops, and by the growing alliance between bishops and "some of the leaders of the great political parties." [3]

Baird was scarcely the first or the last to enunciate these thoughts. But there are other elements which deserve consideration. Ten years before Baird, Alexis de Tocqueville noted them. A man of restoration Europe, he was well aware of the tendency of Catholic clergy to align themselves with reactionary governments. But he did not find such a tendency among priests in America and, with it absent, something else happened. American Catholics of the 1830s had come to "constitute the most republican and the most democratic class in the United States." Tocqueville argued that Protestantism tended to make men more independent, but that Catholicism made them more equal:

> The Catholic faith places all human capacities upon the same level; it subjects the wise and the ignorant, the man of genius and the vulgar crowd, to the details of the same creed; it imposes the same observances on the rich and the needy; it inflicts the same austerities upon the strong and the weak; it listens to no compromise with mortal man, but, by reducing all the human race to the same standard, it

confounds all the distinctions of society at the foot of the
same altar, even as they are confounded in the sight of God.[4]

What Baird saw as threat, Tocqueville saw as advantage. The hole
remained round, and the peg square.

An attempt at analyzing the awkwardness of Roman Catholicism in America would have to go far beyond what we can
attempt here. Baird has suggested some of the underlying religious
problems. Anglo-Americans had inherited the traditions of Foxe's
Book of Martyrs, an abhorrence for the Inquisition and the
mysterious powers of priests in the Roman Church. These
inherited antipathies had been fine-honed in colonial times as
Catholic France and Spain and their Indian allies fought for the
new continent with good Protestant Englishmen. Among later
immigrants from Europe, other inherited antagonisms flourished,
imported from myriad European settings. There have been several
classical periods of violently anti-Catholic persecution: the nativism of the 1830s and '40s is perhaps best known, with memories of
the burning of the Ursuline Convent in Charlestown, of Catholic
and Protestant militia companies fighting it out in the streets of
Philadelphia, and of Bishop Hughes in New York issuing muskets
for defense. Anti-immigrant prejudice, pure and simple, played its
part here, but it would be to avoid reality to ignore the
anti-Catholic bias of nativists or, later, the American Protective
Association, or indeed the somewhat subtler forms of that bias
which one still encounters today. It has helped considerably to
keep the hole rounded and the peg squared.

There is a whole other perspective from which we could
analyze the phenomenon of American Catholicism. The church in
the United States was long an object of both scorn and distant, if
somewhat uncomprehending, admiration on the part of European
Catholics.

There was Canon Jules Morel. In 1857 he produced a
triumphant syllogism which led from the Immaculate Conception
definition, with its emphasis on original sin, to the conclusion that
men "always have need of a preventive and repressive system.
. . . self-government is nothing but a Utopia. . . . the United
States whose success has for a moment disturbed the faith of the

weak, will not delay long in proving this by its history, young as it is." [5] And then there was the influential Belgian Benedictine, Dom Laurent Janssens, who summed it all up so well: "Americanism is the Protestant principle of personal inspiration placed at the service of complete liberalism and of Anglo-Saxon hopes, jealous of the Latin and Roman influence." [6]

On the other hand, nineteenth-century European liberal Catholics generally looked with hope and envy to America, even if they did not quite understand what was happening over here. That was true of Count de Montalembert and his contemporaries. It was true of others at the time of the turn-of-the-century Americanism crisis, and their interest considerably confused the issues.

There are any number of ways in which we can analyze the American Catholic community and its schizophrenia, awkwardness, square-peggishness. I tried once to do so at a meeting of the Catholic Theological Society of America by applying categories developed by Sidney Mead in *The Lively Experiment*. Mead was talking about American Protestantism, but it is amazing how many of the characteristics which he catalogs under such headings as Denominationalism, Voluntarism, and so on, can be predicated of American Catholicism. No religious community lives here for nearly half a millennium without taking on considerable local coloration, whatever its roots and continuing ties with another continent.[7]

THE CONTRIBUTIONS OF SOCIAL HISTORY

There are other historical approaches that shed light on the phenomenon. Most of the historiography of American Catholicism has been heavily institutional, largely defensive, and frequently triumphalist. Henry Warner Bowden summed up a school that extends far beyond John Gilmary Shea when he wrote that Shea's version of church history was concerned with "the duly constituted hierarchy and activities officially sanctioned by them." [8] That is not where we are today.

The contemporary thrust of historians is to people-history. We are less interested in structures, leaders, drum-and-trumpet, than we are in trying to find out who the ordinary people were who lived through a given period, how they managed, how they saw themselves, how their needs shaped structure and thought. At question is the object of the historian's effort. For the church historian, that comes very quickly to his definition of "church." For example, if a significant factor in your definition of "church" is the legal dictum set down by a papal diplomat, "The Holy See is the juridical personification of the church," [9] or if you were to accept Domenico Palmieri's exegesis of 1 Peter 2:9, that the church is a royal priesthood because it is "a kingdom ruled by priests," [10] that would affect your historical judgments. But if your dominant metaphor is that the church is "the people of God," that has something to say also to your emphases and understanding, to the kind of history you do, to what you think the role of historical study is.

There are various routes down which the people-historian of the church travels. Ethnic history is immensely in vogue right now. We've known for some time about early Irish-French fights in the Catholic community here, and later Irish-German ones. Now we are being made more conscious of how Poles were treated and how a quarter-million Carpatho-Ruthenians were effectively dismissed into schism by the assembled American archbishops in 1893 with the remark that "the loss of a few Greek souls" must be preferred to disturbing the disciplinary uniformity of American Catholicism.[11] Staten Island's center for migration studies, the *Journal of Social History*, and other sources are telling us the story of Italian immigrants and what "church" meant to them. The *American Catholic Studies Newsletter* reports dissertations in progress on subjects like study of Irish and German family life in Albany, 1850–1915. In Chicago, Thomas Joyce is doing an oral history project on pastoral care of Black Catholics, 1938–70. Jay Dolan of Notre Dame will soon publish a fascinating study of Irish and German parishes in New York City before the Civil War. Ethnic history is "in," and it is immensely helpful in discovering the religious community's identity. Much has been, or is being, done. But more must be done. Particularly urgent areas are the history of Black Catholicism, Latino Catholicism, and Catholicism among the native Americans.

The ethnic route needs exploration and in doing it there will be challenge to the melting-pot myth, and challenge also to attitudes that have grown in function of that myth. Urban history is another growing field closely intertwined with the history of Roman Catholics in America. Without denying the strength that has come from rural communities of Catholics throughout the nation, it is a fact that one of the unique historical realities about American Catholicism is that in a century—the nineteenth—when urban masses and the workingman were deserting organized religion in both Europe and America, a church was largely built in the United States precisely on that same base. That has had an enormous influence on the way we have grown. We need to study urban history, and at the same time keep in mind that the church which grew so much in cities has now shifted much of its base to suburbs, where needs are different and where structures geared to city neighborhoods do not really suffice. We need to realize that in many ways contemporary American Catholicism must face the problems faced by mainline Protestant churches a century ago when their congregations abandoned the inner city to Irish and German and Jewish and Slavic and Italian immigrants. There are challenges to be met by the Catholic Church in the United States as it confronts both its suburban expansion and an urban permanence, peopled by remnants of the old (and by millions of the new) immigration of our own time.

THE RESPONSE TO ENVIRONMENTS

I once taught a course on the changing structure, thought, and worship of the Christian church as it reacted to changing environmental factors—from tiny Jewish sect in Jerusalem, through its stay in Asia Minor, and then in its European form and, beginning in our own day, its universal incarnation. Environmental theology. We can do the same for the Roman Catholic community in the United States and come up with interesting results.

There are three basic periods in development of American Catholicism: (1) Colonial and Federal, the years up to 1830; (2) the immigrant years of the nineteenth century and, at least psychologically, down to 1945; (3) the present.

Of the Catholic traditions which have gone into forming our own, the Spaniards and the French got here first, if indeed they were not preceded by the Vikings or Brendan the Navigator. But the finally dominant Catholic tradition in Colonial and Federal periods was that set by the Englishmen who founded Maryland in 1634. Quiet, nondemonstrative, careful of their religion, they were a minority in England and even in Maryland, despite their influence and status in the colony. They were papists who had come, out of their own experience, to the conclusion that they could not in conscience accept the authority of a political sovereign in matters of religion. In matters of conscience monarchs and laws were incompetent. This doctrine they carried into effect in Maryland, where their record for religious toleration was unexceptionable, clouded only when they had to compromise with Puritans to win the Act of Toleration of 1649. Colonial and Federal Catholics were hardly totally homogeneous with the general population. They were, after all, papists. But I doubt that there has ever been again a period when the Roman Catholic community shared more fully in the general political, social, and cultural outlook of the citizenry at large.

The great immigration changed all that in the 1830s and after. Forty million odd-looking, odd-smelling people with odd habits— habits that too frequently landed them in jail or on the dole—arrived on America's shores in the century before the first great wave ended. They spoke foreign languages or, if they spoke English, had strange accents. The golden door was indeed there, but there's no need to romanticize it too much. Many of the immigrants were Roman Catholics. They fitted oddly into homogeneous Protestant America, and they fitted oddly into a Catholic Church shaped first by Englishmen, then by French refugees from 1789, then by immigrants like the Irish and the Germans who got here first. Square pegs and round holes abounded, inside and outside the Catholic community.

The Roman Catholic Church which grew in the United States during the nineteenth century was shaped to immigrant needs. What Humphrey Desmond called institutions of "pathological charity" flourished. Immigrants needed them. So did parochial schools and Catholic colleges, and the reason was the same. Most immigrants settled in cities, and parishes took shape according to their needs and demands. We need not run through the litany. The immigrant story is well known. But what should be stressed is that what they created, in response to the genuine needs of one era, is not therefore normative for all time. We are grateful to the immigrants for what they did. The way to show that gratitude is by doing as well in our generation as they did in theirs—and in ways appropriate to our generation.

The present is still a post-World War II present. Political, social, and economic forces dislodged in those years have yet to settle. They are the environmental factors in which church and theology live. Mobility, communication, successive liberations, enormous failures of spirit, enthusiasm alternating with apathy. All these have been reflected and then microcosmed in the community of the people of God. It may well be that Americans have finally abandoned their Puritan-inspired self-image as the new Israel of God or, in its secular dress, as the people with a manifest destiny in regard to the rest of the world. Perhaps Americans have come to the point where, as Larzer Ziff has suggested, they must contemplate a stasis that is alien to America's whole past.[12]

Where do we go? I certainly do not have the answers, but at least we must start by a critical reflection on the elements specific to the American Catholic experience. Such an effort represents a new and necessary liberation from a foreign philosophic and theological imperialism that has had to provide stimulus for too long, because we have been unable to reflect adequately on ourselves.

In a curious way, too, if Puritan-inspired images of God's New Israel and manifest destiny are wearing out, so are images like that of square peg and round hole. The past still has much to tell us because its record is history, and history is the tale of change, of adaptation, of the understanding (theological and otherwise) of that change and adaptation. History does not tell us about the future, except that we know new images will replace the old.

NOTES

1. Department of History, University of Notre Dame, Notre Dame, Indiana 46556.

2. *Records of the American Catholic Historical Society*, 84 (December 1973; published January 1975), pp. 167–95.

3. Robert Baird, *Religion in America*, ed. Henry Warner Bowden (New York: Harper & Row, 1970), pp. 257, 261–62. This is an abridged version of the 1844 edition.

4. Alexis de Tocqueville, *Democracy in America*, ed. Phillips Bradley; (2 vols., New York: Alfred A. Knopf, 1945), I, pp. 311–12.

5. Jules Morel, *Inquisition et Libéralisme: Avis doctrinal soumis à Mm. Louis Veuillot, Albert du Boÿs et cte. de Falloux* (Angers, 1857), p. 165.

6. Janssen's comment appeared in *Revue Benedictine* for 1898.

7. "American History and the Theological Enterprise," *The Catholic Theological Society of America: Proceedings of the Twenty-sixth Annual Convention* (Bronx, N.Y., 1972), pp, 91–115.

8. Henry Warner Bowden, "John Gilmary Shea; A Study of Method and Goals in Historiography," *Catholic Historical Review*, 54 (1968), p. 251.

9. Igino Cardinale, *La Saint-Siège et la Diplomatie* (Paris, 1962), p. 63.

10. Domenico Palmieri, *De Romano Pontifice* (2nd ed.; Prati, 1891), p. 71.

11. Report of the Annual Meeting of the American Archbishops, 1893.

12. Larzer Ziff, *Puritanism in America* (New York: Viking Press, 1973), p. 312.

DANIEL C. MAGUIRE

catholic ethics with an american accent

Ecumenism is a movement that is heavy with romance. It is marked by loving discovery as well as by intellectual reevaluation. Romance is exciting. It has a power to dissolve hostile barriers and to dissipate impediments to the marriage of true minds. But romance also has a power to blur and to deceive, and so ecumenism, as romantic, must beware.

The danger of ecumenism, a unitive movement of an enthusiastic nature, is that in the rush for unity, heritages can be lost. It need not, of course, be so. To transpose a Teilhardian insight, true ecumenism differentiates. We must be true to our differences and hold them close as we explore our commonalities. As Teilhard says: "true union does not fuse the elements it brings together; by mutual fertilization and adaptation it gives them a renewal of vitality." [1] The modern ecumenical movement must cling to this insight both because ecumenism seems to be a development that is strong and irreversible and because its scope is universal. Unitive dialog is being sought across the board, with atheists, Marxists, and non-Christian religionists.[2]

This dialog has produced an honest, persistent but basically confused question among Christian theologians. The question is: Is there a distinctively Christian ethic? [3] The question is stimulated by two concerns: first, by an ecumenical concern that Christian morality has in the past been presented as a privileged gnosis, a morality that is superior to Buddhist, Hindu, and other moralities; second, the question is spurred by the secularization process and the desire to avoid the supernaturalistic error which would make Christian goodness something superadded to a merely "human" goodness.

Both concerns are laudable. Christian life is, as H. Richard Niebuhr said, "one of the distinctive ways of human existence." He continues: "Whether it is better or worse than other styles is a question neither Christians nor others are in a position to answer, since men lack standards by which to judge their standards." [4] Furthermore, the flight from supernature is to be encouraged. If Christianity does not beckon to a fuller, more authentic experience of humanness, it is irrelevant. The question of a distinctively Christian ethic, therefore, is well motivated if, as we shall see, a bit misconceived.

It is, I believe, accurate to say that the predominant answer given to this question has been to maintain that human morality and Christian morality are *materially* identical. There is no specifically Christian content to Christian ethics that is not available to all other human beings. Concrete moral obligations derive from an authentic humanity in any system of ethics. It is not in these obligations that the distinctiveness of Christian ethics is found. Where, then, is it found? John Macquarrie speaks for the majority position when he says: "The distinctive element is the special context within which the moral life is perceived. This special context includes the normative place assigned to Jesus Christ and his teaching—not, indeed, as a paradigm for external imitation, but rather as the criterion and inspiration for a style of life." [5] The Christian believer will be marked by distinctively Christian attitudes, dispositions, intentions, and goals, but this will not yield something distinct from the human.[6]

There is a radical problem involved in saying with Richard McCormick and the majority that "human morality (natural law) and Christian morality are *materially* identical." [7] First of all, the term "human morality" makes no sense. It is adrift, like the man without a country. Morality does not exist without a distinctive context and history. In James Gustafson's terms, " 'ethics' always needs a qualifying adjective." [8] It does not emerge from a cultural void. If it is authentic morality, it is human, but that does not say enough. It will be in many ways distinctive and specific. Humanity does not exist in unspecified generality. Neither does ethics—the art-science of the human. An ethic will be Mahayana Cambodian Buddhist or early Trobriander, medieval French Catholic or Swiss nineteenth-century Calvinist. It will have different heroes and different saints. It will pulse to the rhythm of a Francis of Assisi or of an Attila the Hun. It will have tense, dominant gender, geography, history, historically derived symbols, and specially salient moral themes more or less explicated. It will be in a state of reaction to unique and unrepeatable challenges and it will think and feel in a web of relationships never found before or afterward. It will care about different realities, and caring is intrinsic to knowing. It will have different sensitivities and emphases, different blind spots, and different faculties of perception will be cauterized or dimmed.

If any ethic of any time is successful, it will be because it will have discerned the humanizing possibilities present within its contemporary moral scene. Some of its discernments will probably be translatable and helpful in other contexts. There will be overlaps and complementarities with other ethics. But each ethic will be distinct. Furthermore, it is not correct to say, as Charles E. Curran says, that "what the Christian knows with an explicit Christian dimension is and can be known by all others." [9] The mystery of the *humanum* does not reveal itself in a disincarnate, disencultured way. Only a docetic epistemology could assert that the knowing experiences of different people in different times and circumstances could be equalized. Anthropologists do tell us that certain ethical insights appear to be nearly universal. As Ralph Linton says: "The values on which there is most complete agreement are those which have to do with the satisfaction of the primary needs of individuals." [10] But this does not mean that the variegated cognitive ethical experience of differently circumstanced peoples, ranging all the way from prediscursive appreciations to functional taboos, could ever nicely coincide.

Because our existential differences are intrinsic to our specific reality, and because knowledge cannot be understood "uncontextually," we all know something that others do not know. Ecumenism is rooted in our ontology. Because of the cultural and historical specificity of our being, we all know differently and in part. Ecumenical exchange is of the essence.[11] Ecumenism is a reaction to differences. It explores differences. It does not blur them.

The discussion of Christian ethics is further queered by the separation of the "material content" or the "moral data" of morality from the distinguishing formality or intentionality lent by the Christian ethic.[12] This, however, represents an unfeasible divorce. The intentionality, or formality, or faith posture, or the "how" of my viewing things yields different results at the level of concrete cognitive response. Since Jesus must be somehow relevant to the Christian ethic, let us see whether in him intentionality can be severed from content and moral data. H. Richard Niebuhr speaks of how Jesus reacts to natural events:

> He sees as others do that the sun shines on criminals, delinquents, hypocrites, honest men, good Samaritans, and VIPs without discrimination, that rains come down in equal proportions on the fields of the diligent and of the lazy. These phenomena have been for unbelievers, from the beginning of time, signs of the operation of a universal order that is without justice, unconcerned with right and wrong conduct among men. But Jesus interprets the common phenomena in another way; here are the signs of cosmic generosity. The response to the weather so interpreted leads then also to a response to criminals and outcasts, who have not been cast out by the infinite Lord.[13]

Clearly this interpretive cast of mind would lead to some very concrete "content" about Garrett Hardin's lifeboat ethics, or about what we owe to posterity, or about the preference for force over diplomacy, or exploitative sexual relationships. If someone shares in Jesus' sense of hope and feels that the end of life is not death but resurrection, that love is the heart of the mystery of God, his conclusions in the area of social justice will be implicated. A fatalist could walk by the wounded traveler explaining his lot by a theory of inexorable karma. But whoever believes that God is love and would become "all in all," would be more likely to take the man to an inn and pour oil and pay.

According to one's intentionality or faith attitude one will find Jesus or Ayn Rand more morally relevant, and that will make for multiple differences at the level of "content" and "moral data." To say that everything Christians have learned "is and can be known by all others" [14] is incorrect in theory and contrary to fact. Christians can share with others many things that others did not and could not learn. Then, Christians should be silent and listen to what they have missed. The end result of this dialog can be what has been called "the kingdom of God."

In an ecumenical world, every person and every group will, like the travelers in *The Canterbury Tales*, have a distinctive story to tell. The story that I would tell is Catholic and American. The question I speak to is not: Is there a distinctively Catholic ethic of the American variety? but, What is it?

AMERICAN CATHOLIC

Sociologist Robert Bellah says that when we recognize that there is a civil religious tradition *and* that we may have something to learn from it, it becomes our task to "search the whole tradition from its earliest beginnings on, including its heretical byways as well as its mainstream. . . ." Then we must subject it to "the most searing criticism." [15]

The various Christian religions, resisting the ecumenical illusions of sameness and glorying in their differences, should follow that advice in a positive spirit. What is needed is a vigorous eclectic traditionalism. Traditional in the sense that we must look at everything that is there; eclectic in the sense that we must be prepared to discard and repudiate what is unworthy of the ennobling elements of the tradition.

Within the trying limits of this essay, I will attempt to trace some of the distinctive themes of Catholic moral experience. Given the battering that Catholicism has taken in recent years, I will be spared the charge of triumphalism if I accentuate the positive without blinking before the abundant negative. Taking *Christian* as the genus, I will focus on *Catholic* as a species, with *American Catholic* (where it is notably distinctive) as a subtype of the species. Obviously, I do not contend that none of these themes or emphases is found in any form in Protestant Christianity or elsewhere, or that lines are always neatly drawn. I find these features, however, saliently influential in the Catholic story.

My task is to discover those themes and emphases in Catholic history that can be reappropriated. Sociologist Alfred Schutz tells us that we live in the description of a place, not in the place itself. We live within social constructions of reality. What I suggest is that by a process of selective retrieval we American Catholics reconstruct a better reality that we can offer to a renewing earth.

THE BONIFACIAN STRAIN [16]

An element of Catholic consciousness culminated somewhat outrageously in the *Unam sanctam* of Boniface VIII on November 18, 1302. Of the spiritual and the temporal swords, Boniface said:

> Both are within the power of the Church, the spiritual sword and the material sword. The latter is to be used for the Church, the former by the Church. The former is in the hand of the priest, the latter in the hand of kings and soldiers, but to be used according to the direction and at the sufferance of the priest (*ad nutum et patientiam sacerdotis*). . . . Therefore, if the terrestrial power deviates, it will be judged by the spiritual power . . . if the supreme spiritual power deviates, it will be judged not by man but by God alone.[17]

Though the Christian church was seduced into a counterprophetic marriage with the Constantinian and Theodosian state, it did not really concede that it was a marriage of equals. The popes were vigilant to remind the temporal power of its lower estate.[18] Boniface's Bull was historically related to the investiture controversy. In the eleventh and twelfth centuries, princes who did not know their place, by papal standards, wanted to invest abbots and bishops and to receive homage from them. Popes like Nicholas II and Gregory VII lambasted the offenders and a Council of Rome (1099) excommunicated all who gave or received lay investiture. The matter was finally settled completely in favor of the church at the Concordat of Worms (1122).[19]

Centuries later, the voice of Pius IX was still Bonifacian. In his *Syllabus of Errors* in 1864 he condemned the "error" that kings and princes are exempt from church jurisdiction or "are superior to the Church in deciding questions of jurisdiction." [20] Furthermore, according to Pius it is not the civil power's business to define the church's rights. The church needs no permission from the state to exercise its authority, and woe to those who say the church has "no power of employing force, nor has she any temporal power direct or indirect." In the case of a conflict between the two powers, civil law does not prevail.[21] Boniface would have cheered.

Needless to say, traditions are not found purely and consistently lived. There is also the fawning tradition of Eusebius of Caesarea (the father of church history) and Lactantius (the Christian Cicero), who saw Constantine as a God-willed leader, providentially appointed like the anointed king of the Old Testament. These men sowed the seed of a redivinization of civil power after blood had been shed to strip the magistracy of its divine pretensions.[22]

And, on the American scene, it is not the voice of Boniface (much less of Isaiah or Jeremiah) that we hear in the First Plenary Council at Baltimore in 1852. Said the bishops to the people:

Show your attachment to the institutions of our beloved country by prompt compliance with all their requirements, and by the cautious jealousy with which you guard against the least deviation from the rules which they prescribe for the maintenance of public order and private rights. Thus will you refute the idle babbling of foolish men, and will best approve yourselves worthy of the privileges which you enjoy, and overcome, by the sure test of practical patriotism, all the prejudices which a misrepresentation of your principles but too often produces.[23]

Add to this American story the sad reference of historian John Tracy Ellis to the "almost unvaried policy of support by American bishops to the public authorities in time of war, a policy that continued practically unbroken to the 1960's. . . ." [24] Insecure, immigrant Catholicism does have a sorry American record of fawning patriotism. But even in America another Catholic spirit shows through. At the height of an anti-Catholic crusade, Bishop John Spalding of Peoria let loose with this:

> Our record for patriotism is without blot or stain, and it is not necessary for us to hold the flag in our hands when we walk the streets, to wave it when we speak, to fan our selves with it when we are warm, and to wrap it about us when we are cold.[25]

The retrievable element in Boniface VII, Gregory VII, and Pius IX is a refusal to worship at the civil shrine. Let us grant the egregious excesses of these strongmen, who in their zeal to defend the church from statist idolatry (conceding that there were other motives) actually divinized the church. Still they represent an antidote to the pretensions of statism. Protestant Christianity has proclaimed that the state is under the judgment of God. Catholic Christianity has gone further and said that it was also under the judgment of the community of believers.

Spalding did not come from nowhere. Neither did the Berrigans. They were nourished not only on the soil of Hebraic prophecy but also were rooted in the historical papal refusal to bow before the Leviathan.[26] Boniface and Pius, cleansed of their sins by a good confession, could serve us today. They had something worth reappropriating.

CATHOLIC HOPEFULNESS

Hope has a bad name. It is confused with quietist optimism which inertly trusts that things will work out in the sweet by-and-by. Catholic hope is made of sterner stuff. It is grounded in a firm belief that God is now reigning. A realized, not a futurist, eschatology is Catholic. Catholic hope is also grounded in the belief that nature is not totally corrupted by sin. The Council of Trent declared against its understanding of Protestant doctrine that we are not justified by the imputation of Christ's justice but by the infusion of grace and love by the Holy Spirit. We must do something to dispose ourselves for this infusion. Sins *are* forgiven.

Grace does restore. Nature, though wounded, is not ruined.[27] That is the Catholic credo.

Protestant Paul Ramsey writes that "the most fundamental premise or insight upon which Christian ethical reflection proceeds in the Catholic tradition" is that there is "continuity of grace (love) and 'nature,' of charity and the perfection of the self with others. . . ." [28] He is right, and that is a very hopeful posture that shows up in a variety of ways in the Catholic tradition. I will cite, and discuss below, just three of the ways in which hope unfolds in Catholicism: (1) it finds room for self-love and thus self-respect; (2) it has confidence in reason, which it will not, with Luther, call a harlot; (3) it is confident that God is doing something and thus there is less reason to be crouching and trembling in the upper room.

1. Anders Nygren, in his *Agape and Eros*, writes of the renewal of the *agape* motif in the Reformation. He locates Luther's Copernican revolution in his insistence against Catholic Christianity that *agape* cannot be perverted by self-interest. "In Catholic piety [Luther] finds a tendency which he cannot help regarding as a complete perversion of the inmost meaning of religion: the egocentric tendency." [29]

Self-love, for Luther, must be plucked up by the roots if true Christian love is to find a place in us.[30] Nygren stands stoutly with Luther in this revolt. He indicts the Catholic heroes, Augustine and Thomas Aquinas, for their implicit hedonism: "For Thomas, as for Augustine, all love is fundamentally acquisitive love. . . ." [31] And with a prosecutor's excitement, he cites Thomas's statement: "Assuming what is impossible, that God were not man's *bonum* then there would be no reason for man to love Him." [32]

In the name of Aquinas and all that is Catholic, I would plead guilty to the charge that Catholicism finds room for self-love. It is, of course, not a Catholic discovery that we should love our neighbor *as* we love ourselves, that self-love is a model for agapic love. But Catholics are very at home with this discovery. It spares them the question of why the neighbor is worth what we are not worth. It squares better with experience. It gives a happier basis for ascetical theology and it is congenial to modern psychology that builds on the legitimacy of self-esteem. No apologies for this one.

2. Catholics have trusted reason for the same reason that they have been so long attracted to theories of "natural law." The *eschaton* is being incipiently realized. Neither nature nor nature's inquiring cognitive faculties are totally corrupted or out of reach of divine illumination. Our traditional confidence in God's guidance is at times embarrassingly overdrawn. As the Catholic theologian Yves Congar writes: "We know how, up to and including the Council of Trent, the expressions *revelare, inspirare, illuminare,* and others analogous to them, are continually applied to the Fathers, councils, canons, even to the elections or particular acts of secular authorities." [33] Gradually this accent became abused and limited to the hierarchical magisterium as though the Holy Spirit had an exclusivist penchant for illumining prelates. In its broader reality, however, I believe it accounts for the openness of the Catholic lineage to the insights of Plato, the Stoa, Roman law, and Aristotle. Reason was not broken, nor was it alien to the Spirit.

Obviously there were some intellectual disasters that came from these ecumenical adventures. Still, it was Catholic to think that we *can* think and that God is with us. (At its roots this is what the later Catholic doctrine of infallibility is all about, though there are some who would interpret it more juridico-magically. It is quintessentially a doctrine of hope that God will not let us get entirely lost in our doctrinal pilgrimage.)

3. Catholic sacramental theology is another manifestation of hope.[34] No one will deny that sacraments are prominent in Catholicism. There is no parallel in Protestantism for our elaborate sacramental theology. In this theology, the sacraments function, given all the requirements, *ex opere operato,* independently of the worthiness of the minister. There is a bit of mischief and indeed of magic in the way this has often been understood, but I submit that beneath the theological infelicities there is a confidence that God is at work. The sacraments express a faith that God is reaching for us and will touch us if we will but reach

for him. The sacraments ritualize the hope that such contact is promised and possible.

If Catholics could reappropriate the hopefulness of their tradition, they would be more open to creativity, more ready for risk, more aware that they are, in Thomas Aquinas's language, participants in divine providence.[35] Hope is the precondition of courage, and courage according to Aquinas is the prerequisite for all virtue.[36] With all due thanks to the powerful Protestant sense of sin, it is dynamic hope, without naïveté, that is the undergirding of moral and social evolution.

MIRTH AND DIONYSUS

There is an apocryphal version of a Belloc poem that goes like this:

> Wherever a Catholic sun doth shine,
>   there is lots of laughter and good red wine;
> At least I've always found it so,
>   *Benedicamus Domino!* [37]

The verse is on to something. The Catholic God is capable of both laughter and the dance. Apollo, of course, is prominent in all institutions. (How could Dionysians put and hold anything together!) But Dionysus would not brook excommunication from Rome, and he survived to toast all those Roman Apollonians who ranted and raved at him. And that is good because, as Sam Keen says: "When Dionysus is not given his due, Apollo becomes a tyrant, a god to be killed." [38]

For a witness here I turn again, in proper Dionysian fashion, to poetry. (Apollonian theology has naturally been slow to recognize poetry as a prime theological source.) William Butler Yeats, whom T. S. Eliot said was the greatest poet of our time, was a Protestant. Occasionally, however, and pointedly, Yeats moves into a Catholic idiom with all the symbols and theology thereof. He does this in "The Fiddler of Dooney," to make a point, I think, about the place of Dionysus in the Catholic scheme of things.

The Fiddler of Dooney[39]

When I play on my fiddle in Dooney,
Folk dance like a wave of the sea;
My cousin is priest in Kilvarnet,
My brother in Mocharabuiee.

I passed my brother and cousin:
They read in their books of prayer;
I read in my book of songs
I bought at the Sligo Fair.

When we come at the end of time
To Peter sitting in state,
He will smile on the three old spirits,
But call me first through the gate;

For the good are always the merry,
Save by an evil chance,
And the merry love the fiddle,
And the merry love to dance:

And when the folk there spy me,
They will all come up to me,
With "Here is the fiddler of Dooney!"
And dance like a wave of the sea.

Notice in the poem that the dour clerical relatives will also get into heaven. "He will smile on the three old spirits," but it is the Fiddler who will set the feet of the cherubim, seraphim, apostles, and martyrs a-dancing: ". . . first through the gate," "For the good are always the merry." Whole tomes of "theology" harbor less content than this poem.

The Dionysian element in Catholicism shows up, too, in the attitude toward the body and especially toward sex. Let us hear some Protestant voices on the subject to set the contrast. Tom Driver writes:

> Laughter at sex is the only way to put sex in its place, to assert one's humanity over against that impersonal, irrational, yet necessary force that turns even the best of men into caricatures of themselves. . . . This natural force can no more be made fully "human" than can mountain goats or ocean currents.[40]

Reflecting the Lutheran aversion to self-love, Herbert Richardson writes:

> Let us suppose that one seeks, through a sexual relation, not his own satisfaction and orgasm, but the joy of perfect sharing. Such sexual desire is a totally different thing from eros love. It is an "agapic" love. . . .[41]

For Catholic Sidney Callahan, sex is no goat or alien current to be agapized into respectability. She writes:

> Man can only reach the heights of humanity by going through his anonymous instinctual nature, not by attempting to climb over or around it or to destroy all vestiges of irrationality. . . . Pleasure, irrationality, and automatic activity are necessary to man. . . . The individual personality and mutual unity of the couple can be refreshed by participating in one of the fountains of reality, irrational instinct.[42]

Perhaps our remarks here on mirth, Dionysus, and sex cannot be separated from those on hopefulness. The hopeless, after all, do not dance. If one believes with Luther that we must "pluck up and . . . break down . . . everything that is in us . . . and in ourselves pleases us," if our need is "to be instructed in a righteousness altogether external and alien," then both reason and sex will be damned, for they are quite internal and native.[43] They who ban Dionysus will probably end up making blue laws and condemning drink, sending the Maypole dancers back to England in chains, producing a gloomy Jonathan Edwards, and spawning an austere "Protestant work ethic." A Catholic work ethic is almost unthinkable. Thanks be to Dionysus!

LITURGY

If the survival of Dionysus was related intimately to hope, the development of the liturgy is related to Dionysus. Living liturgy will not issue from the frigid. Liturgy is both a creative and a poetic expression and thus comes hard for Apollonians.

Liturgical expression does what Shelley saw as the work of

poetry; it "defeats the curse which binds us to be subjected to the accident of surrounding impressions." [44] It vaults into the mystery beyond the reach of a merely verbal ministry. It contains what Herbert Marcuse calls "the rationality of negation." [45] In the face of the status quo of insight and of facts, it intimates other dimensions and horizons. It knows that the icon is mightier than the word. Liturgy does what Marcuse saw the cathedrals doing in his *One-Dimensional Man*:

> No matter how close and familiar the temple and cathedral were to the people who lived around them, they remained in terrifying or elevating contrast to the daily life of the slave, the peasant, and the artisan—and perhaps even to that of their masters. [46]

Liturgy has social, political, and religious significance. It is a spur of transcendence.

Catholicism is deeply liturgical. Our icons are of our essence. At present we are in a liturgical wilderness. American Catholicism is an unlikely candidate to respond creatively. We have been too absorbed in building brick enclaves and proving our decency to the "upstairs" people to have that peace which is the prelude to creative inspiration. But who knows what will be, now that the end of the Protestant era has been proclaimed! Maybe liturgical creativity of the sort for which our larger tradition should equip us.

PROBABILISM AND THE FREEDOM OF CONSCIENCE

The one hundred and fifty years before Vatican II have an impressive claim to being the nadir of Catholic moral theology. Unfortunately many know only that period and presume it paradigmatic of the whole. Probabilism is an example of a prior achievement that has been neglected and indeed perverted. It represented a classical way of coping with the undefeatable ambiguity of many concrete moral questions.

Quite simply, it faced the issue of what to do when moral consensus breaks down and a liberal opinion emerges saying that X, contrary to what all had thought, may be moral and good. At what point can one depart from majority rigor and follow an insight favoring a new freedom? [47]

Probabilism was based on the incontrovertible insight that a doubtful obligation does not bind as if it were certain. If, therefore, a liberal opinion is sufficiently probable to establish a doubt, *although the more rigorous opinion is more probable*, conscience may opt for either opinion. The question became: When do you have sufficient probability to be free? Sufficient or "solid" probability was determined by the presence of cogent *but not necessarily conclusive reasons* (intrinsic probability) or by reliance on the authority, learning, and prudence of other people (extrinsic probability). As Henry Davis, S.J., put it:

> In its ultimate analysis, Probabilism is common sense; it is a system used in practical doubt by the majority of mankind. People rightly say: I am not going to debate all day before acting in doubtful matters; there must be some very obvious way of making up my mind. At all events, if I cannot make up my mind for myself, I will act as some good people act, though many other good people might disapprove. That practical solution of doubt is common sense, and it is Probabilism.[48]

What set the stage for the general acceptance of Probabilism, was the condemnation of a competing system known as Absolute Tutiorism (from the Latin *tutior,* safer). This system taught that in a dispute, an opinion that expands one's moral freedom may never be followed unless it is clearly certain, i.e., until *all* doubt is resolved in favor of the liberal option. Alexander VIII in 1690 condemned this opinion as untenable.[49]

Note well the essence of Probabilism. It is all based on moral insight: your own (intrinsic) or that of your authorities (extrinsic). Either you or someone trusted by you (Henry Davis's "some good people") *see* the reasons for new moral freedom. Insight, or the understanding of reasons, however, is not subject to magisterial veto. What is seen is seen—without and independent of permission. (This does not mean that dialog with authorities and others is not always good. It is.)

Whatever became of this genuinely liberating doctrine, which could have forestalled the birth control debate and which could be applied today to debated issues such as mercy death, sexual conduct, conscientious objection to governmental policy, etc.? It was lost in the decadence of moral theology, in the simplistic certitudes of the nineteenth century, and in the heavy-handed infallibilism of the Vatican I period. Moral theology helped do it in by treating intrinsic probability as nonexistent and by assuming that the authorities required for extrinsic probability were those "approved authors" who cautiously and uncritically hewed to the prevailing Roman ideology. This, in effect, established a juridical Absolute Tutiorism which only crumbled with *Humanae vitae*, Paul VI's encyclical which dealt with, among several other issues, morally acceptable attitudes toward birth control.

Humanae vitae succeeded in putting Catholics in the position of siding with Alexander VIII who condemned Absolute Tutiorism or of obeying Paul VI who was enforcing it by attempting to negate voluntaristically the widely perceived reasons for the now dominant liberal position. In effect, Pope Paul tried to overrule the cognitional experiences of innumerable Catholic people. It was a last heroic effort to nullify the view of Alexander VIII. Alexander, however, prevailed.[50]

THE CONTRIBUTION OF THOMAS AQUINAS

Finally, in this suggestive but not exhaustive list of distinguishing Catholic themes, I turn to Thomas Aquinas. Jaroslav Pelikan puts it this way: "Although many Protestants criticize Roman Catholicism for its ignorance and superstition, they must also acknowledge that in Roman Catholic Thomism they confront a system of thought for which there is no equivalent in Protestantism."[51]

Thomas is a victim of bad companions. In proof of the saying that a conservative is a worshiper of dead liberals, ultraconservative Catholics have turned selectively to Thomas. Then in the fervor of recent renewal, Thomas was thrown out with the bath water, and that is a loss. The lapses of Thomas are easily spotted, but the strengths of his far-reaching systemic approach are an enduring service. Baptism by immersion in a great thinker does not commit you to everything that thinker thought, but it does give a base and a field of broad reference from which to relate maturely to newer insights.

Thomas is rich and full of surprises for those who know only the caricature. Ahead of season he said that "the nature of man is mutable." [52] Anticipating the modern realization of the difficulty of teaching morality transculturally, Thomas wrote that law is not everywhere the same "because of the mutability of the nature of man and the diverse conditions of men and of things, according to the diversity of places and times." [53] He saw the cognitive role of affectivity in ethics,[54] and in his treatment of prudence and the moral virtues. He taught the "human actions are good or bad according to their circumstances." [55] He insisted that the primary moral law for Christians was the grace of the Holy Spirit, with all written wisdom cast into a secondary role.[56] He recognized that specific moral principles are open to exceptions and cannot be turned into categorical imperatives.[57] And more.

There are other resources in the Catholic reservoir that can merely be listed in the space available: the message of the contemplative life which, in Christianity, developed only among Catholics; the sense of law and its relationship to morality; the priestly tradition with its stress on the value of personal symbols; the balancing of conciliarism with strong executive power; the effort to collectivize prophecy in religious orders, etc.

Catholics who are putting their house in order should start in the attic. There is a lot there that should be thrown out. But there is a lot that should be brought downstairs where life is lived. For the first time in American history, American Catholics can securely manifest their differentness. This would be a national service. As John Tracy Ellis says: "Conformity of the type which some Americans have mistakenly advocated in religious matters is not healthy for the general community any more than conformity in political shades of opinion is healthy for democracy." [58]

CONCLUSION

My tone thus far has been, by intention, relentlessly positive. I have sought to enucleate the genuine possibilities of the Catholic tradition. Casting a cold eye upon American Catholicism, however, we are brought up short and chastened. What chance is there here for an Easter experience! Do not the indicators show American Catholicism to be a shrinking sect, a decadent dinosaur? Rubem Alves writes of the dinosaurs:

> Their "arrogance of power" entrapped them in the very absurdity of their organic structure. They were thereby made incapable of responding in different ways to the new challenges their environment presented.[59]

The auguries of ill for the American Catholic Church are manifold. The church here, at the management level, is reacting to the twentieth-century reformation as the European church reacted to the sixteenth-century reform. It is battening down the hatches and retreating into the seeming security of nonviable rigidities. Paralleling this retrenchment syndrome is a tendency in many places to pursue the elusive god of relevance, to the point where meaningful identity is lost. Neither path leads anywhere.

Add to this: the de facto excommunication of its intellectuals, the lowering of standards in seminaries, the passion for a tidy propositional orthodoxy that would equate mental paralysis with faith, and the encouragement of anti-intellectual fundamentalist movements in the church.

The proliferation of what could be called social-function Catholics, who, for good and bad reasons, see the church as a place to ceremonialize transition events such as birth, marriage, and death; the fixation of the hierarchical church on issues like abortion—issues where our insistence has put our prestige on the line—to the neglect of other social justice concerns; the inability not only to lead but even to follow in the liberation of women; the frantic clinging to a juridically celibate clergy; the remarkable ability of leadership to believe, like Marie Antoinette and Nicholas II, that what is happening is not happening, and that all is as all was, etc.

And conclude all of these dismal data with:

The lingering effects of the original sin of American Catholicism, its whiteness—its inability, or rather, its unwillingness, to attract black Americans into its lifestream. It is difficult to think of a people more naturally attuned to the best elements of Catholic

Christianity than our Afro-American brothers and sisters. These natural friends should have appealed to us also because they were another, even more fiercely persecuted, minority. Shared plight normally makes bedfellows. Instead, we withdrew xenophobically from a redemptive encounter. The blacks could have given white American Catholics more than we could have given them. They might have given us back our Catholic soul.[60]

American Catholicism is in a winter and it is not clear that it will have a spring. That, of course, is an intellectual verdict and a decidedly hopeless one. It is also un-Catholic. Better, perhaps, to turn to the image of winter wheat which, against all apparent odds, outwits the deadening frost and succeeds in living and giving life. But that image, like every image, falters. For the wheat of this sinful church will not grow inevitably with the passing of the season. It will grow only when action is fused with creativity. Therein lies the question—and the hope.

NOTES

1. Pierre Teilhard de Chardin, *Human Energy* (New York: Harcourt Brace Jovanovich, 1971), p. 63. For a similar insight, see St. Thomas Aquinas, *Summa Theologica* I/II, q. 28, a. 1, ad 1: ". . . those who love desire to achieve unity out of their duality; but because this could cause either one or both to be destroyed, they seek a union that is fitting and proper. . . ."

2. On the dialog with believers and unbelievers, see "Constitution on the Church in the Modern World," *The Documents of Vatican II*, ed. Walter M. Abbott (New York: Guild Press, 1966).

3. The terms *ethic* and *ethics* must be distinguished. *Ethics* is the art-science which seeks to bring method and sensitivity to the discernment of the normatively human. It consists of foundational explorations of the meaning of moral experience, of the presuppositions of ethical discourse, and normative considerations of the methodic interplay of norms, goals, dispositions, linguistic, and empirical analysis of concrete questions. The term *ethic* generally relates to the moral qualities of an individual or a group, as e.g., "the Protestant ethic."

4. H. Richard Niebuhr, *The Responsible Self* (New York: Harper & Row, 1963), p. 150.

5. John Macquarrie, *Three Issues in Ethics* (New York: Harper & Row, 1970), p. 89.

6. See James M. Gustafson, *Christ and the Moral Life* (New York: Harper & Row, 1968), pp. 238–71. Supporting the idea of a dominant position in this regard, Richard McCormick writes: "First, I would agree that these arguments are convincing reasons for saying that human morality (natural law) and Christian morality are *materially* identical. This is what nearly everyone (e.g., Fuchs, Aubert, Macquarrie, Rahner) is saying these days. The light of the gospel does not bring something distinct from the human, but helps us to discover what is authentically human." ("Notes on Moral Theology," *Theological Studies* 32 (1971), pp. 74–75.) There are, of course, differing elements in all these authors. Charles Curran, for example, while fitting under this general umbrella, writes that "Christians and non-Christians can and do share the same general goals and intentions, attitudes and dispositions, as well as norms and concrete actions." "The difference lies in the fact that for the Christian his ethics is thematically and explicitly Christian." Cf. "Is there a Catholic and/or Christian Ethic?" *Proceedings of the Twenty-Ninth Annual Convention: The Catholic Theological Society of America* 29 (1974), pp. 153, 154, 145.

7. "Notes on Moral Theology," *Theological Studies* 32 (1971), p. 74. See note 6.

8. "Response to Professor Curran," *Proceedings of the Twenty-Ninth Annual Convention: The Catholic Theological Society of America* 29 (1974), p. 159.

9. Charles E. Curran, *op. cit.*, p. 145 (see note 6).

10. Ralph Linton, "The Problem of Universal Values," *Method and Perspective in Anthropology: Papers in Honor of Wilson D. Wallis*, ed. Robert Spencer (Minneapolis: University of Minnesota Press, 1954), p. 168.

11. This also explains why no one group could claim an exclusive grip on revelation.

12. Joseph Fuchs, in the chapter "Human, Humanist and Christian Morality" in *Human Values and Christian Morality* (Dublin: Gill and Macmillan, 1970), copes with the problem we are discussing by using the notions of human morality, the morality of man "as man," and a special Christian intentionality and faith. There are at least two problems here: man as man does not exist, and "Christian intentionality" and material content are linked in the knowing Christian.

13. H. Richard Niebuhr, *op. cit.*, pp. 165–66.

14. Charles E. Curran, *op. cit.*, p. 145.

15. "American Civil Religion in the 1970's" *Anglican Theological Review*, Supplementary Series 1 (1973), p. 16.

16. This is a term that I used in a brief listing of some of the themes of Catholic existence in "Death and Resurrection of Moral Theology," *Commonweal* 101 (1974), pp. 145–46.

17. Henrici Denzinger, *Enchiridion Symbolorum* (Friburgi Brisg.-Barcinone: Herder, editio 29, 1953), no. 468. In response to the vigorous protest of Philip IV of France, Boniface seemed to back off from this statement by saying that he did not want to usurp the jurisdiction of the king. However, he concluded and subverted this demurrer, saying: "Neither the king nor any other member of the faithful can deny that they are subject to Us by reason of sin." *Ibid.*, note 2. (Translations by Daniel Maguire.)

18. The neat distinction between church and state was a late achievement. When Gregory VII went to work on reform, the word *ecclesia* meant Christian society, including both the empire and the mystical Body. See Yves Congar, "The Historical Development of Authority in the Church. Points for Christian Reflection," *Problems of Authority*, ed. John M. Todd (Baltimore: Helicon Press, 1962), pp. 136–44.

19. The princes did retain varying degrees of control over elections of prelates, but on the issue of investiture the papal victory was complete. Cf. *The Oxford Dictionary of the Christian Church*, ed. F. L. Cross, 2nd edition revised by F. L. Cross and E. A. Livingstone (London: Oxford University Press, 1974), p. 710.

20. Denzinger, *op. cit.*, no. 1754.

21. Denzinger, *op. cit.*, nos. 1720, 1722, 1724, 1730, 1739, 1742, 1754, 1755.

22. See Karl Baus, *Handbook of Church History* I (West Germany: Herder, 1965), pp. 405–32.

23. Quoted by John Tracy Ellis, *American Catholicism*, 2nd revised edition (Chicago and London: University of Chicago Press, 1969), pp. 81–82.

24. John Tracy Ellis, "American Catholics and Peace: An Historical Sketch," *The Family of Nations*, ed. James S. Rausch (Huntington, Ind.: Our Sunday Visitor, Inc., 1970), p. 17. Ellis explains some of the historical reasons for this. As in the statement from the First Plenary Council at Baltimore, Catholics were reacting or over-reacting to profound anti-Catholic bias.

25. "Catholicism and APAism," *North American Review* 159 (September 1894), p. 285. Quoted in Ellis, *ibid.*, p. 18.

26. There were sad defections from this spirit among those prelates who danced before the Nixon ark of White House civil religion, uttering inoffensive pieties in the presence of the monarch. But there are other stories. Reportedly, two cardinals refused ever to participate in those self-serving services, and Robert Bellah writes that at worship after Nixon's second inauguration, the only prophetic words came from Joseph L. Bernardin, the Catholic archbishop of Cincinnati. Rev. Billy Graham was himself and Rabbi Magnin fawned before "our great leader," "a beautiful human being." See Robert Bellah, *op. cit.*, pp. 13–14.

27. See Denzinger, *op. cit.*, nos. 792a to 843. *The Decree on Justification* was debated almost word for word and the power and coherence of the decree were seen to be a kind of miracle by those who worked on it, given the litigation that attended its composition. It is a monument of Catholic soul-searching.

28. Paul Ramsey, *The Patient as Person* (New Haven and London: Yale University Press, 1970), p. 178.

29. Anders Nygren, *Agape and Eros* (Philadelphia: Westminster Press, 1953), p. 681.

30. *Ibid.*, p. 716.

31. *Ibid.*, p. 642. Augustine, of course, casts a broad shadow. He influenced all forms of Western Christianity.

32. *Summa Theologica* II/II q. 26, a. 13, ad 3.

33. Yves M. J. Congar, *Tradition and Traditions* (London: Burns and Oates, 1966), p. 119. Terms like "revelante Domino . . . rescribamus"; "instruente Spiritu Sancto"; "dictante Spiritu Sancto"; "Spiritu Sancto praedicante," etc. are common. See Congar, *op. cit.*, pp. 119–37 *et passim.*

34. Charles E. Curran, speaking of a distinctively Catholic ethic, stresses the note of mediation. (See Curran, *op. cit.*, pp. 148–54). In my scheme, I think this idea is understood in the context of sacramentality and general hopefulness.

35. See *Summa Theologica* I/II q. 91, a. 2. This article is a splendid example of the continuity between nature and grace that is so typically Catholic.

36. *Summa Theologica* I/II q. 61, a. 3, 4; II/II, q. 58, a. 8, ad 2.

37. The genuine verse is: But Catholic men who live upon wine
> Are deep in the water and frank and fine.
> Wherever I travel I find it so.
> *Benedicamus Domino!*

I prefer the apocrypha in this case.

38. Sam Keen, "Manifesto for a Dionysian Theology," *Cross Currents* 19 (1969), p. 37. Keen, it should be conceded, is a Protestant.

39. *The Collected Poems of W. B. Yeats* (New York: Macmillan, 1956), p. 71. Reprinted with permission of the publisher.

40. Tom Driver "On Taking Sex Seriously," in *Moral Issues and Christian Response*, ed. Paul Jersild and Dale Johnson (New York: Holt, Rinehart and Winston, 1971), pp. 102–4.

41. Herbert Richardson, *Nun, Witch, Playmate: The Americanization of Sex* (New York: Harper & Row, 1971), pp. 106–7.

42. Sidney Cornelia Callahan, *Beyond Birth Control: The Christian Experience of Sex* (New York: Sheed and Ward, 1968), pp. 137–38.

43. Martin Luther, *Römerbrief*, as quoted in Nygren, *op. cit.*, p. 682.

44. Percy Bysshe Shelley, *A Defense of Poetry.* quoted by Jacques Maritain, *Creative Intuition in Art and Poetry* (New York: Meridian Books, 1955), p. 109.

45. Herbert Marcuse, *One-Dimensional Man* (Boston: Beacon Press, 1964), p. 63.

46. *Ibid.*

47. Although efforts were made to trace Probabilism and other moral systems all the way back to the Fathers, it was really in the sixteenth and seventeenth centuries that the "moral systems" took shape, with Probabilism prevailing over a multitude of more rigorous competitors.

48. Henry Davis, *Moral and Pastoral Theology* I (London and New York: Sheed and Ward, 1949), p. 93. Henry Davis, it should be noted, is no young Turk. His four-volume work is all in English until he comes to sexual ethics. Then it plunges into Latin. Not very Dionysian!

49. Denzinger, *op. cit.*, no. 1293. The error condemned was this: "It is not licit to follow a probable or even a most probable opinion."

50. The idea of papal infallibility does not enter in here. It is not a respectable opinion in Catholic theology today to say that the church could be infallible in concrete issues of morality. Such power would require divine comprehensive knowledge and the position is thus reductively idolatrous. See my "Moral Absolutes and the Magisterium," *Absolutes in Moral Theology*, ed. Charles E. Curran (Washington-Cleveland: Corpus Books, 1968), pp. 57–107. I argued there that it is not meaningful to say that the church is infallible in morals.

51. Jaroslav Pelikan, *The Riddle of Roman Catholicism* (Nashville: Abingdon, 1959), p. 143.

52. *Summa Theologica*, II/II, q. 57, a. 2, ad 1.

53. *De Malo*, 2, 4, ad 13.

54. *Summa Theologica*, II/II, q. 15, a. 2.

55. *Ibid.*, I/II, q. 18, a. 3.

56. *Ibid.*, I/II, q. 106, a. 1.

57. *Ibid.*, I/II, q. 94, a. 4, a. 5.

58. John Tracy Ellis, *American Catholicism*, 2nd revised edition (Chicago and London: University of Chicago Press, 1969), p. 156.

59. Rubem A. Alves, *Tomorrow's Child: Imagination, Creativity, and the Rebirth of Culture* (New York: Harper & Row, 1972), p. 2.

60. Underlying this approach of eclectic traditionalism, and thus this entire essay, is the problem of criteriology. How do we know that what we are enucleating is the noblest and best in the tradition? Given the insights of historicism, of social psychology, and what is often called the sociology of knowledge, objectivity here would seem like an unattainable Holy Grail. The problem is the hermeneutical problem of the discernment of the Spirit. It is a problem that besets all exegetical work on Christian sources where selectivity is inevitable. In general, the solution is reached for, if not attained, by a continual and critical process of identification of the specifying themes of Christian existence. Against these, each kind of experience of Christianity must be measured. If we agree to the centrality of themes such as reconciliation, hope, serving and kenotic love, peace, liberty, humility, truth, sincerity, maturity, joy, etc., and, in sum, on the formal centrality of Christ for understanding the Christian ethos, we will be able to make some selections. We will have preferences presumably for nonviolent alternatives, for the conciliar *modus procedendi* of Trent rather than of Vatican I, for the "taught of God" implications of Alexander VIII's condemnation of Absolute Tutiorism, etc. We will be fallible in this task, but, again, not hopeless.

JOSEPH F. GOWER

democracy as a theological problem in isaac hecker's apologetics

A continual interaction between the Christian faith and the life and thought of the cultures in which the church exists is clearly detectable throughout the history of Christian thought. Thus the fact that the situation of the church in the United States differed markedly from every other situation in Christian history gave rise to new theological problems, one of them being the realization that democracy itself is such a problem. The intention of this essay is to examine the significant contribution to American theology that is present in the apologetical writings of Isaac Thomas Hecker (1819–88) especially insofar as he responded to the theological challenge he perceived in American democracy.[1] For Hecker democracy was fundamentally a theological problem primarily concerned with the Christian conception of human nature.

From the nation's inception the uniqueness of the American situation for Roman Catholic theology was distinctly recognized, for the American Catholics knew they were in a predicament unparalleled in the long history of their church. As a minority in a land dominated by Protestants, American Catholics felt compelled to offer a justification for their faith not only on religious grounds but also on social and political grounds. Indeed, it has been remarked that the conflict between Catholic and non-

Catholic ideologies in America has not been simply a conflict of creeds but a conflict over the social and political implications of those creeds.[2]

EARLY CATHOLIC RESPONSES
TO PROTESTANT OBJECTIONS

To diminish prejudice and correct misrepresentation were the modest goals of the first defenders of Catholicism in America. Generally speaking, there were three prominent objections issued by American Protestants to the Roman Catholic Church in America. They charged: (1) that Catholicism is not true Christianity; (2) that it is irreconcilable with democratic institutions; and, (3) that it would lead to the destruction of American social and cultural progress.

Beginning with John Carroll, the Roman Catholic tradition emerging in the United States wholeheartedly embraced the American constitutional system. Though they failed to elaborate an extensive theological rationale, the early Catholic leaders quite willingly accepted the novel situation of the separation of church and state as a practical solution to a very difficult problem. Vigorous approval of this distinctive and unique policy of church-state relations became the standard pattern both in the conciliar documents of the American hierarchy and in the works of the foremost Catholic apologists such as John England, John Hughes, and Martin John Spalding.[3]

During the first half of the nineteenth century, the strictly theological complaints against the Catholic Church diminished and the Protestant attacks were made more for political, economic, and social reasons. The most persistent and notable accusation was that the Roman Catholic Church is essentially foreign in spirit, membership, and allegiance. The celebrated indictment of "double-allegiance" charged that the citizenship of Catholics would necessarily be conditioned by a higher loyalty to the Roman Pontiff and that Catholics would work to undermine the security and prosperity of the nation. As the influx of Catholic immigration continued, nativism gained more momentum and reached its peak in the decades from the 1830s to the 1860s with the political movement known as Know-Nothingism. In response to the fierce anti-Catholic hostility, the Catholic writers endeavored to confirm the loyalty of Catholics to the republic and, by marshaling historical evidence, to exhibit the contributions the Catholic Church has made to civilization, social advancement, and the cause of freedom.

THE EMERGENCE OF BROWNSON AND HECKER

But, after the conversion of the native-born Orestes Brownson and Isaac Hecker in 1844 and their subsequent entry as Catholics into the field of religious controversy, an alternative mode of presenting the Catholic faith to the American people was signaled. For these two intellectual leaders were determined to chart a modified course by promoting a comprehensive and positive apologetics that would reflect an offensive rather than merely defensive quality.

Regarding the place of the Catholic Church within the American civil and political order, Brownson and Hecker deliberately set out to demonstrate that the Catholic religion is the religion that best harmonizes with the American people and fully corresponds with their traditions of esteem for freedom, equality, and human dignity. Indeed, not only was the Catholic faith portrayed as the answer to the spiritual needs of this new nation, it was also represented as the necessary means for the preservation and perfection of the ideals of American democracy. It was with audacious and provocative claims such as these that Hecker and Brownson departed from the usual strategy of American Catholic apologetics by attempting to take the discussion of the role of the church in the United States beyond the legal and historical framework into a more theological setting.

Initially both Orestes Brownson and Isaac Hecker advocated this new pattern even though they differed somewhat in orientation and emphasis. But, in time, Brownson became less sanguine about the success of the Catholic Church in America and inclined his efforts in a different direction. Although he continued to hold and defend the theoretical compatibility between democracy and Catholicity, during the last decade of his life he abandoned all hope for their practical compatibility.[4] Brownson's concern with these issues was not only apologetical, and much of his exceptional work in political theory was devoted to questions regarding the source of sovereignty and the place of authority in the American republic.[5]

Although it certainly does not have to be argued that Orestes Brownson was well prepared to address the native American, that this is also true of Isaac Hecker does require some comment. As a youth Isaac Hecker was active in the cause of social reform. His passionate concern for the amelioration of the economic and social conditions of the laboring class and immigrants brought him to membership in radical socialist movements in New York City. The political group he affiliated with was called the Loco-Foco party, a faction separated from the Tammany Democrats. As uncompromising champions of equal rights, the Loco-Focos considered their party to be the authentic extension of Jefferson's political philosophy and they were steadfastly opposed to all monopolies and vested interests. But, in the aftermath of the 1837 panic and his party's election defeats, Hecker was dissuaded from expecting any effective or enduring social reform through political means.[6]

Fortunately, this interest in political activity occasioned his meeting Brownson. Hecker came to share Brownson's social philosophy as well as his conviction that reform would be achieved only through the agency of religion. As their friendship grew, Brownson encouraged Hecker in the study of philosophy and theology and persuaded him to join the Utopian community of Brook Farm under the leadership of George Ripley.

This opportunity afforded Hecker an association with the intellectual elite of New England that was most formative in his religious development, for he became party to that version of romanticism that flowered in America during the middle decades of the last century. From his time at Brook Farm and Fruitlands, Isaac Hecker was a "critical insider" to transcendentalism both as a religious outlook and as an intellectual movement. He knew well its literary and philosophical achievements, its humanitarian reform proposals, and its communal experiments. It was from this immediate background that Hecker, "the earnest seeker," entered the Catholic Church and was ordained a priest in 1849.

THE INFLUENCE OF "ROMANTIC DEMOCRACY"

It is important to realize that the same romantic spirit and attitudes which were dominant in the philosophical and religious currents of this period also were present in the social and political atmosphere of this time of "freedom's ferment." Americans of this period, as vigorous proponents of their system of government and devoted optimists about the potential and promise of their country, generated a national self-understanding based on the evident success of the democratic experiment. According to Ralph Henry Gabriel, one of the leading contemporary critics of American intellectual history, democracy to them meant more than the principles and organization of their popular government. In addition to that meaning, there was also a romantic overtone to democracy.[7] Gabriel describes "romantic democracy" as a faith characterized by a congenial cluster of democratic ideals. This American national faith has three main tenets. First, there is the concept of the fundamental law which makes up both the natural and the moral laws and provides the basis for American constitutionalism. The second tenet is the doctrine of the exaltation of the free and responsible individual. Recall that this was the Jacksonian age of the advent of the common man and the time of the establishment of universal male citizen suffrage. An unshakable confidence in the divine destiny and special mission of America makes up the third tenet of the democratic faith which resulted from the awareness, perceptively grasped by de Tocqueville, that a new civilization was emerging in America.[8]

It is not surprising that Hecker was affected by this fervent nationalism and ardent patriotism. Even after years of priestly formation in Europe, when he came to promote the harmony of the Catholic religion with the American civil and political arrangement, he incorporated, rather uncritically, the tenets and attitudes of "romantic democracy" as the backdrop to his apologetical theology. To the extent that he was optimistic about the triumph of the church in America, he was also optimistic about the triumph of American civilization in world history.

Motivated by a missionary zeal and determined to forge an apologetics adapted to the unique national religious situation, Father Hecker always insisted that the exposition of religious belief was to be conditioned by the questions and needs of the day. Through his sermons and lectures, articles and books, he fashioned his theology to meet the peculiarities of the American mind, with which he was well acquainted.[9]

But Hecker's desire to serve the religious needs of the American people eventually brought about his expulsion from the Redemptorist Order.[10] While in Rome defending his request for the foundation of an English-speaking house to permit the American Redemptorists to expand their ministry beyond the German immigrants, Isaac Hecker envisioned the formation of a special community with a mission to the non-Catholic American. Along with three other convert priests who also were Redemptorists, Hecker in 1858 founded the Missionary Society of St. Paul the Apostle, known as the Paulist Fathers. The Paulists were the first religious community for men of native American establishment and their principal apostolate was to work for the conversion of the American people to the Catholic faith.

HECKER'S UNDERSTANDING
OF AMERICAN DEMOCRACY

Prior to taking up the theological issues at stake in Hecker's analysis of democracy, it would be instructive to examine his political understanding of the American democratic republic. From a historical perspective, it was his observation that American political thought resulted from the collected political wisdom and experience of past ages, yet he regarded its actual emergence as a providential occurrence. In fact, he saw the very discovery and settlement of this country as an eminently religious enterprise.

At its very roots American republicanism "was shaped by the recognition of man's natural rights and a trust in his innate capacity for self-government." [11] The fundamental document that best expresses the American political creed is, of course, the Declaration of Independence with its cardinal tenets being the theory of natural rights and the notion of government by consent. This firm and abiding trust in the human capacity for self-government was the feature that distinguished the American system from the prevailing political systems of Europe. We find Hecker saying: ". . . if there be any superior merit in the republican polity of the United States, it consists chiefly in this—that while it adds nothing and can add nothing to man's natural rights, it expresses them more clearly, guards them more securely, and protects them more effectually; so that man, under its popular institutions, enjoys greater liberty in working out his true destiny." [12]

The rights enunciated in the Declaration of Independence, Hecker took to be divine, fundamental and practical, having a basis both in reason and in revelation. They are divine in that they reflect the relation and duties of the creature to the Creator. They are fundamental in that without the enjoyment of them a person is not a human person properly so called. Furthermore, these rights are practical, since they guarantee the possibility of the individual's freely working out his destiny as intended by God.

Therefore, the singular excellence of the American political philosophy was attributed to its unprecedented reliance on the natural virtue and native ability of ordinary citizens. Manifestly, such confidence and trust assumed the dignity of human nature and the value of human reason as well as the presence of natural and inalienable rights.

Since the theory of natural rights served as the primary integrating component of America's national political creed, it accordingly provided the formative principles for the state and federal constitutions. The situation of the separation of church and state under the conditions of religious liberty and religious toleration Hecker heralded as the best arrangement for the Roman Catholic Church in the modern world. With pride he pointed to the important contribution of the Catholic Anglo-Americans of Maryland to the formation of the principle of religious toleration. But it was the disestablishment clause of the Federal Constitution that was identified as the keystone in the arch of American liberties. The First Amendment embodies the principle of the state's incompetency to enact laws controlling matters purely religious, and this noninterference in ecclesiastical affairs secures equal rights and privileges for all religious bodies. Hecker's appreciation of the Federal Constitution agreed with Archbishop Hughes's glowing comment that the Constitution was "a monument of wisdom—an instrument of liberty and right,— unequalled, unrivalled, in the annals of the human race." [13]

Although the Roman Catholic Church has flourished under many forms of government, yet in America, unlike elsewhere, the church was uniquely free to exercise its divine mission. Father Hecker's enthusiastic approval of the constitutional arrangement led him to suggest that the form of government in the United States was preferable for the practice of those virtues which constitute the necessary conditions for the development of the Christian life.[14] The wider the range of personal liberty, the greater would be the possibilities for cooperation with the activity of the Holy Spirit. "Intelligence and liberty are the human environments most favorable to the deepening of personal conviction of religious truth and obedience to the interior movements of an enlightened conscience." [15]

Frequently in his writings Hecker drew the striking contrast between the flourishing prospect for the church in America and its persecuted status in some European countries. Though he disclaimed any intention of propagating the American governmental form, he did want to correct the common misunderstanding among European Catholics, particularly Roman authorities, that the republicanism of the New World promoted religious indifference. Assigning a deeply religious character to the American people, Hecker proposed that the situation of the separation of church and state, as a matter of fact, served to enhance the people's concern for and attention to the moral precepts of the natural law and gospel.

Repeatedly in his lectures to non-Catholics, Father Hecker referred to universal suffrage as the clearest illustration of the recognition of the common citizen's native intelligence and personal responsibility for shaping the nation's destiny. Since the whole fabric of American political society rests on the pivotal belief that all citizens, without distinction of birth or rank, have political rights and duties, he concluded that the possession of free will and reason are the necessary presuppositions of popular government. What this implies is that the understanding of human nature embodied in democratic thought amounts to a purely naturalistic conception of the inherent trustworthiness and innate goodness of human nature.

THE THEOLOGICAL FOUNDATIONS OF DEMOCRACY

From this appreciation of the political principles and institutions of American republicanism, Hecker proceeded to render his theological interpretation of democracy. The starting point of his analysis was an insight that became axiomatic in his thinking, namely, that every political society has a religious bearing which involves a theological dogma as its foundational premise; conversely, that every theological dogma has a special bearing on society and in this consists its political principle.[16]

Once Hecker became aware of democracy's essential relationship and necessary dependence on an adequate conception of human nature, he then realized that democracy was indeed a problem deserving attention and study by American theologians. It was evident to him that the anthropological issue is the article on which democracy stands or falls in a theological sense. Therefore, in every theological-ethical interpretation of democracy the foundational dogmas to be considered and tested are the doctrines regarding human nature, that is, the positions advanced concerning: (1) the original state; (2) the fall therefrom; and (3) the consequences it entailed.

What religious bearing does the American democratic society exhibit? Because our political philosophy is based on a highly optimistic estimate of the human person and insists upon his natural rights, American society manifests a religious bearing that Hecker termed "naturalistic." By this he meant to describe a society whose system of order and government was clearly congruent with the natural law, natural justice, and equality. This meaning of naturalism is implicit in the republican beliefs that man is essentially good and capable of free and responsible actions.[17]

Always Hecker emphasized that the American system is based on truths of the natural order. The truths contained in the Declaration of Independence were not the inventions of Thomas Jefferson or the democratic idealists, but simply are evident truths of reason as expressed in the natural law and also as taught by Catholic theologians for centuries. Likewise the rights affirmed were not granted to us by the state, but in fact are natural rights inseparable from our rational nature. Thus our sacred rights and liberties were not begun or instituted by the War of Independence; that war merely secured those rights and upheld those freedoms.

Since the American democratic society manifests a naturalistic religious bearing, the theological dogmas that provide its foundational premises must necessarily yield support to the natural order and uphold the natural law as well as teach the essential goodness of human nature. The problem then is to decide which of the conflicting theological systems can give sufficient justification to democracy's conception of man.

So, in dramatic contrast to the then current polemic that Catholicism was antagonistic to republican government, Hecker submitted the plausible counterposition that Protestantism was the religion incompatible with democratic principles and institutions because of its doctrine of the depravity of human nature and its rejection of natural law. This inherent antagonism results from "the very spirit and doctrines of Protestantism which were derived from an exaggerated idea of the sovereignty of God and the utter nullity of man." [18] "Luther, Calvin and the generality of Protestants teach that man by the fall lost Reason and Free-will, and that his nature became essentially and totally corrupt. . . . Protestantism, in supposing man deprived of Reason and Free-will, is forced to deny natural rights, law, and justice; for what rights, what law, what justice can exist among creatures without Reason and Free-will?" [19]

Surely such doctrines cannot be reconciled with freedom and natural rights. Indeed the democratic ideals could not flourish in the soil of original sin and predestination. The Reformation dogma of the servitude of the will eliminates both personal and political freedom; the Calvinist doctrines of determinism and election disallow the human effort required to make democracies succeed. Both realistic and romantic democracy were postulated upon faith in the intelligence and rectitude of the common man, and the Calvinist doctrine of the corrupt individual was an impediment to faith in man.[20] Hecker, convinced of that judgment's accuracy, asserted: "Protestantism in its political aspect might be defined as a theocratic corporation composed exclusively of regenerate men of orthodox faith, having for its premise the religious dogma concerning the 'total corruption of human nature,' in consequence of Adam's fall." [21] He was assured that nowhere under Protestant ascendancy had there appeared a republican form of government.

PROTESTANTISM IN AMERICA

To buttress this argument, Hecker reviewed the history of Protestantism in New England where he detected its decay and dissolution. From his standpoint, the decline and fall of Calvinism would be the inevitable consequences of the influence of American political principles on Calvinist belief. The religious creed of the Puritans, he stated, was founded on an extreme supernaturalism, with the depravity of human nature as its primary article. So, when the Puritans conformed their government to suit their religious creed, it resulted in the creation of a theocracy which exclusively restricted the rights and privileges of citizenship to members of the "orthodox" church, the elect. Natural or unregenerate man had no political power. Surely this was not the source of religious liberty and religious toleration in the New World.

Now what has become of Puritanism? Hecker suggested that when the New England Puritans joined the other colonists in the Revolution, they unknowingly embarked on a path that would necessarily modify their religious creed. The rights proclaimed in the Declaration of Independence, in effect, represented the dismantling of the entire theological structure of the Reformation built on the cornerstone of total depravity.[22] The descendants of the Puritans, rather than conforming their political principles to suit their religious beliefs, have instead adapted their religious beliefs to accommodate American political principles. This is the key Father Hecker recommended to comprehend the direction of

American Protestantism in nineteenth-century America: ". . . the genius of republicanism is bearing non-Catholic Americans away to naturalism in religion." [23]

This, he believed, accounted for the genesis of Unitarianism, which he took to be a form of deism or natural religion, "the mere republication of the law of Nature." Both Unitarianism and Transcendentalism were the spontaneous developments of the New England mind in protest against the false Christianity of Calvinism. Both were greatly influenced by the American political experience. The Unitarians sought a more rational system of theology which agreed with the dictates of conscience. Calvinism and Unitarianism are antipodal: ". . . the extravagant efforts to magnify man were the natural rebound from the opposite extreme of excessive abasement." [24]

It was Hecker's firm conviction that Calvinism excludes republicanism in politics and that republicanism excludes Calvinism in religion. Thus it followed that the naturalistic bearing of the American democratic society worked to efface the distinctive dogmas of Puritanism. The American mind demanded a theological system that respected natural powers and virtues. To those unacquainted with the Catholic faith, naturalism in religion was the only logical escape from Calvinism. Hecker actually felt that those persons who had "fallen back on human nature" would in time enter the Catholic Church. Robert D. Cross correctly noticed the autobiographical context for Hecker's hope in the coming conversion of America. Cross writes: "Himself once a 'seeker,' Hecker was convinced that masses of non-Catholics were following the road he had traveled to a state of purely natural religion. . . . Hecker hailed it as an excellent preparation for the acceptance of full Catholicism." [25]

THE CORRELATION
BETWEEN CATHOLICISM AND REPUBLICANISM

On the basis of the foregoing analysis that appeals to theological consistency and historical evidence, Hecker was certain that he had demonstrated the insufficiency and impotency of the Protestant doctrinal system as the religious foundation of democracy.

We then find him advancing a recurrent theme of his apologetics: "Republicanism in politics favors Catholicity in religion; and Catholicity in religion favors republicanism in politics." [26]

As you might expect, he argued that the Catholic religion was the only sufficient basis for democracy. Since the Catholic theological system supports the natural order and upholds the natural law, it alone provides the foundational premises for the naturalistic religious bearing of American society. Further, inasmuch as the Catholic tradition teaches that even after original sin human nature is essentially good, this theological system alone propounds the dogmas which harmonize with the democratic conception of man.

"The Catholic religion, by asserting Reason and Free-will, upholds necessarily natural rights, law, and justice, and supposes that man, by the right use of his faculties, may with the assistance of that grace which God refuses to no one, observe this natural law, and come to the knowledge of the Gospel." [27] To Hecker it seemed obvious that American republicanism presupposed the Catholic teaching regarding the present condition and value of human nature. Furthermore, since the natural order of truths which serves as the foundation of the Catholic theological system also underlies the free institutions of America, he posited and affirmed that the sympathy of American civilization was with Catholicity. "There exists a necessary bond and correlation between the truths contained in the Declaration of Independence and the revealed truths of Christianity, since the truths of the natural order serve as indispensable supports to the body of revealed truths of faith." [28] Plainly there is no antipathy between nature and grace, reason and revelation in Isaac Hecker's theology.

Before closing this examination of Isaac Hecker's interpretation of democracy as a theological problem, I wish to consider one very significant corollary of his position concerning the adequacy and sufficiency of Catholicity as the religious foundation of democracy. Here we encounter the truly remarkable claim of the necessity of Catholicity for the very survival of American democracy. That the Catholic faith alone is capable of preserving and perfecting American institutions was a consistent theme in his writings. Several lines of argumentation were adduced to justify this claim.

Not unexpectedly, Hecker employed the traditional Catholic notion that grace perfects nature. Since the natural and supernatural spring from one and the same divine source, it follows by a necessary law of their existence that they "mutually aid, advance, and complete each other." [29] The natural order of our democratic society will receive its fulfillment and perfection exclusively from the supernatural means available in the Roman Catholic Church. By the acceptance of the Catholic faith the American republic will be elevated to partake in the supernatural destiny of the church.

We must bear in mind that the purpose of Hecker's entire apologetical effort was to persuade his contemporaries that the Roman Catholic Church is the authentic embodiment of Christianity. Also, that the church is the prolongation of the Incarnation in time and as such is the historical medium for divine communion and divine communication. He sought to exhibit in a convincing manner his faith that the church's dogmatic teaching and sacramental system best satisfied the demand for a religion consonant with human reason and commensurate with our moral and spiritual nature. Once this was recognized, then Catholicity would be accepted as the religion best suited for the American people, especially for those who were casting off Calvinism and turning to various forms of religious naturalism.

Hecker also indicated a series of pragmatic reasons for the necessity of Catholicity if democracy were to continue and succeed. It was imperative that the American people acquire and make their own the intellectual, spiritual, and moral benefits and resources present in the Catholic Church. In order to correct the tendency to an exaggerated and false naturalism, it was necessary for Americans to adopt the Catholic theological system which was the unique synthesis of Christianity and republicanism and which exactly coincided with the religious bearing of their society. Hecker once again is affirming the position that Catholicity provides the necessary intellectual basis for popular government. Next he went on to attest that Catholic spirituality, piety, and worship contained the means to satisfy the spiritual needs of

Americans and to sanctify their deeply religious character and aspirations. Furthermore, since Catholics insisted that the teaching authority of their church was the source of the correct interpretation of natural and moral laws, Catholic moral doctrine alone could bring the American people to full ethical responsibility and thereby engender the genuine and lasting reform of society. Recall that we noted earlier Hecker's notion that the legitimate religious agency was the indispensable vehicle to sustain the regeneration and advancement of society. Taken together these moral, spiritual, and intellectual contributions from the Catholic tradition fulfill and satisfy the requisite conditions of the possibility of a unity in religion and action for the American people to correspond to the unity they share in the political order. In Hecker's mind the Catholic faith would therefore serve as the integrating factor in a society otherwise divided and segmented by sectarianism. Yet this does not mean that he desired the unity of church and state. On the contrary, the principle of separation would remain even if the Catholics were in the majority.

I wish to mention another warrant Hecker gave to justify the claim of the necessity of Catholicity for American democracy. If, as he argued, the Catholic faith alone is capable of preserving and perfecting the Union, then it must also have the means of guiding the nation to its destiny. With this theme of the mission of America we find Hecker's acceptance of "romantic democracy" fully articulated. The view that their nation represented a decisive turning point in history, the beginning of a new epoch, was commonplace among Americans of the nineteenth century. To them the ordained mission and divine destiny of America was to realize the most perfect society possible on earth. The errand assigned to the American people was to work out a higher order of civilization than has previously existed, to achieve a new level of society in perfect harmony with Christianity. Such a vision of the vocation of America to realize the ideal of Christian society amounted to nothing less than the establishment of the Kingdom.

Father Hecker and also Orestes Brownson shared this understanding of America's destiny and mission but with one significant qualification. Just as the survival of American democracy was conditioned by America's conversion to Catholicity, so too the possibility of America's realizing its destiny depended on its acceptance of the Catholic religion. As Hecker maintained, for America to become the fit instrument for the spread of God's Kingdom, first the Catholic Church had to Christianize the American nation. Once democracy had been elevated to share in a supernatural destiny, then the mission of America "to give to the world a civilization more in harmony with the principles of the Gospel" would be possible.[30] The civilizing mission of the United States demanded the prior conversion of America to the Catholic faith because such a mission was essentially Catholic. Hecker was thoroughly convinced that only under the guidance and assistance of the Catholic Church could America's role as the instrument of Divine Providence be undertaken. The new order of civilization he envisioned was characterized by the synthesis of Catholicity and republicanism. Surely no sectarian form of Christianity could possibly guide the emergence of this higher order of civilization. The Catholic Church, which he considered the source of unity and progress among nations, once reconciled with democracy would effectuate this transition to the Christian ideal of world community. Such is the course determined by Providence. Hecker says, ". . . the discerning mind will not fail to see that the republic and the Catholic Church are working together under the same divine guidance, forming the various races of men and nationalities into a homogeneous people, and by their united action giving a bright promise of a broader and higher development of man than has been heretofore accomplished." [31] With this we can conclude that for Hecker it was indeed necessary that America be converted to Catholicity, for not only would that guarantee the survival of democracy but also would provide the basis for the triumph of Christianity itself throughout the world. Of course the obvious implication of this line of reasoning is that the triumph of Christianity as Hecker portrayed it would also entail the triumph of democracy.

In this essay I have been suggesting that the work of Isaac Thomas Hecker was a formative stage in the history of the theological-ethical interpretation of democracy. He was among the earliest American religious thinkers to come to the significant realization that democracy itself is a theological problem. Despite certain weaknesses and a definite underdevelopment, Hecker's reflections insightfully centered on the fact that an adequate conception of human nature provides the basis for democratic thought. In a plausible and coherent way, Hecker proposed that the Catholic understanding of human nature was not only the sufficient but also the necessary foundation of democracy.

If Hecker's thought signifies a point of departure in American theology in general, then it surely represents a turning point in American Catholic thought. He took the discussion of the church's place in a democratic state beyond a mere justification for the practical acceptance of the constitutional arrangement to a more theoretical level by raising questions about the nature and needs of a democratic community. In so doing, he was forced to deal with the relevant issues concerning the nature and mission of the church and the meaning of human history. Despite these efforts, the traditional pattern of American Catholic apologetics continued, and two of its leading exponents in the last decades of the nineteenth century were James Cardinal Gibbons and John Lancaster Spalding. Although it is true that Hecker's views were widely known among liberal Catholics both here and in Europe, the exact and direct influence of Hecker's positions on the so-called "Americanist party" (consisting mainly of John Ireland, John Keane, and Denis J. O'Connell) is still under debate among historians.[32] It does seem certain, however, that the condemnation of "Americanism" did abort the emerging Catholic theory of democracy.

According to Daniel Day Williams it is altogether unfortunate that Father Hecker's thesis had not been considered seriously by Protestant theologians. Had it been, the long-delayed discussion of the fundamental problems in the theology of the democratic community might have been undertaken. But it was not until the critique of liberalism offered by Reinhold Niebuhr that we had "the decisive turn in the theological-ethical analysis of the democratic faith." [33] Interestingly, Niebuhr's examination of the foundations of democracy was based on a reappraisal of the Christian doctrine of man, although elaborated in a fashion quite different from that of Hecker.[34]

NOTES

1. In my dissertation in progress, I am concerned with Hecker's entire constructive apologetical theology that was forged principally in response to New England Transcendentalism and American democracy.

2. Robert Gorman, *Catholic Apologetical Literature in the United States (1784–1858)* (Washington, D.C.: Catholic University Press, 1939), p. 1.

3. See John Tracy Ellis, "Church and State: An American Catholic Tradition," in *Perspectives in American Catholicism* (Baltimore: Helicon, 1963), pp. 1–8.

4. Brownson's change of attitude regarding the compatibility of Catholicity and American democracy is reflected in his letters to Hecker. The University of Notre Dame Press is planning to publish a critical edition of the Brownson-Hecker correspondence, to commemorate the 100th anniversary of Brownson's death, in 1976.

5. The most complete and systematic exposition of Brownson's political thought is found in his *The American Republic*, published in book form in 1865.

6. Vincent Holden, *The Yankee Paul* (Milwaukee: Bruce, 1958), pp. 1–17.

7. Ralph Henry Gabriel, *The Course of American Democratic Thought* (New York: Ronald Press, 1956), pp. 14–25.

8. See Alexis de Tocqueville, *Democracy in America*, trans. George Lawrence (Garden City, N.Y.: Doubleday, 1969).

9. Hecker wrote three books: *Questions of the Soul* (New York: Appleton, 1855); *Aspirations of Nature* (New York: James B. Kirner, 1857); and *The Church and the Age* (New York: Office of the Catholic World, 1887).

10. Holden, *op. cit.*, pp. 247–68.

11. Hecker, "Relation of Church and State in America," in *The Church and the Age* (New York: Office of the Catholic World, 1887), p. 67.

12. *Ibid.*, p. 69.

13. Hecker, "The Present and the Future Prospects of the Catholic Faith in the United States of North America," p. 12. Hecker is quoting from a lecture that Hughes delivered in New York in December 1843. I am quoting from the typescript of Hecker's original manuscript which is preserved in the Archives of the Paulist Fathers, New York City. It was translated into Italian and appeared as an article in two issues of *Civiltà cattolica* (3rd series) 8 (1857), pp. 385–402, 513–29, entitled "Reflessione sopra il presente e l'avvenire de cattolicisme negli Stati Uniti d'America."

14. Hecker, "Cardinal Gibbons and American Institutions," in *The Church and the Age*, p. 106.

15. *Ibid.*, p. 108.

16. "This truth, then, if we mistake not, has been clearly shown; that every religious dogma has a special bearing on political society, and this bearing is what constitutes its political principle; and every political principle has a religious bearing, and this bearing involves a religious dogma which is its premise." Hecker, "Relation of Church and State in America," *op. cit.*, p. 79.

17. *Ibid.*, p. 75.

18. *Ibid.*, p. 73.

19. Hecker, "Present and Future Prospects," *op. cit.*, pp. 2–3.

20. Gabriel, *op. cit.*, p. 38.

21. Hecker, "Relation of Church and State in America," *op. cit.*, pp. 73–74.

22. *Ibid.*, p. 74.

23. *Ibid.*, p. 79.

24. *Ibid.*, p. 76.

25. Robert D. Cross, *The Emergence of Liberal Catholicism in America* (Chicago: Quadrangle, 1968), pp. 54–55.

26. Hecker, "Relation of Church and State in America," *op. cit.*, p. 87.

27. Hecker, "Present and Future Prospects," *op. cit.*, p. 3.

28. Hecker, "Relation of Church and State in America," *op. cit.*, pp. 79–80.

29. *Ibid.*, p. 91.

30. Hecker, "Present and Future Prospects," *op. cit.*, p. 8.

31. Hecker, "Relation of Church and State in America," *op. cit.*, p. 99.

32. See Thomas E. Wangler, "John Ireland and the Origins of Liberal Catholicism in the United States," *The Catholic Historical Review*, 56 (1971), pp. 617–29. Also, Margaret Mary Reher, "Pope Leo XIII and 'Americanism'," *Theological Studies* 34 (1973), pp. 679–89.

33. Daniel Day Williams, "Tradition and Experience in American Theology," in *The Shaping of American Religion*, ed. James Ward Smith and A. Leland Jamison (Princeton: Princeton University Press, 1969), pp. 481–82.

34. See Reinhold Niebuhr, *The Children of Light and the Children of Darkness* (New York: Scribner's, 1944).

ELIZABETH K. MCKEOWN

catholic identity
in america

The chief ingredients in the American Catholic experience have been the pluralism of American society and the ethnic
diversity of the American church. The formal disestablishment of
religion, the development of Protestant denominationalism, and
the development of American urban-industrialism in the nineteenth century created a society marked by a proliferation of
competing beliefs and institutions, while the immigration of
millions of Europeans to this country during the same period
created an ethnic pluralism which produced lasting internal
problems for American Catholicism. This pluralistic situation
presented the Catholic Church with two challenges: to develop
cohesion among its diverse membership, and to achieve some
effective voice in the direction of American society. Thus the task
of Catholic leaders has been to develop an identity for American
Catholicism, to provide a distinct character that would prevent it
from becoming ineffectual in its pluralistic American environment.

This article will deal with some attempts to foster that
American Catholic identity during the first decades of this
century. It will propose that the first efforts toward such an
identity—through various national federations and societies—
were unsuccessful, but that the solidarity among Americans
engendered by World War I enabled Catholics in this country to

believe that their Catholicism and their Americanism were, at the
very least, compatible.

THE DANGERS OF PLURALISM

In the era prior to World War I, sociologist William Kerby of The
Catholic University produced an excellent analysis of the American church in relation to American pluralism. Giving specific
recognition to the fact of pluralism in a fashion unprecedented
among American Catholic commentators, Kerby discussed the
necessary steps which the church in America must take to provide
"natural social reinforcements of the bonds of faith." [1] His
description of the dangers of pluralism concentrates especially on
the organizational variety of American society. Growing numbers
of social affiliations competed for the attention of Americans, and
their diversity tended to prevent any one institution or organization from commanding the complete loyalty of the individual. The
influence of the church in the lives of its members was thus
seriously threatened, not so much by any one organization,
whether labor union, political party or fraternal society, but by
the combined impact of the organizational diversity of American
life.

Kerby feared the church would play an ever diminishing role in
the lives of Catholics. He noted a growing indifference to religion
in the culture at large, and was aware that religious belief was fast
becoming confined to the personal and private sector of American
life:

> Business, locality, like taste or culture, similar pursuits or
> ambition, these are usually final in fixing our associations.
> . . . There is consequently a tendency to indifference
> concerning a man's religion. . . . The interests and sym-
> pathies which men have in common monopolize conversa-
> tion, attention, while religion and its particular interests
> silently recede from our social intercourse. Hence our own
> religion tends to become a matter of more personal con-
> cern. . . . [2]

This drift toward privatization of religion paralleled the growth in possibilities for social affiliation outside the church and was resulting, Kerby thought, in a situation where the Catholic could expect no reinforcement, positive or negative, for his distinctive religious posture from the larger society that engaged most of his attention. Correspondingly, the church was faced with a shrinking sphere of influence.

For Kerby the pluralism of American society with multiple and competing systems of affiliation and belief was so pervasive as to be inescapable. Because withdrawal from such a structure was impossible, his remedy was to urge church leaders to prepare the church to compete for influence in the lives of Catholics and the culture at large—to organize and fight for attention. Specifically, he encouraged church leaders to improve upon the modes and opportunities for association among Catholics and to develop among ethnically diverse American Catholics a unified viewpoint and common identity. Rational assent to dogma and even participation in sacramental and liturgical functions were not enough. Belonging, he argued, was also a matter of "feeling," of inspirational leadership, a sense of history, evocative symbols, mass demonstrations of group strength, and even common experience of attack or antagonism from the outside world.

By the time America entered World War I, Kerby had specified his proposal even further and was vigorously campaigning with the Paulist John Burke and others for a national organization of hierarchy and laity to implement his vision of a coherent American Catholic identity. Such an organization was advocated for two reasons: to overcome the wide divisions based on ethnicity within the American church, and to enable the church to exercise leverage in public affairs at least commensurate with its numbers. The result of the efforts of Burke and Kerby and their associates was the formation of the National Catholic War Council, the predecessor of the present United States Catholic Conference and its counterpart the National Conference of Catholic Bishops.[3]

Although the formation of a single nationwide organization of Catholics was a difficult task, the first decades of the twentieth century were in fact years during which Catholic societies proliferated. These were generally of a social and fraternal character, often organized along the lines of nationality, and they were of some worth in providing security, charity, and social outlets for the Catholic population. But, precisely because of their ethnic orientation and local scope, they failed to provide Catholics with an adequate notion of their church in its American context, and thus were only of indirect help in meeting the challenges of pluralism.

THE EMERGENCE
OF VARIOUS NATIONAL ASSOCIATIONS

The first effort at forming some association which would bring Catholics together at a national level had actually been initiated by a group of laymen led by Henry Brownson, a Detroit lawyer and son of Orestes Brownson. This group organized a Catholic congress that was held in Baltimore in conjunction with the centennial celebration of the American hierarchy in 1889.[4] The congress was notable for the participation it evoked from the laity and for the few clerical figures it attracted. Without episcopal cooperation any effort to develop a national voice was doomed to failure. A second attempt at a national congress held in conjunction with the Columbian Exposition of 1893 in Chicago similarly failed to provide American Catholics with a lasting form of national organization.[5]

The slight influence of these gatherings underscored one difficulty in the struggle for American Catholic cohesion, namely, the minor role played by the laity in church life. William Kerby stressed the desirability of giving the laity an active share in church government, for although he did not consider such participation to be part of the church's constitution, he argued that it was a necessary factor in the development of Catholic cohesion in the present society: "The age is democratic and practically all great social groups depend on this share in government to foster interest and loyalty among their members." [6]

The editor of *Catholic World*, John Burke, supported Kerby in this view and complained that the existing organization of the church made the layman a complete extern and produced in him a consequent lack of group consciousness. Like Kerby, the Paulist placed the blame on ecclesiastical authorities, whose manner of governing prevented lay participation.[7] Burke was especially aware of the contributions which could be made by members of the laity who had become professionals and who were versed in some specialty. He argued that it should be the responsibility of the clergy to consult with these people and to incorporate their expertise into ecclesiastical decision-making. In every field the priest "should find the material for decisions, not out of his own head—as so often happens—but from specialists and authorities in fields in which he is to decide." [8]

Burke felt that this principle should be applied to financial, sociological, literary, and pedagogical fields. His concern illustrates a growing awareness among Catholic spokesmen in the years prior to World War I of the great diversification going on in American society and of the competence in secular matters made necessary by that diversification. Organizing and incorporating the laity became a major goal of these leaders in their effort to adapt the church to American pluralism.

In general this desire bore little fruit, but in the prewar decades there were a number of organizational efforts among Catholic professionals and the laity at large. In the fields of education, health, social work, and journalism, Catholics formed national organizations which brought both clerics and laymen together to consult on problems within their common professions. In 1904 the formation of the Catholic Educational Association incorporated three groups of Catholic educators—the Educational Conference of Seminary Faculties, the Association of Catholic Colleges, and the Parish School Conferences—into a national organization. John Burke himself became a leading figure in the formation between 1908 and 1911 of the Catholic Press Association, and the Catholic Hospital Association met for the first time in 1915 with a goal of standardizing procedures in Catholic hospitals in the United States.

One of the most prominent of these new professional groups was the National Conference of Catholic Charities, which held its first meeting in September 1910. William Kerby carried his theory into practice in organizing the conference, and remained as its secretary until 1920. In this capacity he continued to emphasize the need for new forms of affiliation among Catholics and for organizations with a scope that would go beyond the individual dioceses.[9] In his often repeated view, the social demands of American society were more complex than anything the church had previously experienced, and an adequate response depended on national unity and a common outlook on the part of Catholics.

Probably the most successful national association of Catholics in the United States prior to World War I was the Knights of Columbus. This organization, or "order," was started in New England in the 1880s, principally among Irish-American Catholics to help them overcome what they felt to be strong social and economic disadvantages stemming from their religious and ethnic backgrounds. A variety of fraternal societies were flourishing during this period, and most of them embodied elements of oath-taking and ritualism which effectively barred Catholic participation. Catholics who enjoyed enough of a socioeconomic achievement to recognize the benefits of such organizations were anxious to initiate something similar for their own church members. As a result, the Knights of Columbus became quite popular and spread across the country and among Canadian Catholics in the first decades of the order's existence. The organization provided insurance and other "temporal benefits" as well as a new basis for social prestige among Catholics who felt keenly the ostracism resulting from their faith.

The earliest rituals of the order emphasized the American character of its Catholic members. In 1903 a ritual was added to provide the membership with an elite corps of "Knights of the Fourth Degree." As with each of the other three degrees of progress through the order, the Fourth Degree had its own particular theme and criteria for achievement. To receive this honor a Knight had to be a proven patriot; his civic contributions were assessed as the basis of his acceptance. At his initiation banquet he received a baldric of red, white, and blue; a sword; and the emblem of the degree. The latter was "a representation of a dove carrying the Cross to the New World," and it underscored the Knights' conviction that with Christopher Columbus, Catholicism became a fundamental element in the American story.[10]

In yet another chapter of Catholic organizational life, the growth of associations of the laity on local and diocesan levels led in 1900 to a movement to form a national federation of Catholic societies.[11] The organizations which dominated this movement were ethnic in character: the Irish-American Ancient Order of Hibernians and Irish Catholic Benevolent Union, and the German-American Knights of St. John and German Catholic Central Verein. These lay groups had some episcopal backing—similarly ethnic—from Bishop James McFaul of Trenton and Archbishop Sebastian Messmer of Milwaukee.

The thrust of the American Federation of Catholic Societies was decidedly political. Bishop McFaul argued, for example, that the church was being overlooked by the larger society because it had remained silent or a-political, and had not advocated measures that would be to its benefit.[12] His views implied that in order to compete successfully for prominence in American society, the church must become overtly political, forming a special-interest group, a bloc of Catholic votes to be levied when necessary in the interests of the church.

Not surprisingly, the Federation ran into opposition and failed to get strong hierarchical support. The reasons given by the bishops for their reluctance were varied. Some feared the movement would alienate public opinion and lead to another of the recurrent waves of anti-Catholicism. Others feared lay interference in ecclesiastical affairs, or suspected that a national organization would eventually challenge the traditional autonomy of the bishops in their own dioceses.

Whatever their reasons for rejecting the Federation, this particular episode brings into focus perhaps the major problem in achieving American Catholic identity, namely, the lack of episcopal consensus on the shape which that identity should assume. Ethnic differences among the bishops accounted for much of the episcopal disagreement and led to intense and prolonged friction among factions within the hierarchy over the proper stance of the church in relation to its American situation.[13] Contrary to the outsider's general impression of conformity among bishops, the history of the American hierarchy is filled with struggle over the problems encountered in adapting Catholicism to American culture. In the late nineteenth century episcopal tempers frequently boiled over and gave rise to acrimonious public debate.

Some bishops during this period demanded that the church be isolated from the larger society, separated as much as possible from potential dangers, internally organized but withdrawn. Others argued that the church must assert itself publicly if it hoped to retain significance in the lives of its members. In the wake of this "Americanist" controversy, which was replete with papal admonitions, the bishops tended to withdraw to their separate diocesan jurisdictions where they enjoyed a great deal of autonomy. Only Rome could interfere with a bishop in his own diocese, and Rome in general was remote. The net result of this pattern of withdrawal was that the challenges of the American environment to the church were not met in any unified or systematic fashion by the hierarchy. A vacuum was created which left the development of a coherent American Catholic identity to chance.

THE INFLUENCE OF WORLD WAR I

The church without an integral identity was immensely susceptible to the influences of the larger culture, to having its own influence co-opted from the outside. Pressures toward social conformity, economic advancement, and the privatizing of moral impulse all weighed from the outside upon Catholics who were not equipped to deal with such challenges. In this vulnerable condition the church was suddenly confronted with the all-absorbing national experience of World War I. The eighteen months of American involvement in that conflict left a deep and lasting mark on American Catholicism.

In the period from August 1914 to April 1917, when the United States declared war, the American hierarchy remained neutral and generally silent on the conflict. Given the ethnic diversity among Catholics, neutrality was an appropriate stance. But President Woodrow Wilson's decision to go to war galvanized the Catholic leadership of the country. The hierarchy, in official pronouncements, sermons, and informal addresses in support of war-mobilization programs, gave overwhelming support to the

policies of the United States government.[14] Urban and rural
bishops, German- and Irish-American bishops, northern and
southern bishops, all showed a startling degree of unanimity.
Occasional criticism of the war by lesser church members of
German or Irish descent (the Irish, of course, were not fond of
England and English enterprises) were opposed and sometimes
suppressed by church officials.

The immediate explanation for this sudden and unprecedented
unanimity among Catholics was the position Catholics occupied in
American society during this period. By and large they were still
second-class citizens, regarded by other Americans as outsiders,
suspected because of their foreign ways and ethnic backgrounds.
In light of the overwhelming public sentiment in favor of the war,
anything less than wholehearted promotion of the war by Catholic
leaders would have undoubtedly led to local reprisals against
church members.

But the response of the hierarchy was not merely prudential or
defensive. Bishops and other leaders grasped the fact that for the
first time the United States government very much needed
Catholic cooperation. Government officials in charge of military
mobilization, loan drive programs, food and fuel conservation
efforts, and other wartime endeavors actively sought Catholic
support. This experience of being consulted and needed was
heady, and Catholics were jubilant over the prospect of winning
for the church a prominent place in public life. In addition,
wartime fervor tended to repress ethnic differences among
Americans in favor of an Americanized nationalism. This, in turn,
tended to soften the differences dividing American Catholics. And
so, in response to these opportunities and advantages offered by
the war, Catholic leaders embraced the American cause. More
than that, there was wide agreement among those leaders that the
war aims announced by President Wilson were decidedly Christian in their intent. Comparisons were frequently made between
the goals of Woodrow Wilson and those of Benedict XV in the
latter's effort to bring peace to the West.

Behind this wartime enthusiasm, an important and uncritical
consensus was emerging. Catholic leaders had increasingly come
to believe that the American experience had a Christian sub-

stance, and they saw that experience as the natural base upon which the supernatural could readily be established. Catholicism, they imagined, was the institution most important in the realization of true Americanism. The church with its traditions of authority, obedience, and doctrinal uniformity could educate millions of American Catholics in the principles of religion, civic duty, and morality, and thereby provide the American experiment with the spiritual core necessary to its success. Protestantism, fraught as it was with the difficulties of denominational life, had failed in the estimate of Catholic leaders to be such a spiritual center for America; and this failure created a vacuum in American life, a vacuum which would be properly filled only by the church. This uncritical equation of America with Christianity and the desire to substitute Catholicism for Protestantism in American society short-circuited the question of American Catholic identity by placing the burden of definition ultimately upon American civic leaders—whatever it meant to be a good American was also, with the addition of doctrinal orthodoxy and conformity to ecclesiastical duties, what it meant to be a good Catholic.

This wartime resolution of the question of American Catholic identity remained a major element of American Catholicism for the next half century, and yet it was seriously flawed. It failed in particular to take into critical account the pluralism of American life. The large divisions of belief and outlook, of economic and social class in America, submerged as they were by wartime fervor, were glossed over or ignored by Catholic leaders, as were the persistent and growing difficulties resident in the conviction that "America was at heart a Christian country." The uncritical Americanization of Catholic identity was, of course, an effective measure for producing conformity, if not cohesion, among ethnically diverse Catholics. By encouraging the transformation of nationalist sentiments of ethnic Catholics into wartime Americanism, Catholic leaders managed to diffuse many of the otherwise troublesome ethnic situations within dioceses and parishes. One need not become an Irishman to be a good Catholic, so the perception now seemed to go; one might become a good American instead.

But while the war was helpful in this sense, creating a certain kind of American Catholic identity and conformity, it set Catholics up to be seriously shaken by every major political upheaval experienced by the country at large and to be uncritical followers of American public sentiment. Catholic leaders failed in general to give proper attention to the basic pluralism of American society which in itself disallowed a unitary view of that society. It was apparent to some observers even before World War I that there was little chance that Americans would develop a uniform and constant character, let alone that such a character could be sustained by the civic devotion of Catholics. And yet the tenuously Americanized Catholicism that emerged from World War I remained a major element in the identity of Catholics for nearly a half century until the events of Vatican II and Vietnam shook church and country to their respective roots. Those events opened a period of painful reevaluation for Catholic Americans as they considered the relationship between commitments stemming from religious convictions and those stemming from patriotic allegiance.

NOTES

1. William Kerby, "Reinforcement of the Bonds of Faith," *Catholic World* 84 (January 1907), pp. 508–22; (February 1907), pp. 591–606.

2. *Ibid.*, p. 515.

3. A detailed study of the National Catholic War Council and its implications for American Catholicism may be found in Elizabeth McKeown, "War and Welfare: A Study of American Catholic Leadership, 1917–1922," Ph.D. diss., Divinity School of the University of Chicago, 1972. The materials discussed in that study are from the archives of The Catholic University of America and from the archives of the United States Catholic Conference.

4. *Official Report of the Proceedings of the Catholic Congress Held in Baltimore, Maryland, November 11–12, 1889* (Detroit: William H. Hughes, Publisher, 1889).

5. Sr. Sevine Pahorezki, *The Social and Political Activities of William*

James Onahan (Washington: Catholic University Press, 1942). See also *Progress of the Catholic Church in America and the Great Columbian Catholic Congress of 1893*, 2 vols. (2nd ed.; Chicago: J. S. Hyland and Co., 1897).

6. Kerby, *op. cit.*, p. 516.

7. John J. Burke to William Kerby, November 7, 1906. *Kerby Papers*, Archives of Catholic University of America.

8. *Ibid.*, January 5, 1907.

9. *Proceedings*, First National Conference of Catholic Charities (Washington: Catholic University Press, 1910).

10. John B. Kennedy and Maurice F. Egan, *Knights of Columbus in Peace and War*, 2 vols. (New Haven: Knights of Columbus Press, 1920). The Knights compiled this two-volume history of their order after the Armistice to explain their part in the war and to furnish proof of having fulfilled all obligations toward country. The work is, in part, a survey of social relations between more prosperous Catholics and their Protestant and non-Catholic counterparts. Because the account is rendered from a postwar viewpoint, it provides an illuminating description of those organizational developments and national self-awareness in American Catholicism which gained precedence during the early part of the century.

11. Sr. Mary Adele Frances Gorman has provided a history of the Catholic federation movement in "Federation of Catholic Societies in the United States, 1870–1920," Ph.D. diss., Department of History, University of Notre Dame, 1961.

12. James A. McFaul, "Catholics and American Citizenship," *North American Review* 171 (September 1900); and James A. McFaul, "Catholic Grievances—Their Remedy," *American Ecclesiastical Review* 23 (December 1900).

13. There were 133 members of the American hierarchy during the years of World War I. Of this number, fifty-three were foreign-born, and many of the rest were of second-generation extraction. A breakdown of those of foreign birth provides an accurate projection of the ethnic composition of the whole hierarchy. There were twenty-eight born in Ireland and one in England. There were six German-born bishops, two from Switzerland and one from Austria. Five were born in France, three each in Belgium and Holland, and one in Luxembourg. There were two Italians and one Canadian bishop. All of these men immigrated to America either prior to or just subsequent to their ordination to the priesthood.

14. In the summer of 1918 George Creel, chairman of the Committee

on Public Information, a government propaganda agency organized to help mobilize public opinion in support of American participation in the war, requested that a collection be made of all sermons, speeches, and pastorals of the American hierarchy that had been or would be issued during the course of the war. Creel's intention was to publish a volume under the auspices of the Committee on Public Information entitled "The Catholic Hierarchy and the War." Although the volume was never published, the Creel request resulted in the assembling of a wide selection of official Catholic pronouncements on the war, as well as an abundance of news clippings detailing episcopal wartime activities.

II.

Religion and American Culture

FRANKLIN H. LITTELL

the radical reformation
and the american experience

The influential role of sectarian Protestantism in America has long been recognized by specialists. William Warren Sweet of Chicago, for many years the leading Protestant interpreter of American church history, wrote in the first edition of his popular textbook:

> The one fact, more than any other, which explains American religion in the period of the colonies is that the colonial churches were largely planted by religious radicals. With hardly an exception, the leaders in the establishment of the American colonies were liberal and even radical in both their religious and political views. Political and religious radicalism naturally went hand in hand.[1]

Kenneth Scott Latourette of Yale and others affirmed a similar interpretation, not infrequently carrying the emphasis upon radical Protestantism in America on through the great century of missions and revivalism.

Although Professor Sweet's elision of "liberal and even radical" positions confuses rather than clarifies, he was correct in assigning a heavy input in America to the men and women of the Radical Reformation. Not only in Pennsylvania, which the beneficiaries of the New England standing order called the "latrina" of the early colonies, but from Plymouth Rock to Ebenezer, Georgia, the

radicals of Protestantism played in America a significant role that
was denied them in the Old World.

WHAT WAS "THE RADICAL REFORMATION"?

A group of scholars operating for nearly a decade under the
unlikely umbrella of an organization called The North American
Committee for the Documentation of Free Church Origins, an
affiliate of the Center for Reformation Research in St. Louis, has
defined the formative period as the years 1525 to 1675—from the
time when the first believers' baptism was introduced at Zurich to
when Jakob Philip Spener's *Pia Desideria* began its wide circula-
tion among pious Protestants. This century and a half saw the
emergence and clear formulation of Anabaptism, Antitrinitarianism, revolutionary Christianity, the individual Protestant spiritualizers, radical Puritanism, and radical Pietism—in brief, the whole
restitutionist melange which contemporary scholarship distinguishes from the "magisterial Reformation" [2] of the mainline
Reformers. The radical reformers were not simply those who took
more seriously than most the concerns of the sixteenth-century
Protestant Reformation. Neither were they simply going beyond it
and moving more rapidly. They had, in fact, an utterly different
position from the Reformers—in world-view, in periodization of
church history, in assessment of Christian priorities, in definition
of a Christian style of life.

There is a geological faultline between the state-church Reformers who continued the medieval territorial and parish definition of the *corpus christianum*, and the radicals, who espoused not
reformatio but *restitutio*, who envisioned the True Church *(die
rechte Kirche)* as a covenant people united in voluntary membership. The conceptualization of the voluntary covenant took
various forms. Three of them have been singled out in the left
wing of the Reformation by James Leo Garrett, Jr.: "covenant-
kingdom" (e.g., Thomas Müntzer), "covenant-community" (e.g.,
Peter Ridemann of the Hutterites), and "covenant-brotherhood"
(e.g., Pilgram Marpeck of the South German Brethren.)[3] But
whatever the model of covenant, and there were many other

schemes as well—and for those who like landmarks and symbolic dates we might mention that the first formal congregational covenant of which we have documentation was sealed at Frankfurt/Main in 1528—the thrust of the adult covenant was subversive of the interlocking and mutually supportive relationships which the post-Constantinian Western world had taken for granted for centuries.

The choice had to be made between "Christendom" and voluntary covenant, although it took generations for the tension to be resolved and some of the major implications of the dissolution of the Constantinian pattern to be perceived. In the Boston area, for example, it was not until the legal split of the Trinitarian Congregationalists and Unitarian Congregationalists in 1819 (the Dedham Case) that the tension between a church style based on adult Christian profession and a church style based on tax support and political appointment worked itself out in schism. In the meantime, as C. C. Goen's classic study has shown,[4] other radical Protestant impulses in New England had already produced nearly one hundred independent congregations which not only stood for the covenant (in theological terminology) and voluntaryism (in sociological language) but also—on Christian terms—advocated separation. "Separation" meant that the church was responsible for her own discipline and that civil government should be secular rather than sacral.

But the historical events are racing ahead of our typological patterns. Let me give a brief outline of the sixteenth-century radical Protestant groups and indicate something of the Free Church chronology which leads from that time to this. During the first decade of protest, from the first adult baptism at Zollikon bei Zurich (January 1525) to the successful siege of revolutionary Münster by the combined forces of the Protestant Landgraf Philipp von Hessen and the Roman Catholic Bishop Franz von Waldeck in 1535, there was a great variety of individual and group radicalism. Fairly early, however, four types emerged which have had permanent historical impact. All four types were as critical of the magisterial Reformation as they were of Roman Catholicism. All four types adopted a primitivist view of history and proclaimed a new periodization of church history which relegated the state-church Reformers—men like Martin Luther, Ulrich Zwingli and Martin Butzer—to the Dark Ages.[5]

The four major types of Christians discernible in the Radical Reformation are the following, and they have their spiritual offspring and counterparts in American colonial and contemporary Protestantism.

First, the *Anabaptists*. Scholars now distinguish four wings of Anabaptism: the Swiss Brethren, whose most important leader was Conrad Grebel; the South German Brethren, of whom Pilgram Marpeck was the dominant figure; the Hutterites, named for Jakob Huter; the Mennonites, named for Menno Simons. There were differences among teachers and groups. For example, the Swiss paid the war tax and the Hutterites criticized them for it; the Dutch *Doopsgezinde* sometimes used shunning *(Meidung)* —the avoidance of all contact with a recalcitrant member—as well as dis-fellowshiping, and the South Germans objected to their "legalism"; Balthasar Hübmaier defended magisterial use of the sword—whereas almost all Anabaptists were New Testament nonresistants; some of the Polish radicals were both Anabaptist in ecclesiology and Antitrinitarian in theology—whereas almost all Anabaptists adhered to what is called the Nicene Creed. But all were agreed that a "fall of the church" had occurred after the golden age of the New Testament church, probably with the union of church and state under Constantine the Great, and that the program for the future was a return to a virtue lost in the past.

Second, the *Antitrinitarians*. For them the "fall" occurred when the scientists of theology replaced the simple, heartfelt religion and ethical concern of the apostolic church with the Trinitarian dogma, the creeds and glosses of Schoolmen. Later, the often highly educated leaders of the Antitrinitarians developed sophisticated systems of critical philosophy, but at first the Antitrinitarians were champions of "the simple gospel." Even Michael Servetus called his program *Restitutio Christianismi*. A parallel transition from New Testament simplicity to rationalism can be traced in the Antitrinitarianism of groups in Holland, England, and America. In the process they lost most of their radicalism and virtually all of their eschatology: in the New England split,

Unitarianism stood for the traditional legal establishment and for Christendom against the "enthusiasm" of the evangelical, covenanting volunteers. The Disciples of Christ or Christian churches, on the other hand, took their stand as a "Restoration Movement" on the original antirationalistic grounds: they condemned philosophical and theological dispute, not dismantling the Trinitarian systems but holding to New Testament language and refusing to speculate. "Where the Bible speaks we speak; where the Bible is silent we are silent."

Third, the *religious revolutionaries*. Here the most substantial documentation surrounds the career of Thomas Müntzer, who died during the Thuringian Peasants' War, and the revolutionary regime at Münster in Westphalia (1534–35). Private property was the chief mark of the "fall." All groups in the Radical Reformation, even the most consistently nonresistant, believed that the Restitution of the True Church was predictive of the "restoration of all things" (Acts 3:21) to the truth and virtue and beauty they had before sin and corruption defaced the earth. Communism and peace and spiritual communication identify both the church at Jerusalem and the lost Eden. Among the revolutionaries, the restitution and the restoration were telescoped, and the rough war harness of David replaced the gentle yoke of Jesus. The final battle of the forces of good and evil was at hand, when those who have opposed God's law shall be slain by his fighting angels. For the wicked live only by the sufferance of the righteous . . . (cf. Exod. 23:7).

Fourth, the *Spiritualisten*—the "Third Type" in Ernst Troeltsch's *The Social Teachings of the Christian Churches*[6]—better translated as "spiritualizers" than "spiritualists." The representatives of this type were individuals who opposed all creedal and institutional controls, for example, internal church discipline as well as supervision of religion by princes and town councils. For them, true religion was inward, hidden and primordial—*unpartheyisch*, anteceding not only contemporary sects and cults but also found among the righteous *(alle guthertzige Leute)* of many nations and cultures. Sebastian Franck, author of the *Weltbuch* (the greatest survey of human history of the sixteenth century), and Caspar Schwenckfeld, great champion of freedom of conscience, were two of the outstanding persons of this type. The "fall" was for them indicated by outwardness—repressive governments, hierarchies, sect rules and regulations, formalism and liturgy. With the triumph of the Ternal Gospel in the Age of the Spirit, God would write directly on the human heart and unmediated truth would redeem the race.

The primitivist motif [7] involved a new periodization of history, and it is here that the contribution of Joachim of Fiore to Western radicalism—political as well as religious—must be noted. From the time of the radical Franciscans' struggle with the papacy, a new and explosive interpretation of the course of history moved outward in ever wider circles. According to the view which had prevailed from the time of Augustine and Orosius, the Ascension of Christ and the Second Coming bracketed a single period of history, a period unmarked by events of any special salvific note. Joachim's disciples broke history into three periods: the Age of the Father, of the Old Testament, of law on tablets of stone; the Age of the Son, of the New Testament, of the *Lex Christi* transmitted in liturgy and sacramental grace; the Age of the Spirit, when creeds and formalism shall pass away and alienation between persons be ended throughout the earth.[8]

Each previous age gives birth to the new in pain and agony. Each new age is introduced by a "man of miracles" (e.g., Moses, Jesus, Francis of Assisi) who proclaims the old truth *(Evangelium Aeternum)* in its new form. It is interesting to note, in this day of vocal feminism, that by the time of "Mother" Ann Lee of the Shakers and "Mother" Mary Baker Eddy of Christian Science, the possibility arises that the *Wundermensch* may be a woman. In other understandings of the New Age, androgynous man reappears. Tension and alienation based on sex will disappear along with war and violence, slavery and exploitation, all coercion of human soul and conscience.

Where did the new periodization arise? Calabria, the center of Joachim's work, was but a generation away from two centuries of Muslim rule. Roger, the first Norman king of Calabria and Sicily, kept many Islamic institutions and struck coins with one side Koranic. Roger II, king of the "Two Sicilies," spoke Arabic, used a Muslim royal seal, ran a court and financed a palace school with heavy Muslim staffing. The threefold periodization, with a culminating spiritual age superseding both Judaism and Christianity, is a standard device of historical interpretation among Muslim teachers. Upon extensive circumstantial evidence of this sort, scholars like Henry Bett and G. G. Coulton have openly attributed Joachim's periodization of history to Muslim influence. According to Coulton, Joachim's main theories "would seem to owe far more to Islam, which essentially rests upon this idea of successive revelations, each complementing and to a great extent superseding its predecessor, and all culminating finally in the Prophet." [9] The matter will be more definitively settled in the next few years by some young scholar trained in the history of religions and using Arabic as well as Latin and German. In the meantime, we know that some of the radicals—including Thomas Müntzer—read both Joachim and the Koran. And we know too that Joachim was the first Christian teacher to break the traditional periodization of church history and that his spiritual progeny are today, like the sands of the seashore, innumerable.

Karl Marx's "withering away of the state" is a secularization of Joachim's "withering away of the church" at the transition from the second to the third age. From Adolf Hitler's "Third Reich" to Theodor Reik's "Third Consciousness," this powerful appeal of the triadic typology is evident. For our purposes here, it is significant that August Hermann Francke (the great teacher and statesman of Halle Pietism) and Cotton Mather (the prodigy of New England Puritanism) could carry on a correspondence for years in which they used without question such Joachimite terms as "Age of the Spirit" and "Eternal Gospel." [10]

Just as unquestioningly, Francke and Mather took for granted the chronological primitivism of the Radical Reformation, with the early church normative, the "fall" identified with Constantine, and the Restitution now beginning—accompanied by all the glorious signs of the return of the Spirit to floodtide.

THE "AMERICAN ISRAEL"

One of the characteristics of most radical Protestant churches, especially evident in Pentecostalism but by no means limited to it, is this significant theological sign: they prefer to speak of divine initiative in the church in the language of the Third Person rather than the Second Person of the Holy Trinity.[11] Sometimes, as in the Hicksite split of the Quakers, they have even moved outside the ancient boundaries set by the *filioque* affirmation and spoken of the light given to the gentiles. Early Quaker leaders carefully identified "the Indwelling Word" with "Christ within," and Robert Barclay even wrote a major treatise on the church as "the Body of Christ," but in later generations the spiritualizing undertow of radical Protestantism led many Quakers as well as other radicals to affirm a promiscuous doctrine of the Spirit and its works.

In many Radical Reformation circles, the restitution of the True Church introduced the Age of the Spirit. Thus the historical perspective of Christian restitutionism was welded to the driving power of a general millennialism. The Age of the Spirit, for them, was that transition period in which the whole earth was filled with the signs and wonders which had accompanied the coming of Christ and the impact of the first Christians. They sought eagerly for the signs of the times.

Francke and Mather agreed that the evidence of the new age was twofold: first, the flowering of worldwide missions, with the predicted first fruits of a multitude of tribes and nations being baptized into the covenant; second, the rising ecumenical cooperation of many previously divided churches in the task of world evangelization, with an impending restoration of the one, undivided True Church. Among many Protestants, other signs of the new age were these: (1) the invention of printing, which made the Bible accessible to the layman in his ministry; (2) the restitution of true Christianity and/or the purification of Christian teaching in the sixteenth century; (3) the discovery of America.

The discovery of America was no factor at all in Martin Luther's thought. It had, however, a striking impact on later Lutheran and Reformed thought, when the import of the discovery finally penetrated theological minds. It took about a century and a half for this to happen. Against the Anabaptist missioners, men of the first generation of the Reformation stoutly maintained that the gospel could not be served by rootless land-rovers, but only by those properly licensed by the authorities, who stayed in the places where they were put. The Great Commission had been exhausted during the time of the Twelve and the Seventy, when the message had been carried to the four corners of the earth and some people had responded and others had rejected the Lord. In the middle of the seventeenth century a Dutchman named Adrian Saravia awoke to the fact that none of the apostolic missionaries could possibly have visited America, and that therefore a new initiative had to be launched in Christian missions. That new initiative finally surged upward in the Reformed and Lutheran churches as a result of Pietism—the missionary societies founded in the territorial churches and the communities of renewal of the Moravians.

The Anabaptists, on the other hand, were from the beginning never impeded by commitments to Christendom: they said that the baptized heathen *(getauftes Heidentum* = Christendom) of Europe were as much in need of hearing, converting, and being baptized on profession of faith as were the Turks or others. Indeed, there is a curious report from Zurich during the imprisonment of leaders of the Swiss Brethren in 1525. According to the handwritten document, some spoke of leaving Europe and going over the sea *zuo den roten -den* (to the red *-den*). Emil Egli's sourcebook of 1879[12] prints *Juden;* Ernst Correll suggested a few years ago that the word was *Inden.* In fact, the iota is written long, and today we cannot be sure which they meant. But they certainly meant America, and they may have meant both *Juden* and *Inden.* For at least by a century later the idea was widespread among radical Protestants, including such men as Oliver Cromwell and William Penn, that the American Indians were descendants of the Ten Lost Tribes of Israel.

The greatest Protestant missionary enterprise during the sixteenth century was, strange as it may seem today, that staffed and supported by the Hutterites. In the following century the most extensive was that of a radical Puritan group, the Quakers. In Boston several dozen Quakers were persecuted—heavily fined, jailed, mutilated, sold into slavery, and some even put to death—for obeying the mandate, "Go ye into all the world and proclaim. . . ." The century after that, the Moravian Brethren

(*Herrnhuter*) and Pietist societies within the Reformed and Lutheran state-churches launched Protestant missions in the form which produced the modern missionary movement: independent societies, governed by special boards, staffed by volunteers, financed by free contributions.

The radical Puritans and radical Pietists were especially important for the American colonies. In their world-views, the dream of a New World and the reality of America sometimes blended and sometimes collided.

Certainly one of the major sources of the idea of "the American Israel" and civil religion's later development is the idea that in America the "new Israel" is both restituting the True Church and restoring the lost Eden. As one preacher proclaimed at the beginning of the republic,

> May we not view it, at least as probable, that the expansion of republican forms of government will accompany that spreading of the gospel, in its power and purity, which the scripture prophecies represent as constituting the glory of the latter days? [13]

Both the church and the general society are being redeemed, and both are in the new age infused with the spirit of liberty. Thomas Jefferson proposed that the Great Seal of the new republic should portray the children of Israel coming out of slavery in Egypt, led by a cloud by day and a pillar of fire by night. Etienne Cabet, Utopian Socialist, anti-Semite and anticlerical, called his program for securing the future of man in the New World through communes ("Icaria") "true Christianity." Today, after Vietnam, Watergate, the Huston Plan and related "White House horrors," there is a special pathos in remembering that for a great many early American Christians the New World was the place where the promises of the new age, the Age of the Spirit, were to be actualized. It is perhaps symbolic that America's present identity crisis, America's loss of innocence, should rotate around the personality, cabals, and activities of a renegade Quaker.

FROM RADICAL REFORMATION TO CULTURE-RELIGION

Radical Protestants taught that major signs of the fall of Christianity were selfish property-holding instead of mutual aid,[14] war and violence instead of peace, the union of church and state instead of separation of the religious and political covenants.

Governments which meddled in religious matters, where the *potestas Christi* alone should prevail, were condemned. Persecuting governments were identified with the Antichrist. Accommodation to the dying age, "the world," was not to be tolerated. Among Anabaptists, radical Puritans, and radical Pietists, at least, sturdy countercultures were in the early generations maintained through cultivation of adult faith and application of church discipline to prune away spiritually dead or diseased members—as proscribed in Matthew 18:15–19.

The question naturally arises how, if internal discipline and vigorous counterculture were characteristics of radical Protestantism, American Protestantism has become so thoroughly blended with "the American way of life" (or perhaps "the southern way of life"). Among the three great denominational groupings of English background—the Methodists, the Baptists, and the Disciples or Christians—the transition seems to have been completed around the turn of this century. Among the Methodists, it was at the 1908 General Conference of the Methodist Episcopal Church that a resolution was passed which virtually eliminated membership training and the special function of the meetings for discipline, i.e., gatherings of the congregation to fix penalties for neglect of religious duties. In the Methodist Episcopal Church, South, open membership had been accomplished thirty years earlier. The 1906 split of Disciples and Christians, of which historians first became generally aware at the time of the 1926 religious census, shaped up on matters of discipline—even, as on the question of musical instruments in church, discipline carrying a heavy load of cultural primitivism. But such "separation" soon withered in the larger groups: today it would be incredible to maintain that Harding College of the "Christians" is more a center of prophetic criticism of the American standing order than—for example—Drake University of the Disciples. And among all the larger denominational communities, the slackening of discipline produced literally dozens of small splits, of people protesting in one way or another the acculturation process. Among these are the Christian and Missionary Alliance, the Church of the Nazarenes, the Missionary Baptist Convention. Above all, the various Pentecostal churches which have expanded in America and abroad since the "Latter Rain" revival movement in the early decades of this century and the Azusa Revival of 1906—such as the Assemblies of God, the Church of God in Christ, the International Church of the Four-Square Gospel—represent in some sense a turn away from formalism and externalism to heartfelt religion, from developed institutions to primitive models.

The irony of the situation is that most of the latter restitutionism seems to have a vision of separation almost always deeply personal and subjective: they are not afraid to be different, but there are few signs of the things that were at the heart of sixteenth-century radicalism: a recovery of the peace testimony, of the communal economy, of a vigorous condemnation of public sin and corruption. Bumper signs such as JESUS HAS THE ANSWER and GOD BLESS RICHARD NIXON on the same automobile are as typical as a sign I saw recently in front of a mainline church in Florida: GET AWAY FROM IT ALL—WORSHIP GOD.

In my earlier interpretation of American religious history, *From State Church to Pluralism*,[15] I had come to the conclusion that the primary thrust toward accommodation and acculturation came as a result of the trauma of the Civil War. The churches of one section seemed to rally around the myth of the antebellum South; the churches of the other seemed to identify with the optimism and expansionism of the industrial North, with Josiah Strong's *Our Country* a typical high-level call to political and religious Americanism.

I believe now that we must push further back, and perhaps the impulse of the Bicentennial will produce enough studies to establish whether or not the "fall" in American radical Protestantism began with the republican religion of the new nation. As closely as I can now read it, the identification of America with the

THE RADICAL REFORMATION 83

new age of Christian glory came early in the history of the republic. Puritanism, of which the Church of the Latter-Day Saints (Mormons) is an authentic product, early interpreted the Age of the Spirit in the language of nativism, antipapalism, republicanism, and Anglo-Saxon destiny. By a few decades into the nineteenth century, Pietism—with a delay largely due to language difference, and with the temporary exception of separatist communes like Economy, Zoar, Bethel and Aurora, Amana—had made the same adjustment.

Oneida of the Puritans is now a successful silverplate corporation. Amana of the Pietists is now an exceedingly prosperous corporation producing woolens, freezers, and microwave ovens. Those who crossed the great water to cultivate the wilderness and make it again the beautiful garden of simple faith and quiet virtue before the fall seem seldom to notice the briars and brambles which choke the harvests, the dying beasts and birds that cannot survive the poisoning of the earth.

The social establishment of the American churches is as successful as the political and legal establishments of the "Old Egypt," Europe, from which Roger Williams and William Penn and Francis Asbury and Alexander Campbell went forth. And the spiritual progeny of these radical Protestants are no more apt to identify the true nature of that "success" than are the spiritual descendants of Samuel Seabury, Henry Melchior Muhlenberg, and John Witherspoon.

With the exception of a few remnants (some of them half-fossilized), with the as yet indecipherable potentiality of the burgeoning Pentecostals, the vision of the Radical Reformation has largely disappeared from the churches. A radical tract of 1526 summarized that vision:

> Three transformations have been seen in history: the first was instituted by God the Father in the Old Testament; the second transformation was instituted by God the Son in the world with the New Testament; the third transformation will be brought about by the Holy Spirit; with this future transformation the world will be changed from the evil in which it finds itself.[16]

For most of the baptized around us, America *is* that new age, that changed world. And this "realized eschatology," with its happy blend of religious and political self-satisfaction, is neither "church" nor "sect" according to Ernst Troeltsch's noted distinction, i.e., neither a structured institution with a positive relationship to the world nor a free union of those who separate themselves from the world. It is an American casting of the spiritualizing thrust in religion, which, like a sky-thrust missile when the fuel gives out, returns to earth to be counted among the dead artifacts of the former times.

The men and women of the Free Church line—Anabaptists, radical Puritans, radical Pietists—fought against *both* the establishment and the spiritualizers, a fact commonly ignored by those who have struggled to apply the typologies of "church" and "sect" to the American scene. And, although Troeltsch himself warned against it, dozens of students have been encouraged to try to apply Troeltschian patterns to English and American and post-eighteenth-century Christianity. Numerous dissertations have been written to show how the Mennonites or the Church of God or the Nazarenes, or some other so-called "sect" have with prosperity and stability in America managed to become "church."

This misuse of Troeltsch by scholars and students has diverted our eyes from the real development in America, which is not from "sect" to "church" at all. "Church," in the European sense, began to disappear in the United States with the First Amendment to the Federal Constitution and related disestablishments of state religion. "Sect," in the Troeltschian sense, disappeared when most of Puritanism and Pietism accepted the vision of "the American Israel." The dominant motif in American Protestantism is fixed by neither John Calvin nor Menno Simons, but by the enlightened, emancipated, nonpartisan inwardness of the "Third Type"—the Spiritualizers.

In the German Third Reich, the *Deutsche Christen* popularized this *positives Christentum* in a debased form, blending Teutonic virtue and something called "the spirit of true religion." Certainly a major sign of our recent crisis of self-identity in America has been the popularity of "White House piety," a blend of Americanism and "the spirit" which lacks both the sacramental and creedal

integrity of "church" and the discipline and lifestyle of "sect."
American "Christendom" is dominated by neither Thomas Aquinas nor Martin Luther, John Calvin nor Menno Simons: its
commanding spirit is a lowgrade apparition of Sebastian Franck,
the sixteenth-century German humanist who incurred the wrath
of Catholics and Reformers alike for his advocacy of complete
freedom of thought and a totally undogmatic Christianity.

Even the language is being destroyed. Recently I heard a
member of Billy Graham's team telling enthusiastically about
their annual week-long retreat for prayer and Bible study. It was
held in the Florida Everglades, I learned, and I was also informed
that they had "a mountaintop experience." It reminded me of a
very common experience in Methodist circles: to have someone
suggest that we join in a circle at the end of a meeting, singing
"Let us break bread together, on our knees"—everyone standing
upright, with no thought of kneeling! Whatever happened to
"plain speaking"? As a Free Church man, confronted by an
establishment which spiritualizes institutions and language and
degrades both, I plead for a restitution of the Restitution.

NOTES

1. William Warren Sweet, *The Story of Religion in America* (New
York: Harper & Bros., 1939), p. 2.

2. George H. Williams, *The Radical Reformation* (Philadelphia:
Westminster Press, 1962), pp. xxiv–vii.

3. James Leo Garrett, Jr., *The Nature of the Church according to the
Radical Continental Reformation* (Fort Worth, Tex.: privately printed,
1947).

4. C. C. Goen, *Revivalism and Separation in New England, 1740–1800*
(New Haven: Yale University Press, 1962).

5. Franklin H. Littell, *The Origins of Sectarian Protestantism* (New
York: Macmillan, 1964), chap. 2.

6. Ernst Troeltsch, *The Social Teaching of the Christian Churches* II
(New York: Macmillan, 1931), pp. 729 f., 949.

7. "Primitivismus," in Franklin H. Littell and Hans Hermann Walz,

eds., *Weltkirchenlexikon* (Stuttgart: Kreuz-Verlag, 1960), cols. 1182–87.

8. Ernst Benz, *Ecclesia Spiritualis* (Stuttgart: W. Kohlhammer, 1934); the classical work on Joachim, it was reissued in 1969 by the Wissenschaftliche Buchgesellschaft, Darmstadt.

9. G. G. Coulton, *Five Centuries of Religion* II (Cambridge: University Press, 1927), p. 120.

10. Ernst Benz, "The Pietist and Puritan Sources of Early Protestant World Missions (Cotton Mather and A. H. Francke)," *Church History* 20 (1951), 2:28–55.

11. Franklin H. Littell, "Some Free Church Remarks on the Concept, The Body of Christ," in Robert S. Pelton, ed., *The Church as the Body of Christ* (Notre Dame: University of Notre Dame Press, 1963), pp. 127–38.

12. Emil Egli, ed., *Actensammlung zur Geschichte der Zürcher Reformation in den Jahren 1519–1533 I (Zurich: J. Schabelitz, 1879), no. 691.*

13. *Nathan Strong, On the Universal Spread of the Gospel* (Hartford, 1801), p. 31. I am indebted to Nathan O. Hatch for this reference.

14. Documents on mutual aid in Free Church history have been published by Donald F. Durnbaugh, *Every Need Supplied* (Philadelphia: Temple University Press, 1974).

15. Franklin H. Littell, *From State Church to Pluralism* (rev. ed.; New York: Macmillan, 1971), chap. 3.

16. Abraham Friesen, "Thomas Müntzer in Marxist Thought," *Church History* 34 (1965), p. 314.

THOMAS O'BRIEN HANLEY, S.J.

church/state relations in the american revolutionary era

The American Revolutionary generation has often been misread by its twentieth-century descendants, including, in my opinion, the Supreme Court of the United States when it has reflected on the state and federal constitutions of the Revolutionary era in a constant mood of present, rather than historical mindedness. In particular, the Supreme Court has imbedded the "wall of separation" mentality in most of the major decisions on church-state questions, using Thomas Jefferson's phrase but outside of its historical context. The thrust of this article is to indicate that we can understand what the "doctrine" of church-state separation meant at the time when our federal and various state constitutions were being written only by penetrating into the concerns and attitudes of that period. The projection of contemporary bias only distorts the historical lessons to be learned.

My line of argument has been pursued before. Years ago, Wilfred Parsons pointed out this twentieth-century mythologizing in a rather clear book.[1] Parsons stated that the First Amendment was put in the federal Constitution expressly to keep the federal government from disturbing the established churches of Massachusetts and some other states. The historical data are readily at hand. Anson Phelps Stokes unfolded all that was known in published primary and secondary studies in his first volume on church and state in the United States,[2] although after Stokes's death abridgments of his work were not as careful to preserve an accurate historical perspective. Yet, in spite of the evidence, Americans go on believing that the first American constitutions radically separated religion from the state.

Nor is this question of historical interest only. The financial plight of church-related schools as well as the theoretic arguments of men like John A. Ryan in the 1920s and, more recently, John Courtney Murray[3] over the optimum relation between church and state make the issue quite current. Murray argued that, contrary to classical European theorists, the religious freedom of the individual is identical with the common good and not secondary to it. The separation of church and state *as embodied in the federal Constitution* was, therefore, the best political structure for the growth of true religion and the fulfillment of a government's responsibilities to its citizens.

THE INFLUENCE OF THE GREAT AWAKENING

The difficulty with the historical basis of Murray's theory, however, is that it failed to reckon with the state constitutions which preceded the federal Constitution.[4] It is here that one may today find a very different orientation to the whole question of separation of church and state. Historians, political scientists, jurists, and theologians have not reckoned with *the two* religious impulsions of the American Revolutionary generation. Americans of that time were not only chaffing under the impositions of the established Church of England; they were also carried along with the religious enthusiasm which the Great Awakening of the 1740s had instilled. There is evidence that John Winthrop's dream of America as a "Wilderness Zion" was deeply grounded in his contemporaries' consciousness, as was the belief that American independence would open the door to the Kingdom of God in the new "promised land." While the lawmakers of 1776 did not turn to specific passages of the Old Testament for their statutes (as did John Cotton, Thomas Hooker, and other seventeenth-century constitutionalists of the New England Bible states), the Great Awakening told them that public morality without religion was impossible. The legislators also understood that only evangelical Christianity deserved the name of religion. Furthermore, the

Antichrist was clearly identified as Deism, that suave seducer of Christianity. There was a striking unawareness that the constitutions of their new states should deny the states the powers to foster public morality through religion.[5]

Before the heat of Awakening fervor had abated, some state constitutions provided for religious tests of Christianity for office, others for established Protestant churches, and several for a government system of tax support for clergy and congregations from a number of Christian denominations. By 1789 this system for the establishment of Christianity was widespread. The American Revolutionary generation believed that they had done away with the burdens of the established Church of England because they had made all religious groups equal before the law insofar as that was possible, and because the religious freedom of the individual was respected so far as the public good would allow. It seemed reasonable to that generation that office holders should profess belief in God and the divine inspiration of the Bible (Pennsylvania), in Christianity (Maryland), in the truths of Protestantism (North Carolina), and in the rejection of any ecclesiastical authority of the Pope in regard to the United States (New York). For its own salvation and that of its citizens, it was also deemed proper for the government to allow taxes to be raised to support congregations and their ministers who served the state by strengthening public morality. There might even be an official church, as in the case of Congregationalism in Massachusetts, which showed that the Commonwealth was a Christian people.[6]

There were various ways in which the state constitutionalists sought to forestall any embarrassment in the face of their proclamations that no one should be molested in the free exercise of his religion. Conscientious non-Christians might by a special enabling act of the assembly be allowed to hold public office without the profession of belief. All denominations were entitled to support from the state through the taxes their members paid to the government, and if a citizen had no congregation he might designate a charity as the beneficiary. These arrangements led to a long and tangled history of litigation reaching into the nineteenth century. A Jew in the eighteenth century failed to get an enabling act to hold public office in Maryland, and by 1825 profession of

Christianity had to be removed in favor of simple belief in God. The last remnant of this practice was removed in 1961 when a notary public refused to take such an oath. In the wake of the great religious revivalism of the early nineteenth century, many states, particularly in the south, had de facto Protestant establishments, which arose from provisions in state constitutions. The reading in public schools of the King James Bible with its Protestant-slanted footnotes was also an expression of this kind of establishment, as was the hiring of many Protestant ministers as teachers in the schools of these states. Bishop John Hughes's protest against Bible reading in the public schools of New York has significant libertarian meaning in this context.[7]

But this militant Protestant mood in the nineteenth century was not precisely that of the Revolutionary generation. The political and military union of the patriots against the king, Parliament, and their mercenaries helped to put religious differences aside, and the era was marked by an ecumenical spirit in drafting and interpreting the new state constitutions. Americans of that time lived out the myth of John Winthrop and the Great Awakening: a holy war was fought and won to enable all Christians to unite in a peace which would hasten the coming of the Kingdom of God. Houses of worship were shared, and colleges were begun under interdenominational auspices. Ferdinand Farmer, the Catholic pastor of Old St. Joseph's in Philadelphia, was on the Board of Visitors of the College of Philadelphia (later the College and University of Pennsylvania). John Carroll served in a similar way at Washington College, and was offered the office of provost of the state College of Maryland. George Washington called upon Americans to put aside old sectarian grievances. Few thought this would require going so far as Thomas Jefferson and James Madison had gone in Virginia, where Christian oaths for office and financial state aid to religion were discountenanced. But even here, public morality without religion was deemed impossible and the College of Virginia would have all faiths represented in its department of religion.[8]

In addition to the endurance of the Great Awakening influence and a newly discovered ecumenism in many states, a rather long-standing political condition accounted for the state's patronage of religion: the interest of fostering public morality. Ironically, the Revolutionary generation, or at least its leadership, was possessed by the idea of an orderly society which the virtuous would lead in offices of government. Paradoxically, this idea was learned from England, which tried to vindicate the power of Parliament over the colonies by appeal to it. England claimed that there must be an ultimate locus of authority in any civilized society, and the overthrow of the Stuarts in 1688 had placed it in the people's Parliament. Theoretically the Church of England under the king was to give order to society in England and in the colonies, while permitting the growth of religious dissidents in America with the influx of Baptists, Presbyterians, and Congregationalists. Without an American bishop, however, the Church of England failed in its purpose here.

But Americans came to discover that they already had a unity as a Christian people, although it was certainly not based on the Church of England. Denominations, rather than warring sects, would now be the elements of the Christian church. The Revolutionary War experience and this gathering ecumenism inevitably led the state constitution-makers to establish Christianity in one way or another. That the subsequent generation would use the state constitutions to ground a Protestant establishment legally was not expected by many nor probably regretted by many more. The Revolutionary generation was satisfied with its basic religious agreement that government would be a patron exclusively of Christianity. They were content that they had disestablished a Church of England without disestablishing Christianity. "Establishment" as a term was not related to Christianity nor religion, but to a sect of either of these. Denominationalism denoted equality of governmental benefit and so religious freedom was assured.[9]

CATHOLIC ADJUSTMENT
TO PROTESTANT ESTABLISHMENT

This, then, was the evolution in Protestant culture through the Revolutionary War experience with which the Catholic community had to adjust. Pennsylvania held the most favorable environment for this, but Maryland was the scene where the best articulation of this adjustment took place. The numbers, wealth, and leadership of the Catholic community were in Maryland. Moreover, Maryland's Catholic aristocratic families had a church-state tradition deriving from their counterparts in England and from the first generation of Catholic settlers in Maryland.

There were two elements of this tradition which put Catholics at odds with the Protestant evangelical thrust of the first state constitutions. One was an extremely strong church-state separationist feature found in the first documents of the Maryland settlement. The pamphlet, *Objections Answered*, published by George Calvert, the first Lord Baltimore, initially enunciated it.[10] What good, it asked, to have the state by its laws compel persons to a particular belief? The establishment principles of European states would, as Charles Carroll remarked in a similar vein to an English friend, bring only knaves and fools to the support of religion. Maryland would show that religion would thrive if untouched by the state. There is strong evidence that the first Maryland Assembly read its destiny in these terms, for its Toleration Act in the Ordinance of 1639 opened the door of equality and religious liberty to all Englishmen, including Jews. Several incidents argue for this interpretation: a Jewish inhabitant appealed to the Toleration Act when brought to court for publicly denying the divinity of Christ, and a dissident missionary appealed to it in defense of his preaching. Neither appealed to a later Toleration Act of 1649 protecting only Christians. Moreover, when Charles Carroll's father joined other Maryland Catholics in protesting a double tax on their land during the war with France in the 1750s, they too appealed to the 1639 Toleration Act. Once the Church of England had been established in Maryland shortly after 1700, Maryland Catholics—deprived of public worship, voting rights, public office holding, and freedom to conduct schools—gave birth to a militant separationism.[11]

The second thrust of the Maryland Catholic aristocrats' tradition was equally radical. The Elizabethan and Stuart Catholic gentry were imbued with antiecclesiasticism, caused no doubt by their years of persecution. The absence of Catholic bishops in England at that time left the laity the sole source of structure for the church, and their manors were the parishes of Yorkshire and other more Catholic counties in England. The system was transported to Maryland and the law of mortmain (forbidding inheritance of land by a religious corporation) was passed by Cecil Calvert, the second Lord Baltimore, to prevent any possibility of a Jesuit-style ecclesiasticism from disturbing the growth of the English model. Interestingly enough, the Jesuits themselves on the eve of the American Revolution were won to this separationist militancy by a different set of circumstances. The suppression of the Society of Jesus by Benedict XIV in 1773 embittered many Jesuits in America against the highly politicized papal court. John Carroll, arriving in America a year after the event, was the most articulate example of this. For him, American independence held the hope of being free from dominance by the Sacred Congregation for the Propagation of the Faith. In this radical separationist spirit, he fashioned in 1783 a Constitution of the Clergy and a civil incorporation of all Jesuit and other church-related property. He challenged the Propaganda to lay a hand on the American church's temporalities. In his many writings he labored to clarify, even for himself, the nature of the American church's spiritual tie with the Chair of Peter in the midst of its political separation.[12]

A CONSERVATIVE TREND

In view of this Maryland Catholic church-state tradition, one would expect Maryland to play a spirited libertarian part in the American Revolution and in the constitution-making that accompanied it. The right of the individual should be foremost. The oath of loyalty, so long a scourge to the English Roman Catholic, would be buried forever. There would be no testing to eliminate Deists, Jews, or anyone else from public office. Religion was a personal matter and the state should not intrude. Least of all should money be directly given to ministers and congregations.

As it turned out, the Maryland constitution of 1776 opened the door to all of these possibilities. Yet only a couple instances can be found where a spokesman for the Catholic community had reservations on the provisions for the establishment of Christianity. Charles Carroll of Carrollton, who was on the committee which drafted the Maryland constitution, indicated his preference for the arrangement of the Pennsylvania constitution in which profession of belief in Christianity was not required of office holders. In the case of the clergy salary bill, which was based on a constitutional provision allowing such measures, John Carroll, at the time Superior of the American Church, demurred. He even collaborated with Presbyterians and Methodists in defeating a measure that would provide a salary by tax for every minister of a Christian congregation. But Carroll did not fear the entry of the state into the affairs of the church. He feared instead the preponderance of the Protestant Episcopal Church which by virtue of its numbers would receive a dangerously large amount of public funds, and thereby destroy any equality in the process of salary payments. On the other hand, he feared that non-Christian elements would also be strengthened by a clergy salary bill. For these religious groups would be free to designate their own charities or synagogues as beneficiaries, and the state would thus be contributing to the growth of non-Christian religious institutions.[13]

What begins to appear in all of this is a conservative trend in the Maryland Catholic community as a result of the Revolutionary War experience. There was considerable resistance to the Revolution in Maryland, some of it in violent form. Some political groups wanted yearly elections to the Lower House of the Assembly (the House of Delegates), and the elimination of the property qualification for voting. Before the close of 1776, Charles Carroll was overwhelmed with forebodings of public disorder and reckless legislation. He actually thought for a moment that it would be a blessing if an adjustment with England for a provincial status could be made. It is not surprising that this stanch conservative in constitutional matters became the backbone of the Federalist Party in later years. John Carroll, the first Catholic bishop of the United States, was of a similar political temper. This is seen in his frank statement that, after his own election to episcopacy by the clergy, the device was unsuited to stable ecclesiastical government in the future.[14]

To such men preoccupied with the need of public morality and order, traditional Christianity was readily seen as the chief means to its attainment. If government in the hands of Christian men "of the better sort of society" would stabilize political life, the Christian religion would make law-abiding citizens follow their leadership. Those who fashioned the new society and the churches that would be independent of the bishop of London and the Congregation for the Propagation of the Faith expected the state to collaborate with them. While they rejected the clergy salary bill, they welcomed other direct aid, particularly for interdenominational colleges, and generous arrangements for civil incorporation of congregational property and exemption from taxes.[15]

Militancy in this Christian collaboration of church and state awakened as early as 1776, when the leading citizens stigmatized Deism and all that led to the denial of orthodox Christianity. There was an accelerated paranoia directed at heterodoxy. The leaders of the Christian state demonstrated in their sermons, gazette letters, pamphlets, and broadsides that the forces of "infidelity" were bent upon diluting the influence of vital religion on society, to the detriment of public morality. The state could not survive this weakened condition, nor could an authentic Christian church. Some even believed that the profession of belief in Christianity by office holders was too vague and that some creed, apparently similar to the Elizabethan Thirty-nine Articles of Belief, should be required.[16]

These then were the terms upon which Marylanders rejoiced in the disestablishment of the Church of England, and Catholics rejoiced with them. In their reckoning and terminology there was no longer an established church, that plague of provincial America and the national states of Europe. There was indeed an emancipation of religion, both institutionally and personally, for the number of Jews and Deists was small and provision for their personal freedom seemed to be fairly provided for, or would be in time. For the present the need for public morality and stability had been secured for the new nation.

From the standpoint of the twentieth century, however, this disestablishment in the state constitutions is a myth. Disestablishment for eighteenth-century Americans meant something significantly different from disestablishment as it is conceived of today. According to the earlier view, a state that was self-denying of authority in religion was self-defeating. In the practical order, the complete religious freedom of the individual did involve the general welfare and could be in conflict with it. In one way or another, freedom of religion was in the seedbed of the Republic and its founding, but so were two other principles: the state's need of vital religion in society and the obligation to foster it in the best possible way.

A past era understood with historical-mindedness has a disturbing way of chiding a later generation which has viewed it with present-mindedness. As the last half of the twentieth century has progressed, the state has progressively deplored the decline of public morality, particularly in the 1970s. But several factors, both economic and legislative, have deprived the state of the means traditionally used to prevent this, i.e., a vigorous and effective religious life. As a consequence, resort to legislation rather than religion has been used to discourage antisocial behavior. But the threat of imprisonment deriving from these laws has not proved effective without religion. Religious public education, which even Jefferson conceded necessary for enlightened citizenship, has been denied Americans. Future generations might judge the present one guilty of establishing agnostic and secular humanism. If the eighteenth century had to wrestle with its own myths, so has the late twentieth.[17]

NOTES

1. Wilfred Parsons, *The First Freedom: Considerations on Church and State in the United States* (New York: Macmillan, 1948).

2. Anson Phelps Stokes, *Church and State in the United States*, 3 vols. (New York: Harper & Row, 1950).

3. John Courtney Murray, *We Hold These Truths* (New York: Sheed and Ward, 1960).

4. Robert D. Cross, *The Emergence of Liberal Catholicism in America* (Cambridge: Harvard University Press, 1958), pp. 222–23.

5. Thomas O. Hanley, *The American Revolution and Religion: Maryland, 1770–1800* (Washington: Catholic University Press, 1974).

6. B. P. Poore, ed., *Federal and State Constitutions* . . . , 2 vols. (Washington: 1878). See also William G. McLaughlin, "The Role of Religion in the Revolution: Liberty of Conscience and Cultural Cohesion in the New Nation," in *Essays on the American Revolution*, eds. Stephen G. Kurtz and James H. Hutson (New York: Norton, 1973), pp. 256–88.

7. Hanley, *op. cit.*, chaps. 2 and 3. See also John Cogley, *Catholic America* (New York: Dial, 1973), pp. 214–15.

8. John Tracy Ellis, *Catholics in Colonial America* (Baltimore: Helicon, 1965), p. 410. See also John Carroll's letter to Charles Plowden, February 24, 1790, in *The John Carroll Papers*, 3 vols., ed. Thomas O. Hanley (Notre Dame: University of Notre Dame Press, 1976), I, p. 431. Also Gordon Wood, *The Creation of the American Republic, 1776–1787* (New York: Norton, 1972), chap. 3.

9. Carl Bridenbaugh, *Mitre and Sceptre: Transatlantic Faiths, Ideas, Personalities, and Politics, 1689–1775* (New York: Oxford University Press, 1962); Sidney Mead, *The Lively Experiment* (New York: Harper & Row, 1963); Thomas O. Hanley, "The Emergence of Pluralism in the United States," *Theological Studies* 23 (1962), pp. 207–32.

10. See Thomas Hughes, *The History of the Society of Jesus in North America: Documents*, 2 vols. (New York, 1917), I, no. 4.

11. Thomas O. Hanley, *Their Rights and Liberties: The Beginnings of Religious and Political Freedom in Maryland* (Westminster, Md.: Christian Classics, 1959), chaps. 3–6; and "Church and State in the Maryland Ordinance of 1639," *Church History* 26 (1957), pp. 325–42; and *Charles Carroll of Carrollton: The Making of a Revolutionary Gentleman* (Washington: Catholic University Press, 1970), chaps. 3–5.

12. Hanley, *Rights and Liberties* . . . , pp. 109–13.

13. Hanley, *Charles Carroll* . . . , pp. 222–61, on Carroll's ties with the libertarian movement. See also *The Declaration and Charter of Rights; The Constitution and Form of Government Proposed for the Consideration of the Delegates of Maryland* (Annapolis, 1776), and *The Declaration of Rights and the Constitution and Forms of Government Established by the Convention of Maryland* (Annapolis, 1776).

14. Ronald Hoffman, *A Spirit of Dissension: Economics, Politics, and the Revolution in Maryland* (Baltimore: Johns Hopkins University Press, 1973). See also Charles Carroll's letter to his father, October 4, 1776 (Maryland Historical Society). Also Thomas O. Hanley, "Archbishop Carroll and the French Revolution," *Records of the American Catholic Historical Society* 71 (1960), pp. 67–72.

15. Hanley, "Emergence of Pluralism . . . ," pp. 230–31.

16. Hanley, *Revolution and Religion* . . . , pp. 160–67, and "Reluc-

tant Witness to Pluralism in Early America," *Theological Studies* 26 (1965), pp. 375–92.

17. See, for example, Martin Marty's review of this writer's book in *Political Science Quarterly* 90 (1975), pp. 465–66. Marty mistakenly imputes advocacy of a Christian state to the writer, who is actually striving for historical-mindedness in understanding the constitutional era.

MARIE AUGUSTA NEAL, S.N.D.

civil religion, theology, and politics in america

CIVIL RELIGION
AND ITS RELATIONSHIP TO THEOLOGY

Biologists, psychologists, anthropologists, sociologists, and theologians all use scientific labeling to discriminate their data: words about life, about the mind and human behavior; words about people by race, physical characteristics, and environment; words about society, social institutions, and relationships; and finally, words about God. All of these sciences approach religion in some way. That is the meaning of *re-ligere*—to bind together. All the sacred words—symbols and myths about life and death; about mystical experience and prayer; about churches and creeds, codes and cults; about worship and ministry, prophets and priests; revelation and Scriptures, sacred music and art, dance and architecture; costumes and houses of worship and prayer; calls and responses, action and passion; immanence and transcendence—all the sacred words are constantly co-opted by even the nonsacred sciences to name the patterns they see clearly in what they study.

Physicists, chemists, and astronomers do the same thing. They use words about substances and their transformation; about matter and energy; about the celestial bodies, their matter, motion, and constitution; and finally, about God. Science stirs the soul with the order it reveals. Most true scientists are philosophers at heart. They love wisdom and they seek a general understanding of values and of reality, by speculation as well as by observation.

Scientists, however, are also people with personal aspirations, social connections, and cultural images. They all speak some language that channels their thinking in categories resulting from a long-developing tradition, from an ordered world as experienced by those who have power to make the labels and to make them stick. It is within this cultural corset and within this range of human experience that the theologians and other scientists reflect upon, name, and rename God. Inevitably, this experience is historically determined, psychically motivated, socially conditioned, and culturally framed. It is therefore a matter of importance who the theologians are who select the names for God, because these theologians are necessarily located somewhere in the social order in terms of time and space, class, race, and sex. Each of these factors limits the vision and influences the perspective. Any point of view short of God's allows for the influence that interest and power factors always, in time, exert.[1]

In *The Elementary Forms of the Religious Life*, Emile Durkheim points out that society compels a loyalty akin to worship, an experience of the transcendent sufficiently real to be defined as the sacred and responded to as a believer responds to his or her God. For most people, says Durkheim, the God they worship is the society that nurtures them. The idea of civil religion names the link between this allegiance-and-protection relationship (associated with territory, birth, and law) and that order in the universe experienced as an ultimate binding-together and expressed in a people's symbols and stories about their origins and destiny, about incorporation and reciprocation, about protection and allegiance, meaning, design, and celebration; in short, the religious experience. The theologian seeking names for God will choose words connoting power if his main focus is civil, and nutrient words (like "providence") if his main focus is familial. A serious problem arises if God is named as male in a cultural context where the male experience is more one of producing than of supporting. When power is perceived as more effective for action than is love, then God becomes king, ruler, lord, and master.

In 1966 the term "civil religion" was applied by Robert Bellah to a type of religion he observed in America, a religion not associated with any specific church but characterizing the behavior of civic leaders on solemn occasions such as inaugurations and holidays. This behavior, he felt, had meaning more capable of binding people in solidarity and of compelling adherence than the simple patriotism associated with citizenship. He called it religious because he believed it was associated more with transcendent aspects of human experience than with the specific functions of governance and citizenship. He defined civil religion as "the subordination of the nation to ethical principles that transcend it and in terms of which it should be judged." He added that he is "convinced that every nation and every people come to some form of religious self-understanding whether the critics like it or not." [2]

Bellah did not mean by American civil religion "the American way of life," nor did he mean an idolatrous celebration of America as a nation; rather, he believed that "civil religion at its best is a genuine apprehension of universal and transcendent religious reality as seen in, or one could almost say as revealed through, the experience of the American people." [3] The qualities of American religion he saw as activist, moralistic, and social rather than contemplative, theological, and innerly spiritual. He claimed that "civil religion has exercised a long-term pressure for the humane solution of our greatest domestic problem, the treatment of the American Negro. It remains to be seen how relevant it can become for our role in the world at large and whether we can effectually stand for the revolutionary beliefs for which our forefathers fought." [4] The biblical archetypes he found informing civil religion in America include the Exodus, Chosen People, Promised Land, New Jerusalem, Sacrificial Death, and Rebirth. He claimed that each civil religion has its own prophets and martyrs, and that the American form is genuinely new: "It is concerned with America being a society as perfectly in accord with God's will as men can make it and a light to all the nations." [5]

My feelings after examining Bellah's essay is that it is not a sociological piece but, rather, a passionate and persuasive plea that America not succumb to the arrogance of power "which has afflicted, weakened, and in some cases destroyed great nations in the past."[6] Bellah hopes that the transition to international organization now needed for humane development will not destroy the uniqueness that characterizes the American nation as he has known, loved, and trusted it. "Fortunately," he writes, "since the American civil religion is not the worship of the American nation but an understanding of the American experience in the light of ultimate and universal reality, the reorganization entailed (by the emergence of a needed transnational sovereignty) need not disrupt the American civil religion's continuity."[7] Bellah quotes with approval Lincoln's and Kennedy's references to God in their public addresses, Johnson's with less enthusiasm and, later, Nixon's with embarrassment. In 1975 he writes of the Broken Covenant with the same passion, but now with a sense of tragedy, a sense of a nation betraying its function in the divine plan.[8] He speaks more as priest than sociologist, but his action raises for the sociologist questions about the sociologist's purposes and their effects.

A word needs to be said about the amazing popularity of this concept, civil religion, and the way some social scientists, church historians, and philosophers have in the past decade assented to Bellah's analysis and elaborated it with critique and evidence.[9]

Richey and Jones, in their collected essays on the topic in 1974, review five different ways in which the concept "civil religion" has been used recently in writing about religion in America. (1) To some, civil religion is "the American way of life" celebrated as a religious value; thus, the "folk religion" approach of Will Herberg. (2) To others, it is a religion of the Republic, a prophetic critique and guide for that way of life (Sidney Mead and Bellah himself). (3) For others, it is the nation as object of adoration, a kind of idolatry. For this position, Archbishop Ireland is cited and reprimanded. (4) For yet others, it is a democratic faith, implicit in the work of Leo Marx, Gunnar Myrdal, John Dewey, and classically in J. Paul Williams. (5) Finally, it is seen as Protestant civic piety, typical of the work of the historian Winthrop Hudson among others, and certainly characteristic of Bellah himself when he admits in the introduction to *Beyond Belief* that "I still believe that some equivalent of Protestant individualism and voluntaristic social organization is necessary for any person or group who would fully participate in the potential freedom of the modern world." [10]

When Sidney Mead writes about America as the nation with the soul of a church, he explains how the Reformed churches became national churches in Scotland, England, Germany, Holland, North Germany, and Scandinavia and that in each case the nation assumed its own form of Christianity, fusing

> the spiritual tradition of the new and secular nation with the spiritual tradition of the old Christian society. Thus the essentially spiritual society of the nation was in effect Christianized by partially digesting into its spiritual core a particularized version of Christianity. For its people the nation became also their church and the church became also their nation: Church and nation being merely different perspectives on the one society to which they belonged.[11]

After these comments, Mead describes how the Nonconformists, not agreeing with the English link of church and state, came to America and had "their view incarnated in the constitution and legal structure of the United States while the Catholic immigrants brought their Catholicism as but one dimension of their ethnicity, and were forced by the American experience to become Catholic in the broadest sense in order to adapt to the American religious situation." [12] He notes that a Catholic in Elizabethan England was as disloyal as was a Protestant Huguenot in Catholic France. Mead's goal in so writing is to come to understand the relationship of the denominations which emerged out of the American experience to the civil authority of the nation. He concludes that "the course of history exhibits the slow, strong power of high generalities to get incarnated in actuality, and our institutions are primarily incarnations of the constellations of myths and ideas that dominated the thinking of the eighteenth century in which the nation was born." [13] He claims that theologians explain and define the concrete modes of thinking and practice that characterize their group, and that the actual study and explanation of the visible church is done by historians, anthropologists, and sociologists whose findings are as distant from the interests of theologians as are the faith and practice of church members and parish ministers. Mead, of course, is a historian.

This discussion raises questions about religion and social structure. Is religion nothing more than the social cement of a society? Whose God do we worship? Who are the "we" who analyze and interpret? In whose interest do theologians speak? To what end?

I think we can clearly answer the first question with a No. Religion is not *merely* social cement. But it *is* social cement, and as such it is one dimension of the culture of a living group. A body of knowledge, expressive symbols, aesthetics, and other normative rules are also part of that culture, but the religious dimension has a moral fiber and content that, from the theological perspective, may be quite naïve. Naïve or not, however, that religious dimension will act as a controlling force in group process. I think that what gets defined as civil religion is that religious dimension associated with the lifestyle of the dominant class in a given society. This association gives that lifestyle a quality of authority, and includes the power to legitimate the existing allocation and control of goods and services within the political economy.

CIVIL RELIGION AND SOCIAL OUTCASTS

In its authentic form, writes John Coleman, "civil religion is a nation's conscience." This sentence follows a crescendo of statements about civil religion:

> If you like, civil religion is the mystic chord of communal memory (always being summoned to re-interpretation in the face of new historic tasks) which ties together both a nation's citizenry and the episodes of its history into a meaningful identity by using significant national beliefs, events, persons, places or documents to serve as symbolic repositories of the special vocational significance of the nation-state in the light of a more ultimate or transcendent bar of judgment: ethical ideals, humanity, world history, being, the universe, or God.

To this crescendo he appends a note saying that "most of these summary symbols when probed deeply serve as God terms." [14] Apparently William Butler Yeats was captured by that same sense of the link of the nation with the universe when he said: "One can only reach out to the universe with the gloved hand—that glove is one's nation, the only thing one knows even a little of!" [15]

It seems to me that the civil religionists are discovering that aspect of social life that Durkheim wrote about in *The Elementary Forms of the Religious Life*, a book that provided one of the major bases for the emergence of modern sociology. Here Durkheim is speaking of what he chose to call the collective conscience or consciousness when he said that a religion is "a system of ideas with which individuals represent to themselves the society of which they are members, and the obscure but intimate relations which they have with it." [16] He claimed this as the primary function of religion. He said further that the God that most people worship is nothing more than the "collective and anonymous force of the clan," the social forces that bear upon people and that each one experiences as coercive and compelling. "In a general way," he says, "it is unquestionable that a society has all that is necessary to arouse the sensation of the divine in minds, merely by the power it has over them; for to its members it is what a god is to his worshippers." [17]

From the sociological perspective, nothing Durkheim has said is more important than these observations. But they are not theological data; they are sociological facts. Used as the basis of research they provide a framework for investigating why individuals come to feel the way they do about the society of which they are members. Many middle Americans involved in the civil rights movement, the student movement, and war protests became disenchanted with the American civil system and, in that same experience of disenchantment, lost their faith. Those who stood firm against them were often self-righteously religious. On the other hand, oppressed peoples turn easily to the prophetic dimension of religion in causes of liberation, yet seldom have a place in established churches.[18] Indians, black Americans, women aware of sexism do not find God through the state of which they are citizens. Anomie, i. e., a disaffection from the norms of their society, a lack of psychic energy to celebrate its achievements, to sing its praises, to be caught up in its anthem, only characterizes those who once believed in the system but now cannot do so. A loss of faith in their God does accompany a failure of faith in society. On the other hand, enthusiasm for society is animated with enthusiasm for God. "Movement people" who discovered new qualities for God could no longer tolerate traditional liturgies, but still sought modes of worship and prayer.

These things point to a basic sociological fact, namely, that social groupings do have a quality of mystical or at least mysterious affectivity that is so deeply associated with personal identity that rejection by one's group is felt in the very depths of the soul. So strong are the psychic bonds that derive from family training, education in the neighborhood school, free associations, and other bondings in the lives of those who have been nurtured and supported by the societal system, that it is very difficult to initiate and persevere in a movement of indignation even against a nation that has violated its own principles of justice toward some of its own members as well as toward nonmembers. The fact is, however, that the very poor and the minorities whose bounds are defined by the affluent and accepted classes have not been socialized to that natural sense of belongingness. Their God, if they have a God, is not the God of the civil religion; and the cries to rally around the symbols of nationalism do not stir latent bonds for them, because the first gestures of inclusion have not been part of their earlier experience. The "effervescence" of civil religion is not a social universal across all class lines, nor across all ethnic lines, but the people of the dominant classes and ethnic groups do not know this. Those who do not experience these stirrings fail to do so simply because they do not know what it is their fellow citizens or fellow humans are experiencing when the civil symbols are invoked. They have never really belonged. And they have never really belonged because they have never had a human share of the society's resources. The human solidarity that stirs a Yeats does not stir the pagan because he has never been welcomed. He is not a boor. He is an outsider.

The peculiarity of Christianity in its scriptural roots is that it claims to be the religion of these outcasts. That is its uniqueness. Accordingly, it could never be genuinely a civil religion unless the nation were a nation of all human beings relating to each other as peers. Using Christian symbols for any particular national solidarity is a co-optation of a religious experience, a religious tradition, and a religious ministry. From the time of Constantine onward nations and states have attempted to make this merger of country and Christianity. As Christopher Dawson so well said in *Religion and Culture*, any religion can be so co-opted and history is full of the records of this process.[19] It is the judgment of the priest that makes the co-optation possible. He decides when and to what degree the religion should celebrate the solidarity that results from the social interaction that becomes the society, produces the common culture, and creates the bonding that is recognized as membership and is expressed verbally as "us" against "them." The priest's is seldom a conscious judgment and this responsibility has been his only since the division of labor provided for separate role-players for priestly tasks distinct from those of ruler, producer, and father of the family. These decisions are made by the priest on the basis of his ideas about who God is and who constitutes the people of God. His decisions are formed not only by his self-interests and clan identification, but even more by his theology, his faith.[20]

A recent article in *Christianity and Crisis* entitled "Whatever Happened to Theology?" defines theology and its tasks from several perspectives and then proceeds to account for its current demise, resurgence, development, deflection, or neo-incubation, depending on the point of view of the writer.[21] These range from theologians to church ministers, from bourgeois white males to women, blacks and Third World viewers. All affirm that theologians in the Christian perspective reflect on God as known in Jesus Christ; some reflect on him as experienced in the life of the church, but all in the light of the biblical story and the history of interpretation. There is real diversity among these people, however, as to the meaning of the contemporary experience. For one respondent, the main concern is the embarrassment of our "frenetic search for social relevance and our pathetic romance with the institutional structures." Another respondent is aware that "in our own generation the dramatic shift of power away from the Western world and the crisis of technological civilization have exposed the roots of that world view" that locates the God concept on the "upper" pole of such polarities as men/women, black/white, spirit/matter, ruler/ruled. This person sees the conquered tribal peoples rising up to new consciousness of self, social and ecological wholeness that renders obsolete the cosmological assumptions that underlie systematic theologies with long and, until recently exposed, respected traditions. Most contributors to the article affirm that theologies are rooted in cultures. It should also be noted that cultures rest on assumptions, usually unexpressed, about the right order of societal, institutional, and social relational exchange. The poor, moreover, do not shape these cultures but are shaped by them in certain significant and alienating ways.

The theologian has to choose a standpoint from which to begin viewing. It makes all the difference in the world where one stands—whether one stands, that is, beside the rich or beside the poor. In a divided world one would have to be God, or at least be standing beside God, to stand simultaneously with both groups. The perspectives are too different to allow one to bilocate. If the gospel is to be the guide as to where one stands, however, then Luke 4:16–20 and the corresponding passages in Isaiah 61:1,2 and 58:6 opt to stand with the world's poor:

> "The Spirit of the Lord is upon me because he has anointed me to preach good news to the poor. He has sent me to proclaim release to the captives and recovering of sight to the blind, to set at liberty those who are oppressed, to proclaim the acceptable year of the Lord." And he closed the book and gave it back to the attendant and sat down; and all eyes in the synagogue were fixed upon him and he began to say to them, "Today this scripture has been fulfilled in your hearing."

In the *Christianity and Crisis* discussion, José Miguez Bonino of Buenos Aires declared that "what is happening is that the great and admirable social and cultural achievement that we call Western bourgeois culture is reaching the end of its run; and consequently, the imposing and noble theological tradition which has accompanied, at times inspired, sometimes humanized and always expressed it, is also running out." [22] "Running out"—that expression suggests another look at Hegel's *Reason in History* if for no other reason than to review his thesis about how a civilization comes to an end and the Spirit moves on to some place that allows for the development of a broader-based freedom for the people.[23]

Gary MacEoin, long a spokesman of protest against the nonfreedoms in Western society, notes in his review of the new eleven-volume history of Ireland that the last volume, *Ireland of the 20th Century*, provides "no real picture of the new colonization of both parts of the country, especially of the Republic, the transfer of decision-making to British and American global corporations, and the distortion of the economy for the benefit of the wealthy few at the expense of the many poor." [24] I cite this criticism because it not only names the central failure of American society, that is, the exporting of the multinational corporations to the oppressed of the world, but it also points to their exploitation of the Irish people in a nation old and close to American foundations. Here is a people involved in a war so local that it touches every home, so related to "religions of the book" that the ecumenical directions of the churches are rendered impotent. This localism parallels the divisions that characterize American cities where not only is the Protestant-Catholic division exacerbated but the whole Third World confrontation of Africans, Latin Americans, and Southeast Asians is set alongside the ethnic divisions of our old European heritage. These divisions fragment the city over simple issues like living together in the same neighborhoods, sharing schools and churches and the available resources of the commonwealth for health, education, and welfare services. In the teeming central city of America the great melting-pot tradition breaks down. The civil religion celebrated and analyzed in the literature of the last decade is not the religion of our cities but the religion of the suburb and the university campus, the religion of the "kept" classes.

What the sociologist can tell us with unambiguous clarity from the results of large sample surveys is that belief in a God standing outside society and remotely brooding over the whole universe correlates (with a mathematical probability far beyond what chance can explain away) with rejection of people who are black, with political indifference, with unawareness of the sufferings of the poor, and with almost total absorption in one's own interests —including ease of life, preference for authoritarian structures, blaming the victim for the conditions of society, and indifference to human suffering. All of which may be accounted for by ignorance, but by an ignorance that ignores what is knowable, by preferring to read only those journals that not only neglect to communicate news of human suffering but—in what is communicated—distort the news to exonerate and even celebrate the activities of the exploiters.[25] When belief about God among large samples of people of the middle and upper classes as well as the employed and churched working classes correlates so highly with indifference to the plight of the poor, then the sociologist can, from the knowledge of her discipline, tell the theologian that the God that these people are worshiping is the very society that serves their advantage in laws that protect property rights rather than human rights.

We are not now looking at the manifest intention of the taught theologies but at their measured effects, the overall influence of the taught theologies on the outcome of decisions made by those who have learned them and used them in their own interests. What this says, it seems to me, is that we have to review what those who are suffering in today's world are telling us about what is happening to them as they interact with preachers of the gospel and with those to whom a "faith conviction" gives energy to act against whole groups of people whom they define as the enemy.[26]

T. Dunbar Moodie has recently published a book about the Afrikaner religion in South Africa entitled *The Rise of Afrikanerdom: Power, Apartheid, and the Afrikaner Civil Religion.*[27] The documents and records he quotes show us that the Trekkers—the Dutch who departed Cape Colony to settle in South Africa—saw themselves as an Exodus people, carrying their entire worldly goods and their idealized women and children into the wilderness in order to escape the aggrandizement of their English confreres, while at the same time they justified for themselves a master-servant relationship with the black population of South Africa. Despite the inspirational quality of this record, it still expresses the religious legitimation of apartheid, making possible the contradiction that today characterizes Southern Africa where a people 94 percent Christian has provided itself with a law system that "justifies" the exploitation of the overwhelming majority of the population of the land. The black South Africans, 71 percent of the population, are without citizenship; colored and Asians are without equal rights under the law; all three groups are separated from the resources needed for their development, and all this on the basis of laws initiated and administered by a controlling white population arguing for separate development as a value while retaining, in their own titles to the land, the property for production and the means of exchange. Religion of the civil variety in South Africa celebrates this system with the same psychic grip and social techniques for retaining it that are used in the case of civil religion in America. In both nations, civil religion can be seen currently to obscure the same type of social contradictions—social contradictions which emerge in America if one looks at the inner city, rural poverty areas, the minorities, the sick, poor, and elderly; and especially if one views the American nation-state in world perspective.

AMERICAN CIVIL RELIGION AND WORLD POVERTY

On May 1, 1974, the sixth special session of the General Assembly of the United Nations adopted a Declaration and Program of Action regarding the problems of raw materials and development. It was entitled "Declaration on the Establishment of a New International Economic Order." [28] It came at the end of a several-week period in which ninety-five of the developing nations of the world presented evidence of their need to participate in the decisions made about the disposal of the resources of their country in order for their people to survive as human beings. For the poor of the world it was a great event, the first time representatives of that 70 percent of the world's population possessing only 30 percent of its income had occasion to stand up and claim what is rightfully theirs: namely, a human share in the planning and use of world resources. Having organized in order to have enough power to speak effectively, they stated clearly what were their basic needs in an emerging world society. The target of attack was the American-based multinational corporation, its European counterparts, and the governments that support them. The question that becomes necessary for all of us to ask ourselves is, Whose side were we on on that occasion? Which perspective have we followed in the development of the struggle that has intensified between the rich nations that consume energy and the poor nations that produce energy? Only six nations voted against that charter; 130 voted for it; twenty discreetly abstained, because of the link of their immediate interests with the six vetoing nations. America vetoed, offering instead a proposal of aid in time of disaster. Vietnam, Cambodia, Western Africa, Chile, Brazil, the Dominican Republic, and Northern Ireland, as well as the Middle East, are examples of the kind of aid we are able and willing to provide to developing nations. These countries, long poor and used in the interests of nonresidents, relate to America in a way similar to America's own inner-city areas, all being places where the expendable people live. Neither the United States nor South Africa has been able to finance free health care, education, and care for the elderly in all their years of affluence, yet China learned how to do it and to carry out what they learned for 800 million poor and alienated people in twenty-two years. The difference in performance is related to a difference in the perception of the worth of people. We learn our evaluations of people in our religious systems. They are informed by our theology.

In early January 1974 I met with the North American Broadcast Section of the World Association for Christian Communications. Twenty-nine denominations, including Catholics, were there. I asked them what coverage they gave to the sixth special session of the United Nations. They asked me what event I was referring to. A show of hands from the delegates revealed five who knew the session had taken place. How do we reflect theologically on the events of our times if we do not know what is going on? Journals and newspapers as well as the verbal and visual media are organized and staffed by those who share a certain vision of what is worth seeing and reflecting on. The daily press scarcely covered this event in the United States. China and Japan did cover it. If the religion is civil, it is done in the interests of those whose interests are protected by the laws of the civil society. Our American conscience as shaped by our civil religion will hold in purview only those people we define as worthy to be viewed and it will do this according to our previous evaluation of who has the right to life and to the resources necessary to sustain that life. The poor are not central to that view.[29]

Two thirds of the world live below the level of subsistence in a world system which has technological potential for resolving this problem in the interests of all the people. Nation-states have adopted an operating rule making international decisions in their own business interests even when such interests jeopardize the lives, the freedom, and the development of the peoples over whom they have economic power, but to whom they have no citizen commitment by law. Some theologies affirm that rule. Some do not. There is a powerful movement in America and other First World countries to rest justice solely in entitlement. What the law defines as the rule of exchange then becomes the basis of justice, so that civil rights take precedence over human rights. A book propounding that rule won the religion and philosophy prize this year in the national book awards in America.[30] Exchange theory in sociology is becoming or has already become the most advocated form of sociological analysis on the university campus. It propounds similar standards for justice. In the words of George Homans:

> A man in an exchange relationship with another will expect that the rewards of each man be proportional to his costs—the greater the rewards the greater the costs—and that the net rewards, or profit, of each man be proportional to his investments—the greater the investments, the greater the profits.[31]

If Leviticus 25:25–28 and Luke 3:7–11 represent our theological perspective on the social order, then the new international economic order, as well as concern to hasten the current activity toward a planned economy for the United States in the national

interest, will be central elements in our theological reflection on
the biblical summons to return the land to the people every
fiftieth or Jubilee Year. These would not be the central concerns
for an American civil religion because the problem can be solved
only in world perspective. Civil religion sets limits to the
alternative social structures it can celebrate and still remain civil.
From a sociological perspective it seems that at this time a world
economy that honors the developing peoples and provides for
their betterment stands outside what American society can affirm.
It certainly stands outside what America did in fact affirm
regarding the United Nations economic charter.

The Hartford Statement[32] gathered signatures from American
theologians who had become concerned that God was no longer
the center of theological reflection because theologians had
become too absorbed in the social, economic, and political order. I
submit that the problems of the social order in world perspective,
that is, beyond the confines of the civil perspective, have scarcely
touched the vision of theology in America in any serious way; in
such a way, that is, that God-language might have come to name a
divine relationship with a world society that goes beyond the
interests of traditionally structured Western society. Since this
traditional society is no longer able to embrace the demands of the
world's poor for what they need for survival, though many of
those poor live either within the confines of the traditional society
or under its control, then its theologies cannot reach to God, that
is, they cannot reach beyond the special interests of the advantaged in the society in which they were developed.

Basil Moore and Sabelo Ntwasa, trying together to clarify why
the God of European theological reflection does no more than
reinforce Southern African white control over the black population, say in part:

> In South Africa the Christian God's whiteness has been
> there from the beginning, if not always overtly. The strange
> white man arrived on our soil with his strange new God, and
> set himself up as the ecclesiastical authority—a position he
> has never relinquished.

Having questioned the usefulness of the emphasis on God-as-person, given its sexual implications, they continue:

> Thus the symbol of God as "Father" reinforces his maleness and authority; God as "Son" reinforces his maleness; God as "Shepherd" or "Guide" or "Lord" or "King" or "Master" reinforces his authority; even God as "servant," like God as "Father," while attempting to express God's loving concern, still carries strong overtones of authority.[33]

Authority is the presence of the oppressor in an apartheid society.

Mary Daly has made similar points from the perspective of women in America.[34] The point is that language about God does not yet reveal space and hope for the oppressed peoples of the world. Because this is the case, theology is experienced by these oppressed peoples as a political act done in the interest of those whom the nations support, that is, the middle and upper classes, whites and males. For oppressed people words about God are merely another factor in the culture they experience as oppression, both within their countries and outside. For them, civil religion is not religious but merely civil.

THE SOCIETAL COMMUNITY

Prior to the current ascendancy of exchange theory in the academic community, structure-functional theory dominated sociological analysis. The current emphasis on exchange theory marks a shift in academic interest from the nation-state to the world trade system as the organizing principle of human intercourse. This shift to exchange theory is a basis of theological anxiety because it focuses the roots of world order in the international trading market and, in the development of international law, gives priority to the production and exchange of goods and services for development over human life and its development.[35] That shift is the reason why we have to test our theological concern for the development and presentation of the United Nations economic charter, a document and a program that would shift the emphasis of world order from the old affirmation of the trade elites to a new affirmation of all the world's peoples. Exchange theory, as well as the newer sociobiology, furthers this elite trading interest.[36] In this essay, I am not pursuing the full implications of these two theories but, rather, will, in this section, indicate a major new understanding of society derived from structure-functional theory applied to this problem of world trade.

Talcott Parsons has been the main exponent of structure-functional theory and his understanding of social systems is the major theory of that school. In his most recent theoretical explication he defines a society as "that type of social system characterized by the highest level of self-sufficiency relative to its environment, including other social systems." [37] Then Parsons proceeds to show how a society maintains itself in the self-sufficient state, through (1) the use of technology and an economy to exploit the physical environment, (2) the linking of the ecology to the division of labor by allocating economic interests among the various subgroupings of the population, (3) the political function, which means controlling action within the territory by the use of physical force (police and military) to prevent undesired action, (4) control of its membership by being able to count on the members to perform adequately the tasks needed for this self-sufficiency (rather than be alienated from the ways the institutions operate). This commitment of membership requires that the cultural system of the society be internalized in personalities, that the social system also be internalized, and that the cultural system be institutionalized in the social system.[38] These tasks of conditioning human psychic energy to the performance of the jobs that need doing for a society to maintain its self-sufficiency bring us to the heart of the uses of sociology within a given society. Finally (Parsons's fifth point), for self-sufficiency he notes that the society's institutions must be legitimized in two ways: (a) by the values its members hold in common with relative consensus, and (b) by congruence with the other components of the cultural system and especially that component he calls the system of constitutive symbolism. Constitutive symbolism is the core of the religious system, he declares, and he ends this formula for self-sufficiency by noting that ultimately values are legitimized in religious terms.[39]

Here, then, is the point of confrontation of the theologian and the sociologist. I fully realize that the last paragraph may be, from a theological perspective, boring and even meaningless, but it is still, from a sociological perspective, the heart of the matter. Parsons is saying that unless a social geographical entity can be self-sufficient, as he defines self-sufficiency, it is not a society. If you work back through his criteria, neither America, nor Germany, nor England, nor any other nation-state can by his criteria any longer be a society, because none is any longer self-sufficient in this sense. Once it uses its technology to control the resources of the world in its own interests, then a nation-state invades the sociocultural systems that define other societies. If each is struggling to be self-sufficient in the sense defined here, then each is overstepping the boundaries of the other. If, then, the religion that is operative in any one of these systems is maintaining the values that honor self-sufficiency as the yardstick of societal status for a rich nation-state, then the religion, along with the other institutional units of that so-called society, is acting against some people of the world in the interests of others.

This poses a problem for Christian theologians. Theoretically, Christianity stands with the poor of the world against all established interests that work to the manifest advantage of the rich man seeking to get through the eye of the needle. Historically, then, it should always be in judgmental tension with societal systems, especially as these systems have come in time to institutionalize the interests of advantaged segments of the society. Such, however, has not been the case. When Christianity remains true to its scriptural base, it is prophetic with respect to institutionalized exploitation. Membership, then, in organizations defined as Christian—that is, churches or mentalities that are distinctly Christian—should provide people with an affiliation alternate to their citizenship groups, in order to assure space for psychic solidarity that is not either easily co-opted into citizenship enthusiasm or repressed as defying the law. As civil religion, cultural enthusiasm and solidarity—by its very identification with established authority and even when it stands in criticism of that authority—collapses the social base for a prophetic stance and perhaps also decreases the possibility of creativity in the expressive modes, having limited the basic assumptions about social structures from which ideas about those structures might develop. From this perspective it appears that civil religion reduces tension and in so doing provides for the experience of a pseudo-divine assurance that the cultural norms associated with established civil power are closer to the will of God than is critical judgment passed on them, even when these cultural norms provide not for the life but for the death of the people.

The idea of civil religion is popular today because, for any nation to assert its right to program the world economy in its interests, those in power need the assurance of a naïve, spontaneous, uncritical, "religious" celebration—in Durkheim's term, an "effervescence"—to mask the mass exploitation that such a program requires. Religious enthusiasm uncritically expressed and charismatically released is one of the most effective ways of delaying the deluge.

Theologians are faced with a serious task in developing words about God that are not analogous to exploitative relationships, and yet are as effective as those of other sciences when they categorize substance, matter and energy, mind and behavior, people by race and location, society and social systems. If the sociologist discovers that there is now no society in our world because there is no self-sufficient geographical unit, that is, no people grouping in its own interests that does not by that very fact exploit other people whose interests are not its established concern and whose rights are not protected by its laws, then national gods become incredible. Language about gods corresponds to language about law, and both change as we become aware of other people whom we previously ignored. Throughout history people have changed their perspective from household gods to tribal gods, from tribal gods to national gods, from national gods to class gods. Karl Marx challenged the classism of religion and Max Weber demonstrated its existence, as has the research of sociologists in America since Liston Pope named the denominations by class in 1948.[40] Today, American blacks ask us, "Is God a white racist?" [41] The research of the 1960s on religion and prejudice, surveying the opinions of the majority of practicing Christians, suggests that the answer to that question is Yes.[42] Our cities overwhelmingly affirm that minister and people alike are still racist. Today, in pleading with us to move beyond patriarchy, women reach out for language about God that is nonfamilial; and we scarcely hear their reasons because they come so close to our personal identities and private gods.'[43]

In a year when we are asked to deal with justice as a program of social action we can well recall the historical development according to which Roman law affirmed only the rights of household heads in its *paterfamilias*. The Middle Ages dealt with the divine right of kings, which Dante immortalized by locating in hell (in the perfect ordering of the *Divine Comedy*) the popes who challenged this divinity of kingly rights—though the political implications of this scarcely touch our consciences. Modern nations began their religious activity under the rule of *cuius regio eius religio*; the religion of any territory was dependent upon the choice of its ruler, not the people. A concern for civil rights moved us to affirm in the 1950s that separate education is never equal. And today, human rights—affirmed by no law but stirring the new collective consciousness of a world of people newly aware of their own power and the processes of empowerment—seek a law, an ethic, a religious affirmation that our sciences have few words to name, a divine law neither modeled in the image of powerful civil systems nor proclaiming the same values, but standing in tension with such systems.

There was a time when civil religion was holy. This was during the period of the development of nations. It is still holy for developing peoples. But in America today it is a rationalization for the status quo—as the plight of our cities reveals only too painfully. American theologians, like all First World theologians, are called upon to develop a theology of relinquishment as the peoples of the world reach out to grasp what is rightfully theirs. For theologians, patriotism cannot be a primary virtue. Nation-states are today important societal units and nations are often cultural units that can and should celebrate their solidarity. However, if the God the advantaged people worship continues to be the society in which they live, then the anomie and alienation generated by disenchantment with an unjust social system will increase among the poor of the land. We can no longer afford to do theology—that is, to generate words about God—in any context which is less than global, or within the mental framework that defines peers as children, no matter who is called father. Transcendence, immanence, and spirit need affirmation—but not in the language of family, community, or society. God is not American no matter how much we would like this to be. Neither is God male, nor white, nor civil, nor economic, nor human. One cannot speak about God, however, without including these elements. What words, then, can we use to speak about God? That all depends on who the "we" are who do the speaking and for whom it is done. Politicians will try to convince believers to unite as they try to bind together—*re-ligere*—the units in which they have power, so that they can control the reflection and enthusiasms of the people. For some, yes, God is society; for the person of authentic religious faith, that is at least a moot question. Listen to the speech of the people.

NOTES

1. Max Weber, *The Sociology of Religion* (Boston: Beacon Press, 1963), pp. 80–137, for a graphic description of religion by social class, with all this implies for power and the uses of religion.
2. Robert Bellah, "Civil Religion in America," in *Beyond Belief* (New York: Harper & Row, 1970), pp. 168–86.
3. *Ibid.*, p. 180.
4. *Ibid.*, p. 183.
5. *Ibid.*, p. 186.
6. *Ibid.*, p. 185.
7. *Ibid.*, p. 186.
8. Robert Bellah, *The Broken Covenant* (New York: Seabury Press, 1975).
9. The significant literature regarding civil religion includes the following: Russell E. Rickey and Donald G. Jones, eds., *American Civil Religion* (New York: Harper & Row, 1974); Sydney E. Ahlstrom, *A Religious History of the American People* (New Haven: Yale University Press, 1972); Donald R. Cutler, *The Religious Situation: 1968* (Boston: Beacon Press, 1968); William G. McLoughlin and Robert N. Bellah,

Religion in America (Boston: Houghton Mifflin, 1968); Patrick H. McNamara, *Religion American Style* (New York: Harper & Row, 1974); Winthrop S. Hudson, *Religion in America* (New York: Charles Scribner's Sons, 1973); Sidney E. Mead, *The Lively Experiment* (New York: Harper & Row, 1963); Will Herberg, *Protestant, Catholic, Jew* (Garden City, N.Y.: Doubleday, 1955); Michael Novak, *Ascent of the Mountain, Flight of the Dove* (New York: Harper & Row, 1971).

10. Robert Bellah, *Beyond Belief*, p. xx.

11. Sidney Mead, "The Nation with the Soul of a Church," in Richey and Jones, *American Civil Religion*, p. 49.

12. *Ibid.*, p. 50.

13. *Ibid.*, p. 53.

14. John A. Coleman, "Civil Religion and Liberation Theology in North America," unpublished paper prepared for *Theology in the Americas: 1975*, Conference of North American and Latin American Theologians, Detroit, Mich., August 1975.

15. Quoted from Martin Marty, "Two Kinds of Civil Religion," in Richey and Jones, *op. cit.*, p. 142.

16. Emile Durkheim, *The Elementary Forms of the Religious Life* (London: Allen & Unwin, 1915), p. 225.

17. *Ibid.*, p. 206.

18. Gustavo Gutierrez, *A Theology of Liberation*, trans. Caridad Inda and John Eagleson (Maryknoll, N.Y.: Orbis Books, 1973), pp. 102–19; Max Weber, *op. cit.*, pp. 46–59.

19. Christopher Dawson, *Religion and Culture* (New York: Sheed and Ward, 1938).

20. National Opinion Research Center, *American Priests* (Chicago: NORC, 1971); prepared for the United States Catholic Conference.

21. "Whatever Happened to Theology?" *Christianity and Crisis* 35 (1975), pp. 106–20.

22. *Ibid.*, p. 111.

23. G. W. F. Hegel, *Reason in History* (New York: Bobbs Merrill, 1950).

24. Gary MacEoin, "Eleven-volume History of Ireland," *National Catholic Reporter*, May 23, 1975, p. 13.

25. Marie Augusta Neal, "Cultural Patterns and Behavioral Outcomes in Religious Systems," a paper delivered at the International Conference on the Sociology of Religion, September 1, 1975.

26. Charles Y. Glock and Rodney Stark, *Christian Beliefs and Anti-Semitism* (New York: Harper & Row, 1966). See also "The First Year: An Account of Boston School Desegregation: the Students, the

Officials and the Public," *Boston Globe*, May 25, 1975, section A, pp. 1–24.

27. T. Dunbar Moodie, *The Rise of Afrikanerdom: Power, Apartheid, and the Afrikaner Civil Religion* (Berkeley: University of California Press, 1975).

28. United Nations, *Declaration on the Establishment of a New International Economic Order* (United Nations, 3201-VI, May 1, 1974).

29. Francis Scott Piven, *Regulating the Poor* (New York: Random House, 1971); Harry Magdoff, *The Age of Imperialism* (New York: Monthly Review Press, 1969); Felix Greene, *The Enemy* (New York: Vintage, 1970).

30. Robert Nezick, *Anarchy, State and Utopia* (New York: Basic Books, 1975).

31. George Homans, *Social Behavior, Its Elementary Forms* (New York: Harcourt, Brace & World, 1961), p. 75. See also "Social Behavior as Exchange," *American Journal of Sociology* 63 (1958), pp. 597–606.

32. The Hartford Statement, "An Appeal for Theological Affirmation." See *New York Times*, March 9, 1975, for a report on the January meeting of eighteen ecumenists seeking a more theological basis for social action, having found the social movements of the 1960s too secular. The statement itself is reprinted in *World View* 18 (1975), pp. 39–41.

33. Basil Moore and Sabelo Ntwasa, "The Concept of God in Black Theology," in *The Challenge of Black Theology in South Africa*, ed. Basil Moore (Atlanta: John Knox Press, 1973), p. 23.

34. Mary Daly, *Beyond God the Father* (Boston: Beacon Press, 1973).

35. Pope Paul VI, *The Development of Peoples* (Boston: St. Paul, 1967).

36. The publication of Edward O. Wilson's *Sociobiology, the New Synthesis* (Cambridge: Harvard University Press, 1975) brings Social Darwinism again to the fore with new prestige and interest.

37. Talcott Parsons, *The System of Modern Societies* (Englewood Cliffs, N.J.: Prentice-Hall, 1971), p. 8.

38. *Ibid.*, p. 9.

39. *Ibid.*

40. Liston Pope, "Religion and Class Structure," *Annals of the American Academy of Political and Social Science* 256 (1949), pp. 84–91.

41. William R. Jones, *Is God a White Racist? A Preamble to a Black Theology* (Garden City, N.Y.: Doubleday, 1973).

42. See Charles Y. Glock and Ellen Siegelman, *Prejudice USA* (New York: Praeger, 1969).

43. Marie Augusta Neal, "Social Encyclicals: Role of Women," *Network Quarterly* 3 (Spring 1975).

MARY L. SCHNEIDER

a catholic perspective
on american civil religion

The scope of this essay is a limited discussion, from a
Catholic perspective, of some of the major problems inherent in
the current debate concerning American civil religion, particularly as the problems concern the Catholic community and
tradition in the United States.

One of the recently published landmarks in the field of
American religious history is Sydney Ahlstrom's monumental
work, *A Religious History of the American People*. Notwithstand-
ing its excellence, however, the book follows the basic pattern of
most Protestant histories of religion in America. Ahlstrom devotes
the bulk of the book to the various Protestant traditions, leaving
four chapters to Catholicism, two apiece to Judaism and black
religion, with an extra chapter thrown in for the "harmonial"
religious strains on the American scene. The structure of the book
reveals the basic and implicit assumption that when it comes to
the formation of a normative American culture, the primary input
has been the Protestant influence. Catholics have written their
own histories of Catholicism in the United States, very often as
though they were dealing with two parallel histories which
intersect and interact most frequently at the sad junction of
nativist attitudes and activities. American Catholic history has
been as much concerned with nativist confrontation and Catholic
response as it has with the basic facts of Catholic religious and
institutional development in the country. Thus, whether or not

one holds that the nation is still a "Protestant" nation culturally or has succumbed to a secularity that may be even more rigorous in the price it exacts from all religious traditions, it is clear that Catholicism, despite its numerical advantages, is not regarded as either the formative or the normative influence in the development of an American self-image.

With some exceptions, then, the problem of an American self-image and self-understanding has been the concern of the mainstream Protestant groups out of which the image of a "Protestant" nation fully emerged in the first half of the nineteenth century. Thus H. Richard Niebuhr, Sidney Mead, and Martin Marty, notably, have been among the first to raise the subject of the gradual penetration within the developing national self-image of certain biblical images—the Kingdom of God, the Promised Land, the Wilderness, the holy people of God—derived from the self-understanding of the early Anglo-Saxon Protestant immigrants.

They raise the subject from the point of view of how these images have been interpreted within the framework of the American experience. They are rightly concerned with the manner in which the images have been subject to abuse in certain periods of American history. But while these images have played an important role in the formation of an American self-image, they are not simply equated with an American civil religion. The various definitions of civil religion that have been proposed usually include the aspects of Protestant typology mentioned above, but go beyond them to incorporate certain secular motifs as well, which then take on religious overtones.

ATTEMPTS AT A DEFINITION

The primary problem which still exists in the discussion concerning civil religion in America is the problem of clarifying and defining terms. While the area of civil religion has been basically the domain of the social scientists and only relatively recently has invited the interest and concern of religious historians and theologians, the amount of study concluded so far by both groups lacks any common fund of definitions and terms. We are faced with various uses of such words and phrases as "civil religion," "nationalism," "patriotism," "the American way of life," "civic piety," "democratic faith," "transcendent values of the Republic," "overarching symbols of national unity," and "the American self-image."

Primacy has generally been conceded to Robert Bellah's definition of civil religion as "a collection of beliefs, symbols and rituals with respect to sacred things and institutionalized in a collectivity," [1] a collection which "at its best is a genuine apprehension of universal and transcendent religious reality . . . as revealed through the experience of the American people." [2] This view assumes a positive and normative role for an American civil religion. It becomes, in Sidney Mead's view, "the transcendent universal religion of the nation," [3] functioning in a prophetic capacity, calling national life and policy to a realization of cherished values and ideals and standing in judgment over both policy and practice. This definition presupposes nationhood as an implicit if not explicit given. The common set of symbols, beliefs, etc., arises out of a sense of unity and peoplehood which postdate any prior loosely conceived and expressed self-image. We can perhaps define the term "American self-image" as referring, in its early stages, to the Protestant self-image whose normative typology derived from the Puritan emphasis on the concepts of the Kingdom of God and a holy people, a new Israel.[4] This is not yet the mature civil religion which Bellah describes, but it is the beginning of the phenomenon. To this can be added the heritage of Anglo-Saxon constitutional law and the contribution of Enlightenment thought concerning God, man, and society.

This pluralism of sources forms the composite belief system and symbols which Bellah identifies and is at the root of one of the problems in defining civil religion. American civil religion is at once both deistical and Protestant, rational and religious, legal and nonlegal. It is the concern of the Protestant community precisely because the Protestant typological component has been so prone to demonic distortion in the development of the nation. It is the concern of the Catholic community insofar as that community has historically been on the receiving end of the distorted hope, characteristic of nativism, for a religiously segregated Kingdom of God. In addition, the Catholic community has been faced with the task of demonstrating its loyalty to the nation without falling into the pitfalls of a simple acceptance of that Protestant typological component.

This amalgam of rational and religious sources within an American civil religion has given rise to several alternative definitions. These definitions of civil religion are not as inclusive and general as Bellah's definition, but they emphasize one or more of the working components of the civil religion. Emphasizing the Protestant component, one definition that has been proposed is that of civil religion as *Protestant civic piety.* The Protestant emphasis on moralism, activism, pragmatism, individualism, the sense of national destiny are the object of focus in this meaning of civil religion which includes strong emphasis on an Anglo-Saxon coloring and interpretation of American history.[5]

Another definition which seems to stress the Enlightenment contribution as well as the contribution of Anglo-Saxon constitutional law is that of civil religion as the *democratic faith,* emphasizing the various concepts of justice, liberty, equality, without any necessary transcendent or divine reference. Democracy itself becomes the object of exaltation. Similar to Dewey's "common faith," [6] it is perhaps a variation that is relatively recent, having affinities to the democracy-as-religion theme of the Eisenhower era.[7] The definitions of civil religion as Protestant civic piety and as the democratic faith appear, then, to be simply several aspects of a far broader phenomenon of symbols and beliefs which have been termed civil religion. Bellah's definition remains the most inclusive, yet this very inclusiveness lends itself to a vagueness which makes it necessary to give closer scrutiny to the reality which it purports to identify.

The fact that we are dealing with a sociologist's definition points to the reality that is being identified as one which manifests itself as a *functional* element in American society, an element that is at once both observable and capable of functional interpretation. That Bellah can identify this as a "civil religion" reflects his sociological background. Most, if not all, sociologists (Durkheim, Luckmann, Berger) will agree that every functioning society has a common set of symbols, values, ideas. Even though definitions of "religion" vary, most are generic enough to encompass both the particular (denominational) and the general types of "religion" in the United States. Thus it is possible to equate the denominational and the general types of religion as having similar characteristics, regardless of whether or not both have a transcendent reference, an "other" as the object of worship.[8]

This lack of precision in defining "religion" is perhaps at the heart of the problem of an adequate understanding of the phenomenon termed "civil religion." Resolving this problem is the first necessary step toward formulating any acceptable Catholic approach and attitude, much less offering any theological contribution which can serve both the Catholic and the Protestant communities in their search for a satisfactory position to adopt toward civil religion.

SIGNIFICANCE OF ROUSSEAU'S CATEGORIES

As Bellah indicates, the term "civil religion" is derived from Rousseau's *Social Contract*. In chapter 8 of Book Four, Rousseau outlines the nature and qualities of a civil religion, while distinguishing between three types of religion. The first type is the religion of man, a purely internal worship of God without external rites, a worship rendered in terms of keeping the moral law. He labels this as the true theism, the divine right or law. The second type of religion is termed the civil or positive divine law or right and it consists in external rites or dogmas centering on the god(s) of a nation. Such was the religion of the Roman empire. The third type of religion offers two codes of conduct, two rulers, two "kingdoms," and sets up a dichotomy between loyalty to the earthly nation and obedience to a priestly caste. Such is the religion of Roman Christianity. In this third type, there is no possibility of social unity, no possibility of loyalty to both religion and citizenship. For Rousseau, this is by far the least acceptable of the three in terms of fostering a political and social unity.

The other two also have their defects: the first is so interior that it has no bearing or relationship to the body politic and cannot serve as a source of unity for the state. In fact, it would foster an indifference to the possible effect that one's actions would have on the body politic. The second type of religion is defective in that it creates superstition, allows the state to foster false religion in the name of expediency and unity, and produces an intolerant people who are prone to waging holy wars in the name of their god(s).[9]

Since the type of religion that exists in a society has such an important bearing on the existence and well-being of that society, Rousseau desires the good general beliefs and values of the first type of religion, but applied as the civil or positive divine law imposed by the sovereign (the second type of religion), thus having an applicability to the body politic.

The sovereign is limited in the imposition of this first type of religion, however, to beliefs which "have reference to morality and to the duties which he who proposes them is bound to do to others." [10] These are not exactly religious dogmas, but "social sentiments without which a man cannot be a good citizen or a faithful subject." [11] These sentiments are few and simple, such as the existence of a benevolent Providence, the existence of a future life in which there will be rewards for the just and punishment for the unjust, and the moral obligation to uphold the social and political unity of the state by obedience to its laws insofar as they are legislated for the general welfare of the community. The right to private religious beliefs is upheld insofar as these are one's opinions and insofar as they do not adversely affect the state's welfare and maintenance.[12]

It is clear that Rousseau's concern is with the function of religion in society, its ability to foster or destroy civil unity. Relegating specific doctrinal beliefs to the area of private opinion, he proposes a broadly conceived and sparsely categorized natural theology as the foundation of civil society, reflecting the basic Enlightenment penchant for the general, the natural, the rational, and the ethical.

While Bellah is careful not to posit any *direct* relationship between Rousseau's concept of civil religion and the founding of the American Republic, it appears that he does accept Rousseau's Enlightenment (and personal) bias regarding the relationship between religion and the state, i.e., that for a "rightly constituted government" there must be a unity between what Hobbes described as the two heads of the eagle,[13] and that this understanding has been in some manner reflected and incorporated into the founding of the American Republic. From that starting point Bellah can move to an investigation of the Republic in which all public phenomena (rites, symbols, speeches, etc.) can be viewed as a manifestation of that civil religion as Rousseau has defined it. Thus there is an uncritical acceptance that the public phenomena is "religion" because it manifests a religious dimension, and that it is a civil religion because it has characteristics similar to Rousseau's religious content.

The problem lies in ascertaining whether or not what Bellah (and also Rousseau) has described as a civil religion is in fact anything more than the religious dimension that is an indispensable aspect of the cultural ethos or character of a nation.[14] "Nation" here would mean a single entity which we could perhaps best describe as what Ernst Troeltsch would categorize as an "individual." An "individual" is a term referring to units of various kinds that can be identified in history; units possessing a unique, individual, and unrepeatable character. These can include classes, nations, historical epochs, religious communities, in fact, any entity which has an inner unity and which carries its own immanent meaning and value. It is a phenomenon which is unique to its own time and place and the complex of factors which influenced and shaped it. Each individual exists in a state of becoming much like an organism which has potential for both growth and decay. What is important in this concept is that the individual has potential for the formation of meanings and values, of a culture with its own self-understanding and beliefs which it values, maintains, and expresses as the source of its inner vitality and uniqueness.

Close to Bellah's definition, Michael Novak defines civil religion as "a public perception of our national experience, in light of universal and transcendent claims upon human beings, but especially upon Americans; a set of values, symbols and rituals institutionalized as the cohesive force and center of meaning uniting our many peoples." [15] This understanding includes a mature self-image, the formation of a set of values and behavior which become the norms and criteria by which we foster and continually re-create a "more perfect union."

Thus it is at the very least debatable that what has been defined as civil religion is anything other than a reified set of beliefs and values held by the nation as a whole. The people of the nation maintain and express these values and beliefs as the criteria and norms for their own self-understanding and self-criticism. These beliefs exhibit a religious dimension as an integral aspect of the total ethos of the nation.

It is possible, then, to argue that a national ethos, by its very nature, includes the development, maintenance, and expression of values and beliefs that become the inheritance of the people. This inheritance takes on a transcendent and normative function vis-à-vis the people, constituting their peoplehood or nationhood. This unity is expressed by the public phenomena which Bellah identifies as civil religion.

The term "civil religion," however, does not have these exact qualities when applied to the American republican ethos. But there existed enough similarity to warrant Bellah's use of the term. The crucial difference between Bellah and Rousseau lies within the context of the state as Rousseau proposed it. In his conception, beliefs and rites imposed on the citizens by the sovereign are ultimately supposed to derive from the citizens themselves, albeit in a quite different manner from what we are familiar with in the American Republic.

> The myth of the *Volonte Generale*—which is in no way a simple majority will, but a nomadic superior and indivisible Will emanating from the people as one single unit, and which is "always right"—was only a means of having the separate and transcendent power of the absolute king transferred to the people while remaining separate and transcendent, in such a way that by the mystical operation of the General Will the people, becoming one single Sovereign, would possess a separate, absolute, and transcendent power, a power from above over themselves as a multitude of individuals.[16]

The civil religion imposed by the sovereign in this conception appears to be the same as the ethos (character, values) of the people understood as a single unit. But in this situation, it is an ethos which contains within itself the ingredients for a demonic and heteronomous self-imposition on the body politic. The ethos of the American Republic, on the other hand, contains within itself, in its concept of unalienable rights, rights ultimately *not* derived from the body politic itself, a built-in bias which successfully militates against any apotheosizing of a "national Will," at the expense of the individual or the people as a whole.

It is perhaps also possible to argue that Rousseau simply accepted and utilized in a novel manner the traditional word *religio* which had assumed a broad, generic interpretation in the seventeenth and eighteenth centuries. Wilfred Cantwell Smith has traced the definitions of the term and the gradual historical change in the meaning of the word which allowed it to become synonymous with a system of beliefs, ideas, and rites. The question of what people believe and what they value became identified in Rousseau's period as the task of ascertaining their "religion."

In the Enlightenment view, religion became defined as a "systematic entity," [17] allowing for the distinction between natural religion and revealed religion to become popular as a means of distinguishing and classifying beliefs. Along with this there arose the concept of a "generic religion" to designate as an "external entity the total system or sum of all systems of beliefs, or simply the generalization that they are there." [18] It is this generic conception which Rousseau utilized and which he applied as the functional mechanism for national unity within the secularized type of society he proposed. In reality, what he succeeded in describing, from the general ingredients of the natural theology of his day, were the pertinent foundational beliefs and values for the ethos of his particular type of society or "individual."

A CATHOLIC PERSPECTIVE ON CIVIL RELIGION

From this discussion of the generic use of "religion" and the national ethos which appears to be the phenomenon to which the term "civil religion" refers, it becomes possible to formulate a Catholic perspective on the phenomenon and to formulate some guidelines that would also be of interest to the Protestant community whose typology is such a vital component of the American republican ethos.

The national ethos contains the beliefs, values, and rites which become and reflect the public self-perception. Various degrees of apprehension of that ethos are of course present within a nation, depending on ethnic multiplicity and a wide range of other factors—including historical changes in the self-image that occur as the result of national corporate experience. But one aspect of that self-understanding is that the public perception becomes in a reified manner the object of veneration, a cult of the nation.

This cult of the nation has provided some embarrassment to the Protestant community in particular. The Protestant typological component with its biblical imagery has proved to be a mixed blessing. On the one hand, it is an aspect of the national self-perception which has been responsible for much of the benevolence that has characterized American history and the rationale for much of the positive self-criticism of American life and policy. On the other hand, it has been the basis for most, if not all, of the nativism, imperialism, religious and racial bigotry which has also characterized American history. The imagery of America as the new Israel or the Kingdom of God has, under various circumstances, given rise to a zealous nationalism which has gone beyond the bounds of a "nation under God" and has bordered on a deification of the nation.[19]

This negative aspect has also created a problem for the Catholic community, which cannot simply be reduced to the nativist issue. For the Catholic, there is the broader problem of having to come to terms with being a cognitive minority, a non-Protestant presence in a Protestant environment. The question became how and under what circumstances the Catholic community could demonstrate its loyalty to the Republic, how become "Americanized" without an uncritical acceptance of all aspects of the ethos.

Dorothy Dohen has examined the various approaches taken by key members of the hierarchy to create a Catholic apologetic that would demonstrate the congeniality of Catholicism with a republican form of government.[20] Depite her conclusion that there has been (with the exception of John Lancaster Spalding) a gradual fusion of Americanism and Catholicism that has been achieved by

the hierarchy and which culminates in Cardinal Spellman's overly
zealous patriotism,[21] there exists within the Catholic tradition
several primary justifications for the attempts to reconcile the
community and the national heritage.

The first of these, which affords a Catholic argument for the
validity of patriotism, lies with the distinction which can be found
in the thought of Thomas Aquinas between the worship of God
and the veneration or cult of the nation. Under the broad
discussion of justice in the *Summa Theologica*, Aquinas enumer-
ates nine potential parts of justice[22] and utilizes the distinction
offered by Cicero between two of those parts, *religio* and *pietas*.
This distinction affords the possibility of distinguishing between
the worship that is owed in justice to God and the veneration or
reverence that is owed in justice to one's family and one's nation.
Following both Cicero and Augustine, Aquinas posits *religio* as
properly denoting only the worship of God, whether that mode of
worship is expressed by commanded acts or elicited acts.[23] God is
the end to which the virtue is directed.[24]

This restricted meaning of the word enables Aquinas to limit
the virtue without necessarily limiting the scope of man's
tendencies and obligations of reverence to God alone. There is
another term which properly denotes the debt owed to family and
nation—*pietas*. Again following Cicero, *pietas* is defined: "to
fulfill one's duty and conscientious service towards our own flesh
and blood and those having the interests of our country at
heart." [25] Thus the end of *pietas* is clearly distinguished from
religio and is given its own rationale and distinctiveness. The
nation can be the object of reverence without usurping the
primacy accorded to the worship of God.

The distinction between these two terms as potential parts of
justice serves the Catholic community as an apologetic. Contrary
to the nativist interpretation of Catholicism as a threat to the
nation, it becomes, instead, a source of patriotism which, in
maintaining the distinction between *religio* and *pietas,* can act as a
corrective element in American society, as a counterweight
against the tendency to deify the nation. The genius of Aquinas in
making the distinction was to place the two in a hierarchical order
based on the degree and quality of indebtedness owed to God and

to family and country. Justice is rendered according to the benefits derived from these sources. In no way can the benefits derived from belonging to a nation demand more loyalty or service than the benefits derived from God or even the family. In all cases, "the duties of piety are to be set aside in favor of those of religion." [26] This hierarchical framework can serve as a more viable way of speaking about the element of veneration—allowing for its existence, setting its limits, and tempering the apotheosizing tendencies of the Protestant typological component.

The second justification that exists within the Catholic tradition for the attempts to reconcile the community and the national heritage lies in the harmonious relationship between, on one hand, the Enlightenment and British constitutional law aspects of the national ethos and, on the other hand, the Catholic tradition of natural law. Here, again, the tradition has not only a contribution to make, but offers a standard which can serve as another corrective element of the national heritage.

John Courtney Murray's remarkable work *We Hold These Truths* argues persuasively that the immediate and complete acceptance of the form of government and the views of man and society which were incorporated in the governmental form of the United States was due to the fact that there was an "evident coincidence of the principles which inspired the American Republic with the principles that are structural to the Western Christian political tradition." [27] These Western Christian political principles are the product of medieval natural law. They include the following:

> . . . the idea that government has a moral basis; that the universal moral law is the foundation of society; that the legal order of society—that is, the state—is subject to judgment by a law that is not statistical but inherent in the nature of man; that the eternal reason of God is the ultimate origin of all law; that this nation in all its aspects—as a society, a state, an ordered and free relationship between governors and governed—is under God.[28]

These elements are part of the complex of truths which are

formulated and accepted as the public philosophy. As such, they are a major part of the nation's distinguishing character.[29]

Held as truths belonging to the philosophical and political order, these principles appear to have the same *functional* task as Bellah posits for a civil religion. They are held as truths derived from reflection on human experience and thus are seen to have a universal validity. They "determine the broad purposes of the nation as a political unity," a determination that is a moral act. They furnish standards for judging means and ends, and they furnish the basis for intranational dialogue. They are the content of the public philosophy and the object of support and veneration.[30]

Murray offers a critique of the Lockean concept of the natural law by listing the basic points in Locke's uncritical assumption of an Enlightenment understanding of man and society. Murray argues that this was, in reality, a naïve and degenerative conception which had value only insofar as it reflected, in a superficial manner, an underlying heritage in medieval natural law. This heritage ultimately rescued Locke's philosophy from its own worst practical conclusions, a rescue which was not effected in the case of Rousseau's philosophy where the medieval intellectualist idea of law as reason totally degenerated into the voluntarist idea of law as will.[31]

It is precisely this corruptive element of law as will which is capable of destroying a republic founded on the possibility that rational debate can lead to universal beliefs and values (a public philosophy) which in turn become the basis of a limited form of government. Law as will translates into a majority rule as the political technique for resolving all issues, disregarding any underlying national ethical and political principles. Murray observes that "the structure of the old idea of natural law follows exactly the structure of the problem of human liberty." [32] The function of natural law in political philosophy lies in resolving the "eternally crucial problem of the legitimacy of power, its value as a norm for, and its dictates in regard to, the structures and processes of society." [33]

There is a sense in which the United States owes the origin and stability (and perhaps ultimately its maintenance) of its political structure to the Catholic medieval natural law heritage. This is, of the two justifications offered in this essay, the most persuasive argument offered for the reconciliation of the Catholic community and the national heritage.

CONCLUSION: THE NEED FOR RELIGIOUS INTEGRITY

While it may be appropriate to indicate the theological justifications for Catholic participation in American society, there still exists a fundamental problem with an American civil religion. Alexis de Tocqueville observed in his *Democracy in America* that religious liberty and disestablishment have given an impetus to a vaporous blending of the secular and the religious in American life. This blending may prove the most serious problem for the Catholic and other religious traditions. It poses the dilemma of preserving the integrity and moral freedom of the traditions in a nation in which it is assumed that, in the absence of a state church, the various churches will assume the function of inculcating, along with the school systems, the values and beliefs that constitute the national identity. Under certain circumstances this can and has resulted in the gradual loss of the critical and prophetic element that rightly belongs to religious groups. Martin Marty in *The New Shape of Religion in America* and Will Herberg in *Protestant, Catholic, Jew* have discussed the shift in the 1950s in which the churches were called upon to support the American self-image and understanding. The churches' assumption of this function, however, led to deemphasizing not only their prophetic and judgmental rights, but also doctrinal differences in the effort to present a religious foundation for the "American way of life." Religion, particularly in its tripartite mold of Protestant-Catholic-Jew, was justified in terms of its function to create solid citizens, i.e., those whose sense of loyalty and patriotism almost always led to an unquestioning veneration of the state.

But no religious tradition can allow itself to be judged or defined in terms of its function in society. This tendency to reductionism is not limited to the American scene, but it is amenable to America in ways that are perhaps more subtle and therefore all the more dangerous than elsewhere. Therefore in this country especially, the limits placed on the indebtedness owed to the *patria* must counterbalance the demands for a nationalism in which the state is accorded the right to make moral decisions by some manner of corporate and/or divine right.

The American Catholic tradition cannot merge its religious faith and its patriotism. The submergence of one in the other would be the type of vaporous blending that much of the Protestant tradition has experienced in American history. Since the Catholic tradition finds itself somewhat removed from participation in the biblical typology found within the ethos that characterizes mainstream Protestantism, it is possible to divorce itself from the excesses of that identity between religious and national values. Yet Catholicism can also justify its compatibility with the best aspects of a biblical self-understanding and patriotism and offer a natural theology which deepens and clarifies both.

In conclusion, the definition of civil religion is crucial to the formulation of any Catholic perspective. While the area of a national spirit or soul is always an ambiguous one that can legitimately sustain a number of definitions of civil religion, the one I have offered does supply a starting point for developing a Catholic perspective stemming from the contributions of Aquinas, John Courtney Murray, and others. Starting from the definition of civil religion as the ethos and its veneration, one can assume a middle position that prevents both an uncritical acceptance or an equally uncritical rejection of the phenomena Bellah has singled out for investigation.

NOTES

1. Robert Bellah, "Civil Religion in America," *Daedalus* 96 (1967), pp. 1–21. The substantively identical article appears in Bellah's *Beyond Belief* (New York: Harper & Row, 1970).

2. *Ibid.*, p. 12.

3. Russell Richey and Donald Jones, eds., *American Civil Religion* (New York: Harper & Row, 1974), p. 15.

4. Michael Novak has pointed to the existence of at least five civil religions within the Protestant tradition alone, determined by the cultural histories of the various Protestant groups. Perhaps what Novak (and Bellah, as we shall see) are really describing is simply the various self-images of the nation which are varied and selective in terms of what beliefs, symbols, etc. are the frames of reference for the various group understandings of the national identity. Cf. *Choosing Our King* (New York: Macmillan, 1974), pp. 111–36.

5. Richey and Jones, *op. cit.*, p. 17.

6. There are significant differences, however. Dewey had a vision of the school as a "living community out of which there emerged common morality and a common faith," an other-directed social ethic that created and preserved an American democratic community. Education was to provide the experience and articulation of democratic community and as this experience was treasured, social progress and reform would make possible the greatest good for the greatest number. While he held that religious particularism could become divisive, he did not advocate uniformity. Cultural and religious diversity was to be valued as enriching experiences, even though the common faith of the nation, a faith in the democratic experience and ideal, did transcend and take precedence over ethnic and religious boundaries.

7. Richey and Jones, *op. cit.*

8. For an example of the generic approach to defining religion, see Clifford Geertz's definition which is equally applicable to particular (denominational) religion and the general type of religion that is usually associated with societal religion. Cf. "Religion as a Cultural System," *Anthropological Approaches to the Study of Religion*, ed. Michael Banton (New York: Praeger, 1966), p. 4.

9. J. J. Rousseau, *The Social Contract and Discourses*, trans. G. D. H. Cole (London: J. M. Dent, 1973), pp. 272–74.

10. *Ibid.*, p. 276.

11. *Ibid.*

12. *Ibid.*

13. *Ibid.*, p. 271.

14. "Ethos" is defined as "the character, sentiment or disposition of a community or people; the spirit which actuates manners and customs, and especially moral attitudes, practices and ideals," in *Webster's New International Dictionary*, 2nd ed., 1949.

15. Novak, *op. cit.*, p. 127.

16. Jacques Maritain, *Man and the State* (Chicago: University of Chicago Press, 1951), pp. 44–45.

17. Wilfred Cantwell Smith, *The Meaning and End of Religion* (New York: New American Library, 1964), p. 43.

18. *Ibid.*

19. One of the definitions of American civil religion offered in Richey and Jones's work is that of zealous nationalism. In this case, as with the definitions of American civil religion as Protestant civic piety or as the democratic faith, one aspect of the total ethos is singled out and emphasized. See also Robert Jewett, *The Captain American Complex* (Philadelphia: Westminster Press, 1973) for a study of the positive and negative uses of biblical imagery in American history.

20. Dorothy Dohen, *Nationalism and American Catholicism* (New York: Sheed and Ward, 1967).

21. She uses the word "nationalism" in a pejorative sense. It is something *more* than mere patriotism. "Nationalism is the ideology which permits the nation to be the impersonal and final arbiter of human affairs . . . , nationalism encourages the nation to view its common value system as ultimate, at the same time that it conceives of the nation as the single interpreter of the common creed or value system." This gives the nation "a role in human affairs which has priority over the role of religion, since in cases of value conflict it is the nation—not religion—which has the ultimate right to interpret its own creed, as well as to judge its own actions." (*Ibid.*, pp. 6–7.)

22. Thomas Aquinas, *Summa Theologica*, II/II, q. 80, a. 1.

23. *Ibid.*, II/II, q. 81, a. 1; see also ad 1, ad 2.

24. *Ibid.*, II/II, q. 81, a. 5, ad 2.

25. *Ibid.*, II/II, q. 101, a. 1; see also a. 3, ad 1.

26. *Ibid.*, II/II, q. 101, a. 4.

27. John Courtney Murray, *We Hold These Truths* (New York: Sheed and Ward, 1960), p. 43.

28. *Ibid.*, p. 42.

29. Murray defines "public philosophy" as emphasizing "an objectivity of content"; the term "public concensus" as emphasizing "a subjectivity of persuasion." (*Ibid.*, p. 79.)

30. *Ibid.*, pp 80–81.

31. *Ibid.*, p. 41. For the critique of Locke, see pp. 302–20.

32. *Ibid.*, p. 320.

33. *Ibid.*, p. 332.

JOHN J. MAWHINNEY, S.J.

h. richard niebuhr and reshaping american christianity

In studying the history of American Christianity, H. Richard Niebuhr sought to discover the values inherent in its tradition and learn how they could be reshaped to meet the needs of the present. His objective was to enhance the American cultural and religious tradition out of which he personally had come and with which he continued to find his identity. In this essay we focus primarily on the method and central thrust of three of his writings that deal explicitly with the history of American Christianity. Our study is prefaced with some preliminary observations on Niebuhr's chief theological principles.

INTRODUCTION:
NIEBUHR'S METHOD OF THEOLOGIZING

Niebuhr never attempted to be a systematic theologian. His many essays and even his books resemble "occasional pieces" written to give *his* response to the mood and temper of the time and place in which they were written. There are, of course, certain themes and convictions which appear throughout his works and reveal the unity and consistency of his thought, but they, too, have their origin in how Niebuhr saw himself related to his times. Niebuhr never attempted to relate these themes and convictions in a

systematic way. In this introduction we discuss the most important ones for understanding Niebuhr's approach to the reshaping
of American Christianity.

1. A general methodological conviction runs through all of
Niebuhr's work. It is the conviction of the radically historical
character of human existence. Niebuhr explains this conviction as
follows:

> I am certain that I can only see, understand, think, believe,
> as a self that is in time . . . . I do not see that faith comes to
> me or to my fellowmen through any doctrines about what
> lies back of the historical event. It comes to me in history,
> not in doctrines about history.[1]

This conviction is clearly central to Niebuhr's interpretation of
Christianity as movement and life, to his way of relativizing its
institutional forms and historical expressions and to his theological
and historical relationalism.

2. Neibuhr's primary and fundamental interest was ethical. He
saw modern Western civilization in serious crisis and was
concerned about its fate and what could be done to save it. He
held that one of the major and never ending responsibilities of the
church was the reformation of society, the uplifting of culture,
and the revival of the human spirit. His approach to the problem,
however, was indirect, for he was also convinced that the
fundamental reformation of society lay in the reformation of the
church.[2]

Yet, in line with his conviction about the radically historical
character of human existence, he held that the Christian life was
continous with other modes of human existence and so could not
be understood apart from human life in general. Hence, in his
ethical reflection he sought to explore human moral life in general
and not simply the Christian life.[3]

Thus there is a certain humanistic and universal thrust present
in almost all Niebuhr's work even though, as we shall see below
(point 4), he always writes as a Christian. What he says of his
methodology in *The Responsible Self* might be said of much of his
work: my work "is more philosophy than theology in the current
understanding of theology, because my approach is not Bible-

centered, though I think it is Bible-informed." [4] Or, as he says in another passage: his reflections are those "of a Christian who is seeking to understand the mode of his existence and that of his fellow beings *as human agents.*" [5]

3. Niebuhr's ethical thinking is theocentric and radically monotheistic. It "takes as its starting point men's existence as lived in relation to God," or in other words, "posits that in all man's seeking he seeks God." [6] This God is not just a being, a good, but Being itself, Goodness itself, "the constitution of all things, the One beyond the many, the ground of my being and of all being, the ground of its 'that-ness' and its 'so-ness,'" and the basis of all valuing, for "man exists and moves and has his being in God." [7] For Niebuhr this radical monotheism implied that God alone is absolutely sovereign and trustworthy.

4. Niebuhr approached all his work as a Christian.[8] Again in line with his conviction about the radically historical character of human existence, Niebuhr could not think about God's relation to man in the abstract but only as it appeared in his personal history. For Niebuhr this history was the history of Jesus Christ as known in the Christian community in which Niebuhr was nurtured and with which he identified. The life and history of this community was linked with the life and history of Jesus Christ. It was through this community that Jesus Christ revealed the Father as loving and trustworthy, as redeeming and purposeful.

As far as Niebuhr knows, the full revelation of God and of his miraculous gift of healing and saving grace has occurred only in Jesus Christ. Niebuhr has no evidence to say that such a revelation has also occurred outside the sphere of Jesus' working, but wherever it does seem to have taken place, Niebuhr feels the need to "posit the presence also of something like Jesus Christ." [9] As for Luther, so for Niebuhr: God and faith belong together. Therefore Niebuhr does his reflection *as a Christian* "seeking to understand the mode of his existence and that of his fellow beings as human agents." [10]

Thus we can conclude that, in line with the universalism and theocentrism of his thought, Niebuhr's theology is not Christocentric. The God whom Jesus reveals is not only a Christian God, for there is only one God and he is the Ground of all being and the

Lord of all men. It is only Niebuhr's relation to this God that is Christian because, as a radically historical being, he finds his way of thinking about life, himself, his companions, and their destiny has been so modified by the presence of Jesus Christ in their history that he cannot escape his influence. Nor does he wish to escape it, since he has identified himself with Christ's cause.[11] Again in line with his universalism and theocentrism, Niebuhr understood this cause as the reconciliation of man to God in the sense of universal redemption.

THE SOCIAL SOURCES OF DENOMINATIONALISM

The Social Sources of Denominationalism[12] clearly reflects the universalism and ethical thrust of Niebuhr's theology. The major portion of this work is given over to a careful, detailed inquiry into the impact of various social forces and sectional interests on men's faith and their churches. Niebuhr shows how social and historical factors, rather than theological and creedal formulas, determine the structures, beliefs, ethics, and polities of the divided churches and sects of American Protestantism. He concludes that they are in large measure merely reinforcing the social, economic, racial, ethnic, and political loyalties of the secular culture which surrounds them. They substitute the ethics of caste-organization, class domination, and self-preservation for the ethics of the gospel of Christ. Consequently, in time of social and political crises, they can contribute nothing toward the work of social reconstruction, since they "function as political and class institutions and express that code which forms the morale of the political and economic class each represents" (pp. 22–24, 264–66). In brief, the history of Christian denominationalism is the history of the ethical failure of the churches. The churches do not preach the ethics of Jesus because Christians have failed to transcend the social conditions of their environment (p. 279).

In *Social Sources* Niebuhr's concern about the ethical powerlessness of the Christian churches is closely related to his concern about the fate of Western civilization and the inability of Christianity to effect the cultural integration of the West. "The problem of the world," he writes, "is the problem of the synthesis of culture—of the building up of an organic whole in which the various interests and the separate nations and classes will be integrated into a harmonious, interacting society, serving one common end in diverse manners" (p. 266). Writing in the decade following World War I, Niebuhr saw the West standing aghast before the destructive possibilities of its own handiwork and in need of "some compelling and integrating ideal." This ideal would create the common mind and devotion to divine ends which alone make for unity among men. But Western civilization faced a serious problem; "the only religion available seems incapable of establishing, even within its own structure, the desired harmony" (p. 268).

In *Social Sources* Niebuhr is convinced that the ideal necessary for the synthesis of human culture and the integration of mankind can still be found in the Gospels. There the revelation of the Kingdom of God is not made in terms of dogma but of life and movement, above all, the life of Jesus Christ (p. 278). This kingdom is "nothing less than the eternal harmony of love in which each individual can realize the full potentiality of an eternal life in self-sacrificing devotion to the Beloved Community of the Father and all the brethern" (p. 279). Thus the mission of the churches is the transformation of the whole of society into the Kingdom of God. The churches have often failed to carry out this mission, but Niebuhr is convinced that many of the movements that have arisen within the churches have served this mission quite well. He mentions in particular George Fox and his Friends and the friars under the leadership of Francis of Assisi. Each of these movements has functioned as a church within a church, but as each became institutionalized, it lost the creative spirit that had given it birth and power.

Despite his recognition of the sorry plight of both the world and the churches, Niebuhr speaks in *Social Sources* as an idealistic and optimistic liberal. He makes no mention of the radical sinfulness of man and understands repentance in human terms: the willingness of both individuals and churches to sacrifice their security and pride in order to find a brotherhood of love. He clearly believes that the churches are capable of throwing off their secular character and incarnating the Gospel ideal of the eternal harmony of love and the brotherhood of all men under the Kingdom of the Father. Thus, redemption is social as well as individual and begins on this earth. The ideal of this Kingdom is to be sought through "a self-sacrificing devotion to human brotherhood." The ideal aims to promote "the creative synthesis of human culture" and "the organic integration of mankind into a functional whole" (p. 280).

The full revelation of this ideal was made in Christ, but even apart from Christ the ideal has been sought and worshiped in an obscure way by all men. The ideal has been adumbrated in ethics, illustrated in the family at its best, allegorized in the nobler aspects of patriotism, tried in endless political experiments and "seen in the dark glass of reason by philosophers and prophets" (p. 279).

Niebuhr rejects a "crisis theology" which would condemn human effort and await the arrival of the Kingdom through an "eschatological miracle." Religion is both a divine and human enterprise and has an obligation to penetrate human culture with as much saving knowledge as its best insights can provide.

However, the final significance of the Kingdom of God transcends all mundane versions of it. Ultimately, salvation comes by faith alone, and men must rely on God's mercy rather than human effort to attain peace with him. Thus, although Niebuhr severely criticizes the "crisis theology" of his day for its extreme otherworldliness and its rejection of the human elements in religion, he recognizes that certain elements in "crisis theology" provide a necessary complement to a frequently provincial social gospel. He proposes the ideal of an eternal harmony of love among all men as a middle ground between the extreme anthropocentric understanding of religion (with an almost purely human social ideal) and an excessively otherworldly interpretation of Christianity. His exposition of this position in *Social Sources* appears to be more by way of exhortation than by way of argument.

THE KINGDOM OF GOD IN AMERICA

Eight years after the publication of *Social Sources*, Niebuhr published a second interpretation of American Protestantism, *The*

Kingdom of God in America.[13] He had come to the conclusion that the strictly sociological approach of *Social Sources* did not allow the whole story of American Protestantism to emerge. *Social Sources* was concerned primarily with the static, passive, institutional structures of Protestantism and the interrelationships between these structures and other social and cultural forces. Its focus was on the divisive pluralism within Protestantism and the consequent ethical failure of its churches. *Kingdom of God* focuses on Protestantism as a religious movement rather than on its institutions. It seeks to explain the power, independence, aggressiveness and communality of the religious faith that Protestant churches share as a common possession.

The sociological approach of *Social Sources* explained the dependence of religion on culture but not the independence of religious faith from culture. Unlike *Kingdom of God*, it gives the impression that even though Protestantism, in its institutional expressions, is greatly affected by social and cultural forces, it lacks, as a religious movement, the power to impact significantly on society and culture. Finally, the only positive ethical solution to the problem of denominational disunity that *Social Sources* could propose was an exhortation to good will to overcome stubborn social divisions and to incarnate the ideal of Jesus. In *Kingdom of God* Niebuhr develops the principle of the absolute sovereignty of God as a sophisticated constructive principle of a creative and dynamic Protestantism.

In *Kingdom of God* Niebuhr is searching for meaning in America's past because he believes that the present has continuity with the past and that unless one understands what is retrospect, he can have no sure direction for what is prospect. He hoped to discern within the multifarious history of American Christianity a pattern of meaning, a principle of unity, a law of development and movement that can assist us in making present critical choices.

His method is to interpret American Christianity by taking his stand solidly within the Christian tradition. "No movement," he argues, "can be understood until its presuppositions, the fundamental faith upon which it rests, have been at least provisionally adopted" (pp. 12–13). These presuppositions may later be rejected with good reason, but if from the start we make some extrinsic standpoint the absolute criterion for judging the object of criticism, we beg the question from the beginning and erect a major barrier to real understanding. Only after we have sought to understand from within may we compare our results with those yielded by the opposite approach. Thus, in *Kingdom of God*, Niebuhr writes *ex fide ad fidem*. As a Christian he seeks to understand the mode of his existence as an American and that of his fellow countrymen. He can be most critical of his American Christianity, but it is the criticism of one who has great faith in its ultimate and fundamental vitality, a vitality that springs from his deep, abiding faith in the one all-sovereign God and his love for his creation.

Niebuhr rejects the suggestion that the pattern of American Christianity is to be found in its economic or total social history. The faith of American Christianity is not just a cultural epiphenomenon, a defense mechanism or a belief that has enabled Americans to endure the trials and tribulations of life. It is not simply a social faith, though such a description of the pattern of religious life in the United States has an obvious pertinency. But such a description is far from telling the whole story. Niebuhr believes that there is a revolutionary, dynamic, creative strain to American faith which does not fit into the pattern of a merely social faith. For men like John Cotton, Roger Williams, Jonathan Edwards, William Channing and many others, the Kingdom of God is prior to America, to its politics and economics. Its God is not a protecting, henotheistic deity of the United States, but the God of all men who passes divine judgment on all men and demands repentance and rebirth. America and its people are required to conform to his will and, for so doing, God promises not human victory but eternal salvation. In Niebuhr's view, American Christianity has value as a social faith only insofar as this faith maintains the conviction that it is something more than a social faith. We can understand such a conviction, he argues, only if we first seek to understand this faith from within the movement we call American Christianity.

Niebuhr contends that the meaning and pattern of the multifarious history of American Christianity is found in the idea of the Kingdom of God. Throughout their history American Protestants have employed this idea as the ultimate principle for understanding the characteristically Protestant way of insisting on the absolute sovereignty of God. However, this idea has been interpreted from various perspectives in the course of American Protestant history. In the colonial period we find primary stress placed on the absolute sovereignty and initiative of God. Later, during the creative periods of the Great Awakening and other revivals, the emphasis was on the reign of Christ. During the last century the stress was on the coming Kingdom. Although American Protestants emphasized at different periods one or other of these interpretations, they always recognized that all three were essential for a full understanding of the idea of the Kingdom of God.

In all three periods of American Protestant history, the idea of the Kingdom of God involved two affirmations. Negatively, it meant the relativization of everything human: "no plan or organization could be identified with the universal kingdom since every such plan was product of a relative, self-interested and therefore corrupted reason" (p. 23). Positively, it affirmed God's direct, immediate, present, and sole rule over all men and over all creation without the mediation of any person or institution, ecclesiastical or temporal.

As a protest movement Protestantism was most effective. It found it relatively easy to challenge the absolute claims of all relative powers in the name of God's absolute and sole kingship. In this sense Protestantism was a revolutionary power. But this is the negative side of Protestantism. On the positive side Protestantism faced a serious dilemma which Niebuhr refers to as the problem of constructive Protestantism. The dilemma arose out of the fundamental faith-stance of Protestantism. First, since supreme power belonged to God alone, Protestantism could have no will-to-power. Second, since God's rule over men was a present reality and was exercised in sovereign freedom, the future lay with God alone, and Protestantism could not pretend to know precisely where God might lead men. Thus, the Protestant movement was strong on God's role in the construction of human life, but (unlike Catholicism) it was weak on man's role in this construction. Yet men had to do something to respond to the divine action. They could not just sit back passively and wait, for they lived in a crisis. God's Kingdom was pressing upon them, and they were hastening either to destruction or to life. They had to press forward into his Kingdom. This dilemma appeared in the areas of morality and in the structures of political, economic and ecclesiastical life (pp. 28–34).

American Protestants faced this dilemma in a way quite different from that of their European forebears. At the time the first settlers came to America, European and English Protestantism was still seeking to establish its independence. But in America there was no established church, Roman or royal, and no prince or government of any kind to protest against. As the Puritan Francis Higginson put it: "We do not go to New England as separatists from the Church of England; though we cannot but separate from the corruptions in it; but *we go to practice the positive part of church reformation, and propagate the gospel in America*" (as quoted by Niebuhr, with his emphasis, pp. 43–44). America was truly a place where Protestants were free to make an experiment in positive and constructive Protestantism. "What they did not foresee," Niebuhr tells us, "was that the positive part of church reformation was not a structure but a life, a movement, which could never come to rest again in secure habitations, but needed to go on and on from camp to camp to its meeting with the ever coming kingdom" (p. 44).

This quotation points to the basic thesis of *Kingdom of God*—that Christianity is a life, a movement, and what makes it a life and a movement is its adherence to the principle of God's absolute rule over all men and over all creation. American Protestantism, Niebuhr contends, has been most vital where and when its commitment to this principle was strongest. When and where this commitment has weakened, it has tended to sink into a form of cultural Protestantism.

Niebuhr's study of the history of the Kingdom of God in America left him with three convictions which manifest themselves in all his subsequent writings. First is the one we have already mentioned, the conviction that Christianity is a movement, not an institution or a series of institutions. "It is gospel rather than law," and the true church is "the organic movement of those who have been 'called out' and 'sent' " (p. xiv). Consequently, the real meaning and genius of the Christian movement can never be expressed in organizations, laws, ethical programs, and doctrinal creeds, but only in a life or movement directed toward the infinite, eternal, and transcendent God. Human efforts to capture and crystallize Christian movements in ideas and institutions, in conservative creeds and liberal programs are probably inevitable, but always, even at their best, ambiguous. "We shall look in vain," Niebuhr writes, "if we seek to find in the Protestant ecclesiastical institutions the characteristic features of the Protestant movement; if they are there at all they appear in a form which denies as much as it represents the original intention" (p. 28, note). All efforts at institutionalization are only halting places between Christian movements. "The Franciscan revolution not the Roman Catholic Church, the Reformation not the Protestant Churches, the Evangelical revivals not the denominations which conceived its fruits—and denied it—show what Christianity is" (p. xiv).

Yet because Christians have always wanted to transmit the insights and "white-hot" convictions of their most vital and revolutionary periods, they have tried to consolidate and conserve them. Although these efforts at conservation may at first preserve the content of the dynamic movement that gave them birth, they do not preserve its spirit and inner vitality. The parent movement derives its dynamism from its ability to free men from bondage to a static past by pointing them forward, while efforts at conservation look to the past and tend to become defensive and more fearful of loss than hopeful of new insight and strength. They easily become content with the achievements of the past and lose the spontaneity and power to generate new ideas. They seek, and often quite successfully, to put the insights of their creative parent movement into the symbolic forms of formulas, rituals, and creeds. A symbol, however, is never the reality itself. It only points to the reality, and so, much of the original experience is necessarily omitted from it. As time goes on, the symbol becomes increasingly obscured and even lost, since it becomes wholly substituted for the reality of the original experience. Thus "by limitation and loss of symbolic reference and by the substitution of the static for the dynamic, institutions deny what they wish to affirm and become the antithesis of their own thesis" (p. 169). In this way, they lose the inner vitality of the creative, revolutionary movement which gave them birth. Niebuhr doubts that there is any escape from this process of institutionalization and subsequent deterioration or petrifaction.

The second conviction is connected with the first. As a movement Christianity is a dialectical process that comes to expression in many ways. Theologically, Christianity recognizes that in redeeming the world, God not only draws men to himself, but also moves toward the world, since in his only begotten Son he seeks to restore the whole order of creation to its original righteousness. Therefore, in its worship of God, Christianity must seek to move toward God in its pilgrimage toward the eternal Kingdom. At the same time, in its work, Christianity must move toward the world (which is loved in God) by making his will real on earth. This dialectical movement never reaches a synthesis as long as history remains incomplete, for only God can provide the synthesis for it. Thus no one age, no one society, nation, or civilization ever "can set forth the full meaning of the movement toward the eternal and its created image" (p. xv). The recognition of the dialectical character and continuity of the Christian movement should, therefore, promote tolerance, understanding, and love of those representing other phases of this movement.

The third and final conviction is that apart from a faith in a sovereign, living, loving, and forgiving God, American Christianity and culture is meaningless and destructive. When nations or Christian churches fail to recognize their own finitude and dependence on the one all-sovereign God, they make themselves into gods and become temporary, destructive obstacles to the realization of God's final plan for the whole of creation. Niebuhr hopes that his work in writing about the idea of the Kingdom of God in America might serve as a stepping stone for "the work of some American Augustine who will write a *City of God* that will trace the story of the eternal City in its relations to modern civilization instead of to ancient Rome, or of Jonathan Edwards *redivivus* who will bring down to our own time the *History of the Work of Redemption*" (p. xvi).

THE PROTESTANT MOVEMENT
AND DEMOCRACY IN THE UNITED STATES

Niebuhr further develops his conviction that Christianity is a
movement in his 1961 essay "The Protestant Movement and
Democracy in the United States." [14] In the first part of the essay
he discusses Protestantism on its own terms, as existing between
the polarities of movement and order, process and structure, but
drawn more to the dynamic pole of movement and process than to
the static pole of order and structure. In the second part he
discusses Protestantism in relationship to democracy. Niebuhr
sees Protestantism in polar tension with democracy—standing
between the dynamic forces of movement and countermovement,
at one time producing disorder and dependency at another time
leading to unity and renewed dynamism.

A. *Protestantism as Movement and As Order*

Protestantism as Movement. In *Kingdom of God* Niebuhr expressed the conviction that Christianity as a movement is
dialectical, moving both from God to the world and from the
world to God.[15] In this 1961 essay he develops the idea of
Christianity as a movement from a somewhat different, though not
conflicting, viewpoint. He stresses the polarities of movement and
order, process and structure, which are to be found in American
Protestantism (p. 22), and indicates that "in human history the
dynamic seems always to be followed by the static, and there is a
requirement for order in every movement" (p. 36). Thus, though
they stand in polar tension to one another, both movement
(process) and order (structure) are not only present in Protestantism but are essential to it. In *Kingdom of God* Niebuhr was quite
negative toward institutionalization. In 1961 he is far more
positive toward the forces that make for order and structure, and
finds even in them considerable dynamism.

The 1961 essay, like *Kingdom of God*, puts the emphasis not on
God's past activity in history, but on his present activity; not on
the visible, historical church, but on faith, hope, and love as
essentially invisible movements of the spirit that must seek
constantly new incarnations. The pattern Niebuhr has in mind as

he looks on general and church history is not that of a new creation continuing in enduring structures, but that of creation, fall, and re-creation. Everything is in constant process and movement. Everything is becoming. The church and life itself must be constantly created anew.

This process of becoming is particularly evident in the United States. The American Protestant churches for the most part trace their origins not directly to a sixteenth-century conflict with Roman Catholicism but to a constant stream of reform movements that never seem to stop flowing. Although few of these churches use the term "Protestant" in their official titles, all seem to be content to be called "Protestant." These churches accept this common designation, Niebuhr suggests, because they believe that the term refers to a spirit and faith that constantly is ready to protest against any established order of Christian faith.

Niebuhr finds the source of this protest not in some antiauthoritarian will-to-power, the desire of every man to be God, but in the affirmation of a new life that requires no external ordering because it is ordered from within by the attractiveness of the good. The protest is against the acceptance of mediocre moral and religious existence, but the goal is regeneration, awakening, renewal, and liberty for a new life. The protests are expressions of a revived confidence that a new quality of life is at hand—a confidence that involves a new moral seriousness, a hunger for righteousness, an increased sensitivity to false and divided loyalties and a hope for increased integrity in the self and in the common life (pp. 33–35).

Protestantism as Order.[16] The orders and structures of Protestantism generally emerge from one of two types of situations. One is the conflicts that occur when any reform movement seeks to free itself. The other is the need to conserve the insights of the reform movement for a new generation. These orders and structures are quite secondary in Protestantism—means rather than ends. For the most part they were not envisaged by the founders of Protestantism. Some clearly have their origin in the inspired reading of the Scriptures. Others, particularly liturgical practices, the sacraments, and preaching, though authorized and even rooted in the Scriptures, were inherited from the long

Christian tradition. Still others arise from the interaction of various Protestant movements and groups. They account for the many creedal, cultic, and organizational similarities in diverse Protestant churches. Finally, others have emerged under the influence of the common cultural and political environment of the United States.

Niebuhr stresses that the major elements of Protestant order, especially in America, have retained a certain fluidity and dynamism of their own. For example, although the Bible is an order, its authority is more prophetic than legal. It is not a list of imperatives to be obeyed, but a record of promises, a call to repentance, to change of heart, and to joy in the hope of redemption. Thus its authority has the power of promise in process of fulfillment rather than the power of law. Only in a secondary way do Protestants appeal to it as a constitutional authority for principles of "faith and order" and church polity. Even then, the principles to which they appeal are almost always the ones inherited from the Christian tradition.

Similarly, the common political and cultural environment of America has contributed to the fluidity and dynamism to be found in Protestant order. The chief element of this common environment is the steadfast, though often unconscious, confidence of all believers that "all their religious and secular movements and institutionalizations take place within a world actively governed as a universal commonwealth" by the rule of an all-sovereign God (p. 36). This rule of God is an actual and present affair. However obscurely and mysteriously, divine justice and mercy is being exercised even in the midst of the worst turmoil and suffering. At the same time, although believers are confident that the world is ruled by divine Providence, they possess considerable freedom, not on ultimate issues, but within limited spheres of action. They must constantly wrestle seriously, though provisionally, with the problems of the ordering of life as a temporal affair. Rather than wait for the enforcement of some moral law of nature, they find that they must anticipate, with repentance, the impending judgment of God for such sins as slavery, racial discrimination, international conflict, and Protestant disunity.

B. *Protestantism in Relation to Democracy*

Everywhere, but especially in America, Protestantism has developed in constant interaction with other social and political movements. Niebuhr believes that arguments can be made to show that democracy has promoted both disorder and dependency as well as unity and dynamism in American Protestantism.

Increasing Protestant Disorder and Dependency. From one point of view the conditions of American democratic freedom have meant for Protestants "anarchic pluralism and dependency on the voice of the people rather than the word of God" (p. 51). Religious freedom has not only freed the churches from governmental and political interference but also made them dependent for members and financial support on popular good will. In the case of American Protestantism this dependency on popular support has combined with Protestantism's lack of a long tradition in America and its weak ties with its European heritage and origin to produce unfortunate results. All too often American Protestantism has felt forced to surrender its own essential character in order to adapt to the wishes and felt needs of those who support it. Regrettably, this adaptation has encouraged the debilitating and often contentious pluralism called denominationalism. In addition, it has produced some most undesirable forms of "culture Protestantism." Among the prosperous classes, for example, Protestantism has often been made just another ingredient of "gracious living" and has become "a luxury faith that neither challenges the mores of secular life, nor deeply affects men's sense of their fundamental orientation in the world, but supplies them with special though mild ecstasies" (p. 57).

Niebuhr, however, sees an even more fundamental way in which the Protestant churches have adjusted to the spirit of American culture. The spirit of a people is expressed in their social faith. In the United States, as in most societies, this social faith is the dominant religion of the people and sees society both as the great cause to be served and as the source of the people's identity and significance. Democracy, for this social religion, is not a form of government but a way of life and salvation. The hope of this social faith "appears as the American dream, or as the fulfillment of Manifest Destiny, or simply as progress toward peace, prosperity and plenty" (p. 58). As others have done, Niebuhr points out that this religion has its sacred scriptures, its doctrines, symbols, and rites. Protestantism has not been the only source of this social faith, but the development and progress of both have been so closely intertwined that the one is often indistinguishable from the other. In Niebuhr's words:

> Not infrequently Protestants have defined Christian freedom in democratic terms, not as freedom from sin and death and as that bondage to God which is perfect freedom, but as liberty to worship as one pleases or, better, as deliverance from political tyranny, from want, and from fear. The gospel of a love that seeks out the lost and lowly . . . is translated into the doctrine of equality. The Word of God, and the voice of the people; the hope of the kingdom of heaven, and the American dream; the forgiveness of sins, and toleration; the grace of our Lord Jesus Christ, and affable manners are confused and confounded (pp. 58–60).

Cultural Protestantism has many forms, but whether liberal or conservative, nationalist or internationalist, they are expressions of this social faith. From one viewpoint, therefore, the inherent weaknesses of Protestantism are fully revealed in the situation of democratic freedom.

Increasing Protestant Unity and Dynamic. From another point of view Niebuhr sees in American Protestantism a tendency toward unity and a dynamism springing from an awareness of man's absolute dependency on God rather than on man or any human institution, religious or secular. Under the conditions of democratic freedom, Protestant denominations in America have been free to seek unforced unions and otherwise join together in spontaneous cooperation in the pursuit of common social and religious goals. Out of these trends toward union and integration there has emerged a kind of "core Protestantism" that is still too loosely knit to be called a church. Although the core unity and the dissent surrounding it are distinctly American, Niebuhr does not believe that this "core Protestantism" manifests any greater degree of cultural dependency than Christianity generally.

In this context, Niebuhr criticizes the way terms like autonomy and independence are often used to describe the pluralism of Protestant denominationalism. These terms are frequently understood in a sense that derives from the context of democratic faith, but they have a different meaning when used in the context of Protestant faith in God's absolute sovereignty and the Christian's consequent freedom and relative independence from all human authority. American evangelical Protestantism has always asserted these doctrines in its endeavors both to reevangelize itself and to Christianize American society. For this reason it has always been ambivalent in the presence of a democracy based on a doctrine of inherent human rights. Since God alone is sovereign, evangelical Protestantism opposes the assertion of the divine right of the people as much as it does that of the divine right of kings. Men have the right to freedom of worship and of speech not because they are equal but because they have a duty to worship God and testify to his truth as they know it. Thus, evangelical Protestantism derives all human rights from man's duty to obey and worship God (pp. 66–67).

Niebuhr argues that as long as American Protestantism witnesses to the absolute sovereignty of God, it will retain its ability to challenge American social faith. Whenever it fails to bear this witness, it becomes the passive representative of culture. Yet Niebuhr believes that Protestantism's witnesses to divine sovereignty have been more frequent than its failures (pp. 67–68).

Protestantism has often challenged the way democratic institutions are used and interpreted. In themselves these institutions are logical expressions of neither democratic nor Christian faith. What is important is how they are interpreted and used. Representative government can refer to the ultimate authority of the people or the majority it represents; but it can also refer to the selection of persons who will be obedient to ultimate principles of right and concerned for the welfare of all men and all nations rather than just that of their constitutents and their nation alone. Separation of church and state and religious freedom can mean indifference toward religion; but they can also mean recognition that religion is too important for individuals and society to be put into the hands of short-sighted politicians. The Bill of Rights can be seen as an assertion of the philosophy of individualism as well as an assertion of the individual's obligations in a universal commonwealth. The Constitution of the United States can be interpreted as the expression of the will of a democratic majority, and as such subject to change; but Protestantism, together with Catholicism, has interpreted it as an expression of divinely established natural law that is knowable, however obscurely, through human reason. Political realists have often charged that Protestant interpretations of democratic institutions have been overly moralistic, but Niebuhr believes that Protestants have been as self-critical as they have been self-righteous in making these interpretations.

Protestantism has often been criticized for being more concerned with the moral conversion of individuals than with changing the fundamental assumptions and habits of society at large. Niebuhr acknowledges the justice in this criticism but goes on to make an important theological point. He begins by pointing out that the effectiveness of this effort at individual moral conversion and its impact on the general quality of life in a democratic society can probably never be evaluated. However, Niebuhr emphasizes that from the viewpoint of the Protestant principle of faith in God's absolute sovereignty, this evaluation is not fundamentally important. The value of an independent Protestantism does not depend on the effectiveness of its service to democracy, to society, or to the high god of social faith. Such an evaluation of Protestant faith would be its betrayal and would result in a false utilitarian evaulation of God, faith, and religion. For this reason, in this 1961 essay, Niebuhr assesses only the effect of democracy on Protestantism and not vice versa.

CONCLUSION

The central theme running through all three of Niebuhr's interpretations of the history of American Protestantism is that Christianity is a life, a movement. In *Social Sources* the theme is implicit in such expressions as "seeking universality," the need for "organic integration," "the road to unity," and a revelation "made not in terms of dogma but life." Christianity is in process, moving along the road to fulfillment, but not yet there. In his later two works Niebuhr makes this theme explicit.

The term "movement" came, of course, from Henri Bergson, but it is also deeply rooted in two of Niebuhr's major convictions: the radically historical character of human existence and the absolute sovereignty of God. The conviction of the radically historical character of human existence implies that life is a constant becoming. Life loses its vitality, degenerates, and petrifies when men try to capture it once and for all in fixed beliefs, unchangeable moral codes, and other static forms and institutions. All efforts at institutionalization are static expressions of man's historical conditionedness. Man must be constantly alert, and ready to respond to his ever changing historical situation. The conviction of the radically historical character of human life is the origin of what is sometimes referred to as Niebuhr's historical relationalism.

The theme of movement is also deeply rooted in Niebuhr's conviction of God's absolute sovereignty. Everything human, including religion and its ecclesiastical structures, is in process of becoming and thus historically conditioned. God alone determines the destinies of men and nations. He alone is absolutely trustworthy. He demands that men accept his decisions for the government of the world and that they put their trust in him alone and regard all else as ephemeral. This conviction gives rise to what is spoken of as Niebuhr's theological relationalism.

Niebuhr is concerned to develop the theme of movement in both its historical and its theological senses because he is concerned about man and his destiny, about the relationship of religion and culture and, above all, about God's design in universal creation and his plan for universal redemption. Niebuhr's vision, therefore, is centered on God, but on a God that looks in judgment and mercy on men. Thus Niebuhr's horizon and ultimate concern is a universal one that embraces all men.

His concern with the Protestant Christian churches arises in part because that is where he finds himself; in part because he believes that "the fundamental reformation of society is the reformation of the church"; and in part because it is his view that the God-given mission of the Christian churches is to penetrate culture with as much saving knowledge as their best insights can provide.

At this time when our nation is celebrating the bicentennial of its independence, we may wonder that Niebuhr might say today about reshaping the values of the American religious tradition. Niebuhr recognized that the crisis facing our times is serious and deep, and he did not pretend to know how to solve it. But I think that he could say this much. First, no matter how powerful our nation is—politically, militarily, and above all economically—we must recognize that there is still One who is more powerful and before whose absolute and all-sovereign rule we must ever bow. Second, we must repent for our sins against this one God, whether our sins be those of henotheism or idolatry. Henotheism, because we have on occasion allowed ourselves to believe that he was our God first and foremost rather than equally the God of all men. Idolatry, because we forgot him and substituted for him our wealth, our international power, and our military strength to secure advantages for ourselves and our friends and to perpetuate the disadvantages of the weak and the poor. This repentance must be genuine, which means that it must hurt, and upset us deeply, and even cause us great agony.

Third, we must acknowledge that the rule of this God of all men is a present and active affair, and that the destiny he has for us is hidden and mysterious. Yet we must be ever ready to harken to his will. So, if he commands us to sacrifice our power and our wealth so that other nations and other peoples, or even the weak and poor of our own nation, may have more, we must obey—even if it means that we have to lower our standard of living or allow others to carry away some of our power and wealth. Only if we do all these things will we escape his judgment. If we fail in any one of them, our nationality and even our Christianity becomes destructive rather than creative.

NOTES

1. "Reformation: Continuing Imperative," *The Christian Century* 77 (1960), p. 249. (Hereafter referred to as *RCI*.)

2. *Ibid.*, pp. 250–51. These ideas appear in many of Niebuhr's works, e.g., *The Church against the World*, by H. Richard Niebuhr, Wilhelm Pauck, and Francis P. Miller (Chicago: Willet & Clark, 1935), pp. 1–13; and chaps. 1 and 10 of *The Social Sources of Denominationalism* which is discussed below.

3. See H. Richard Niebuhr, *The Responsible Self: An Essay in Christian Moral Philosophy* (New York: Harper & Row, 1963), p. 45.

4. *Ibid.*, p. 46.

5. *Ibid.*, p. 42.

6. *Ibid.*, p. 44.

7. These ideas appear often in Niebuhr's writings. The two quotations in this sentence are respectively from *RCI*, *op. cit.*, p. 248, and *The Responsible Self*, *loc. cit.* See also his important 1952 essay "The Center of Value," reprinted in *Radical Monotheism and Western Culture* (New York: Harper & Row Torchbooks, 1960), pp. 100–13.

8. For the points made in this section see *RCI*, *op. cit.*, p. 249, and *The Responsible Self*, *op. cit.*, pp. 42–46.

9. *RCI*, *op. cit.*, p. 249.

10. *The Responsible Self*, *op. cit.*, p. 42.

11. *Ibid.*, pp. 43, 45.

12. H. Richard Niebuhr, *The Social Sources of Denominationalism* (New York: Henry Holt, 1929; reprinted, New York: Meridian Books, 1957). In 1954 Niebuhr wrote a brief (one page) preface for a reprint of this book published by The Shoe String Press (Hamden, Conn.). Niebuhr tells us in this preface that he still believes in the essential soundness of its thesis, though he would now emphasize certain theological ideas more than he had done. We refer to this work as *Social Sources*. Page references within the text of this section are to the Meridian reprint edition.

13. H. Richard Niebuhr, *The Kingdom of God in America* (Chicago: Willet & Clark, 1937; reprinted, New York: Harper & Row Torchbooks, 1959). We refer to this work as *Kingdom of God*. Page references within the text of this section are to the Harper & Row Torchbooks edition.

14. H. Richard Niebuhr, "The Protestant Movement and Democracy in the United States," in *Religion in American Life*: vol. I, *The Shaping of*

American Religion, ed. James Ward Smith and A. Leland Jamison (Princeton: Princeton University, 1961), pp. 20–71. We refer to this article as his 1961 essay. Page references within the text of this section are to this 1961 essay.

15. When in *Kingdom of God* (published 1937) Niebuhr spoke of Christianity as a movement, he clearly had in mind Protestant Christianity. His 1961 essay, however, shows the influence of the ecumenical movement. In this 1961 essay he sees both Protestant and Catholic Christianity as movement—moving between the polarities of movement and order, process and structure. The difference is that Protestantism is oriented more toward the pole of movement and process; Catholicism more toward the pole of order and structure. Compare what he says in his 1961 essay (*op. cit.,* pp. 22–25) with what he says in *Kingdom of God* (*op. cit.,* pp. 17–24).

16. By "order" Niebuhr means a collection of Christian organizations with habitual modes of government and obedience, with doctrines, methods of economic support, officers, forms of ritual and prayer, and established modes of education. See 1961 essay, *op. cit.,* pp. 36–37.

A Crossroad Book

The Seabury Press
815 Second Avenue
New York, N.Y. 10017

This book comes to you, with our compliments,
for review or evaluation use.

Author: Thomas M. McFadden, Editor

Title: AMERICA IN THEOLOGICAL
                        PERSPECTIVE

Price: $9.95

Publication Date: 28 June 1976

Please send two copies of your review.

FRANCIS SCHÜSSLER FIORENZA

american culture and modernism: shailer mathews's interpretation of american christianity

The American bicentennial has renewed our interest in the meaning and spirit of American Christianity. It has led to a renewed study of the emerging pattern of American religious thought, its formation out of the crucible of immigrant traditions, and its distinctive contribution to religious life and Christian theology.[1] But underlying all the historical studies and descriptive investigations of the meaning and significance of American Christianity is a systematic issue. The reflection upon the theological meaning of America raises the question of the relation between theology and culture or, more specifically, between Christian theology and American culture. This issue has become acute in the diverse assessments of American "civil religion," [2] as the essays by Marie Augusta Neal and Mary L. Schneider in this volume indicate. In the wake of the Vietnam War and its shattering of American cultural illusion, American civil religion has come under fire. No longer seen as transcendent, it too is judged as a cultural faith that absolutizes America and idolizes its national ideals.

This critical assessment of civil religion raises anew the problematic relation between theology and culture with all its implications for the nature of religious thought. It is not a new question but represents the basic problem of nineteenth-century theology and especially of the Modernist movement. Although Modernism is commonly defined as the "tendency of theology to accommodate traditional religious teaching to contemporary thought," its fundamental presupposition is its conviction that religion and culture are so intertwined that traditional religious teachings should be seen not only as abstract doctrines but also as expressions of particular cultures. It is precisely this insight into the cultural entanglement of religious doctrines which lies behind its conviction that new cultural situations call for revisions of a religious tradition.[3] Since this demand for revision was inextricably based upon its view of the interrelation between culture and religion, it is no wonder that the neo-orthodox critics of Liberalism and Modernism have challenged the Modernist conception of this relation. In Europe, Karl Barth contended that the cultural differences between Paul's time and our time are so "trivial" that Paul speaks to men of every age and culture.[4] In America, Reinhold Niebuhr labeled Liberalism as the capitulation of religion to the thin soul of modern culture and called for a Christian ethic independent of culture.[5] His brother, H. Richard Niebuhr, likewise saw the church as having lost its independence. It thereby became captive to nationalism, capitalism, and anthropocentricity.[6]

The parallelism between these two critiques suggests that a new examination of American Modernism with a view to the problem of civil religion might provide a perspective for understanding how Modernism in its theological evaluation of America perceived the relationship between theology and culture. This examination can illuminate a significant theological movement within America, namely, Modernism, and at the same time shed light upon the thorny problem of the relation between theology and culture.

To understand Modernism, it is necessary to note that in the United States theological Liberalism consisted of two distinct strains: evangelical and modernistic.[7] Evangelical Liberalism represented a Christocentric position which sought to validate Jesus' preaching as universally and permanently valid. Its ethical and social concern to relate the gospel message to the world was evident in the works of William Adams Brown, Harry Emerson

Fosdick, and Walter Rauschenbusch; whereas its personalistic and pragmatic side was evident in A. C. Knudson and Eugene W. Lymann respectively. In contrast, modernistic Liberalism was not as Christocentric. Although the uniqueness of Jesus was asserted, he was more the exemplar than the norm. The Modernists were more concerned with the development of a methodology and looked to modern science, philosophy, psychology, and social thought for their guidelines. Evangelical Liberalism was the product of men who were pastors; whereas modernistic Liberalism flourished in the theological seminaries.

The great center of Modernism was in Chicago where William Rainey Harper and John D. Rockefeller had established anew the University of Chicago. In giving financial support for the founding of the University, Rockefeller stipulated that the Baptist Union Theological Seminary of Morgan Park should become the Divinity School, and as such it became the first professional school of the university. On October 1, 1892, the new University of Chicago opened its doors. Eri Baker Hulbert was the Divinity School's first dean and he was followed by Shailer Mathews, who joined the faculty in 1894, became dean in 1908, and remained in that position for twenty-five years. During these years a distinctive approach to theology, known as the Chicago School, developed. As the church historian Winthrop Hudson has noted, "the dominant emphasis [of the Chicago School], exemplified by Mathews was upon a socio-historical approach to theology which viewed all doctrinal statements as reflections of historic cultural patterns, and consequently were functional and not normative, changeable and not permanent." [8] Although the Chicago School did not reassert traditional values, the influence it exerted in the life of the church was significant mainly because a very large percentage of professors in other theological seminaries received their graduate training at Chicago. Moreover, many of the key figures, especially Dean Mathews, played leading roles in ecclesiastical affairs. Mathews was president of the Federal Council of Churches from 1912 to 1916 and of the American (Northern) Baptist Convention in 1915. Moreover, a program of adult education known as the American Institute of Sacred Literature widely distributed its ideas by means of books, pamphlets, and study courses which were used in the Protestant churches of the Middle West.

The modernistic Liberalism characterizing the Chicago School of Divinity is usually divided into two periods, the sociohistorical and the naturalistic.[9] Whereas the sociohistorical period coincides with the deanship of Shailer Mathews and was concerned with the relation between theology and sociocultural experience, the naturalistic period is often dated with the arrival of Henry Nelson Wieman in 1927. The latter period extends to the end of World War II and is marked by a concern with the natural sciences and process thought. In this essay, however, we shall deal with only the sociohistorical phase.

The development of this phase was undoubtedly due to the influence of the illustrious colleagues that the theological faculty had at the University of Chicago. John Dewey, Albion Small, James H. Tufts, and George Herbert Mead were among the scholars at Chicago. They not only made an enduring contribution to social analysis but forced their theological colleagues to come to terms with the theological issues raised by empirical, social, and psychological approaches to religion. Stressing the qualitative difference between social acts and mere physiological adaptation to the environment, their analysis provided a genetic theory of social existence. John Dewey underscored the importance of occupation and moral interest in the evolution of human experience; Albion Small developed a dynamic sociology; James H. Tufts applied an evolutionary method to ethics to give new meaning to the idea of self-realization; and George Herbert Mead argued for the social formation of the self by an analysis of language and symbolic processes.

This evolutionary approach and genetic social philosophy dominated the University of Chicago when Shailer Mathews (1863–1941) first joined the theological faculty. A native of Portland, Maine, he had attended Colby College and Newton Theological Institute. After briefly teaching at these institutions, he attended the University of Berlin (1890–92), where he studied history under Hans Delbruck and Ignaz Jastrow and economics under Adolf Wagner. Two years after his return to the United States, he became professor of New Testament History at the

Divinity School. At first he was an evangelical Liberal but he soon came to elaborate the sociohistorical method which became characteristic of the school. As Charles Harvey Arnold has noted in his history of the Chicago School, Mathews elaborated "the dominant and unifying methodology of the Chicago School; in time others would add refinements and new dimensions to it, such as Case, Smith, Ames, but Mathews has stated it and exemplified it in its 'classic' form." [10] The thread uniting all the members of the Chicago School at the early part of this century, however, was the sociohistorical method and the attempt to elaborate an empirical and functional understanding of religion. They all sought to reinterpret Christianity from the viewpoint of modern culture. They were all Modernists and Dean Shailer Mathews was their outstanding spokesman.

In view of Mathews's role as the leading exponent of American Modernism, I should like first to investigate and analyze how he understood the relation between theology and culture. The central point and basic insight of Mathews's Modernism was the functional relation that he posited between social mind-sets and theological doctrines. Second, it becomes important to observe how he applied this insight to the task of understanding American Christianity and Americanism. Third, against this background, the systematic question can be raised as to the value of his modernistic and functional method in relation to his understanding of America and in the context of the present debate about the American civil religion.

SOCIAL MIND-SETS AND CHRISTIAN THEOLOGY

The Modernism represented by Mathews contends that theological doctrines are produced by the dominant social mind at work in religion during a particular time and culture. For an understanding of Christian doctrines, it is not sufficient to analyze them abstractly. Instead they must be seen in the context of the social mind-set of the period of history in which they were elaborated and produced.[11] The notion of social mind as used by Mathews should be carefully distinguished from the more commonly known sociological concept of group mind, which is generally rejected by sociologists today. In no way does Mathews understand social mind as a group mind.[12] The meaning of social mind is elaborated with reference to the distinction between analogy and pattern. Since according to Mathews a belief has a theological meaning only when it is understood and interpreted, it is necessary that this understanding take place by means of an analogy between the theological belief to be interpreted and some object of common experience. Interpretation, however, is not limited to such conscious analogies. Often the descriptions are not seen as analogical but are taken as constitutive elements of the religious concepts themselves. In such instances they are "patterns rather than metaphors." [13] As such these patterns give intelligibility to beliefs. The relation between analogy and pattern is that "an analogy becomes a pattern when it is so generally used as to become a presupposition of thought and action." [14] When an analogy is unconsciously and uncritically employed due to its general acceptance, then it becomes a pattern and is understood literally rather than figuratively. The total complex of such patterns in any period or age is what Mathews calls a "social mind."

In his analysis of the history of Christianity, Mathews suggests that Christian doctrines can be divided into seven successive, though overlapping, social minds: Semitic, Greco-Roman or Hellenistic, imperialistic, feudal, nationalistic, bourgeois, and modern or scientific-democratic. The teachings and doctrines developed during each of these periods reflect the dominant social mind of the period. Mathews extensively analyzed the understanding of the notion of God and of the atonement in terms of these patterns.[15]

The *Semitic* social mind saw and organized society in terms of an oriental monarchy. Although Mathews acknowledges the significant influence of Hellenism upon the New Testament, he maintains that the fundamental insights of primitive Christianity are derived from Hebrew religious, social, and political experience. The messianic hope is seen as the dominant social and political mind-set in which Christianity came into existence—so much so that Mathews maintains that "Christianity considered theologically perpetuates the transcendental politics of the Hebrew," [16] which interpreted the significance of Jesus precisely in a messianic framework. Jesus was sent and empowered by God to establish the Kingdom, which his future coming will bring to fulfillment. These beliefs and the scenario of the world drama between God and Satan, between Christ and the Antichrist were all a part of this messianic hope that developed from Judaism. Christian messianism can be interpreted as a religious expression of oriental social and political mind-sets.[17]

The *Hellenistic* social mind characterizes the next period of Christianity in which the notion of the conquering messianic king is replaced by that of the incarnate God as the central pattern for understanding Jesus. In this period, the difficulty of seeing love in the natural order was just as great as it is now, and the identity between God the Creator and God the Saviour was a central question. The growing Catholic orthodoxy stressed that the one God was both Creator and Saviour and appropriated the concept of the logos for this purpose. To the Hellenistic mind the notion of logos appears to have the same position as evolution in nineteenth-century thought, and appeared to fulfill the same practical function as law today. Christianity recast its messianic oriental formulas into terms of the Greco-Roman mind and asserted that the logos was of the same substance as God. The incarnation of the logos made contact with God's substance possible, as well as salvation from death. The religious need of the Greco-Roman period was hereby met much more adequately by orthodox Christianity than by Arianism.[18]

The *imperialistic* social mind characterizes the western part of the Roman empire with its legal genius and social organization. As Christianity developed more and more into a separate religion, it attained its necessary organization under the influence of the Roman imperial system. The church's hierarchical structure witnesses to the influence of this social mind on the growing church. Augustine represents the creative genius of this social mind. His *City of God* provides a conception of Christianity modeled on the imperial political ideal, and his elaboration of the doctrine of original sin in the face of the pessimism engendered by the collapse of Roman civilization can be seen as an attempt to salvage the sovereignty of God. But the imperial ideal lived on after Augustine. It became the ideal of the Middle Ages. Not only was God conceived of as a universal emperor, but his church was an empire struggling against the empire of Satan.[19]

During the Middle Ages the *feudal* social mind developed alongside the imperial ideal. Anselm's theory of satisfaction-atonement was interpreted as an expression of the feudal code. Jesus satisfied the honor due to God, and since he did what he was not obliged to, he has the right to claim the salvation of others. The notion of ransom to the devil played no role in Anselm's theology, which stands under the influence of the imperial ideal of God and the feudal mind-set of his time.[20]

The *nationalistic* social mind emerges in the sixteenth century. The rise of cities, the new capitalistic dynasties, the effects of the crusades upon the feudal system, and the rise of monarchies are all constitutive elements which lie behind the rise of modern political Europe. This creative social mind expressed itself in religion. The rise of monarchies and national states finds its expression in a reinforcement and legitimization of a monarchical conception of God. The maintenance of order by punishment was an important element in the conception of the monarchy. The feudal theory of the atonement held by Anselm was replaced especially in Calvinism with a new punitive justice-satisfying theory.[21] The growing sense of law of which Grotius is an example leads to a conception of the death of Christ as a vindication of God's respect for his law more than his honor. Mathews also sees a correlation between the growth of the monarch's authority and the increasing respect for the authority of God expressed in the ecclesiastic institutions of Catholicism and in the word of the Bible for orthodox Protestantism. The rise of the national churches is another illustration of the influence of the nationalistic social pattern. The necessary limitations of sovereign power also had their effects. The bargains made by the rising monarchs with various parliaments or city states find their theoretical expression in political notions of social contract and the religious understanding of covenants with the Lord.[22] This limitation of monarchical power goes hand in hand with the rise of the bourgeois class and its social mind.

Although the *bourgeois* social mind is an outgrowth of the

municipal development in the twelfth and thirteenth centuries and, more directly, the emergence of cities as trading centers in the ensuing centuries, Mathews sees the bourgeois social mind as beginning with the sixteenth century and culminating in the eighteenth century.[23] The bourgeois mind-set was a major factor in overthrowing the monarchical political order, and the commercialism characteristic of the bourgeois movement finds its expressions in Christianity. The atonement is still understood as substitutionary, but is now conceived according to a commercial pattern. "Jesus paid it all," was one of the favorite hymns of Evangelicism.[24] The Evangelical movement is seen as an expression of this period, along with Unitarianism's stress on natural rights and the repudiation of the depravity of man. The stress on individual religious experience in Wesleyanism also indicates the influence of the bourgeois social mind.[25]

The seventh and final social mind is called the *scientific-democratic* pattern. Mathews sees democracy and capitalism as the two great poles of social history in the latter half of the nineteenth century.[26] Whereas capitalism lacks a creative force and can serve only to preserve the patterns of imperialism and feudalism, democracy as a countermovement to capitalism needs to find its expression in theology if it is to be a creative force for humanity today. The social mind of democracy is not yet complete and it is being influenced by the dynamic rise of modern scientific methods. The task of producing a theology that both represents the creative forces of this social mind and meets its needs is the task that Mathews has undertaken with his constructive proposals for understanding the traditional concepts of God and atonement according to new patterns. Whereas in 1915 the predominant pattern was the democratic one, in 1930 the scientific pattern as well as that of process provide the prevailing criteria.[27] But to understand Mathews's constructive position, it is first necessary to see how he understands the contemporary social mind of America within the development of American history and American Christianity.

MATHEWS'S MODERNIST INTERPRETATION OF AMERICAN CHRISTIANITY AND CULTURE

Shailer Mathews's correlation of the development of social mind-sets and the growth of Christian theological doctrines provides the horizon for his interpretation of American Christianity and its theology. It also provides the framework for his analysis of American culture and the ideals of Americanism. Since the origin and growth of American Christianity and American culture have taken place and continue within specific periods of Western history and civilization, they both participate in and share in the formation of the social mind-sets of those periods. This participation and contribution provide the only adequate perspective by which to analyze first Mathews's understanding of American Christianity and then his interpretation of the ideals of American culture.

American Christianity as Modifying Divine Sovereignty. Mathews locates the beginning of American history around 1600, and thereby places it within the general social mind of that period. American history has its origin in the nationalistic period with the emergence of various nation-states and the end of the imperialistic period. During this time the rise of the middle class led to certain limitations upon the sovereignty of the monarch, but to an affirmation of national hegemony. This political pattern was repeated in the realm of religion and theology with God as sovereign, but now as national sovereign.

Mathews illustrates these modifications by reference to three significant theological positions within America's formative period: covenant theology, the thought of Jonathan Edwards, and Deism. The development of Calvinist theology in America is seen to parallel the political tendency of limiting the absolute sovereignty of the monarchy. This tendency is present in Europe and especially in America. The debate in Europe between the Calvinists and the Arminians revolved basically around the question of God's sovereignty. The Arminians attempted to adjust God's sovereignty to man's free will and to limit that sovereignty by affirming free human choice and the existence of traces of an original righteousness. Although the Synod of Dort represented a decisive reaffirmation of Calvinism, from then onward either a liberalizing of the idea of divine absolutism or its frank abandonment took place.[28] The development of covenant theology by the Anglo-New England Puritans is interpreted by Mathews as a paradigmatic illustration of this limitation of absolute sovereignty. Just as the king or sovereign had to guarantee personal rights in bargaining with the parliament, so too God does not act in an absolutely arbitrary manner, but enters into contracts with humanity. God's revelation to humanity is conceived as a history of contracts or covenants. First there was the covenant with Adam and then the covenant of grace. This theology certainly modifies the absolute sovereignty of God because the covenant sets limitations upon God's action. Mathews sees as an interesting historical question the inquiry into the precise relation between this covenant theology and the contract philosophy of government that will later play a revolutionary role in the political life of the eighteenth century.

Jonathan Edwards represents a second example of the modifications of the pattern of sovereignty. Although Edwards was a thoroughgoing Calvinist and lived in the heyday of absolute Protestant orthodoxy, his thought betrays a complex ambivalence. On the one hand, there is an absolute affirmation of the sovereignty of God. But on the other hand, the influences of the bourgeois social mind-set can already be seen in his theology, even if not yet fully developed. Edwards's discussion of sin and atonement reflects very clearly the differences between the societal patterns of his time and, for example, those of the feudal order. He interprets sin as a debt which Jesus paid, and he depicts Jesus as purchasing redemption by his obedience, virtues, and death.[29] The interplay of two different mind-sets is evident in this understanding of the atonement. Although God is formally understood as a sovereign, the relation between God and humanity is increasingly conceived by Edwards and the ensuing New England theology in creditor/debtor terms. The debt was still regarded as one of obedience to the sovereign's law, but redemption was increasingly seen as the paying of a debt rather than undergoing punishment.[30] Thus Edwards combines the economic and political patterns, and speaks of the death of Christ as a vindication of God's laws. Yet here again Edwards limits sovereignty insofar as God is under obligation to punish sinful mankind or else rebellion would take the place of law.

Deism, popular in England and in the United States, is seen as another example of limited sovereignty. Just as the rise of parliamentary government led to the limitation of the sovereign's powers in England, Deism transferred to nature some of the powers that had originally been attributed to God. Eighteenth-century Deists maintained that God did not interfere with the laws of nature and they distinguished natural religion from revealed religion in order to give credence to the natural religion.[31]

If theology in America during the formative periods of the seventeenth and eighteenth centuries reflected the transition from the nationalist to the bourgeois social mind-sets, the period from the eighteenth century to the middle of the nineteenth century reflected its mature expression. Unitarianism, Universalism, and Evangelicism are singled out by Mathews. In an age characterized by the rise of democracy, American independence, and the rejection of Bourbon sovereignty in France, the Unitarians established "the same rebellious, self-respecting attitudes in the presence of God. Humanity, in their belief, was not born damned but, certainly in New England, it was sufficiently respectable to demand its right from a sovereign God." [32] The underlying trend of Unitarianism and Universalism not only rejected the pessimistic attitude of Calvinism toward humanity and suppressed any notion of punitive justice as central to the image of God, but it also placed almost exclusive emphasis upon the beneficent nature of God. This beneficence was so underscored in early nineteenth-century liberal theology that fatherhood became the dominant characteristic of God and the atonement came to be seen much more as an expression of God's love than as an object of God's justice. Similarly, the revivalist movements of the nineteenth century were significantly different from those of previous generations insofar as less emphasis was placed upon the punitive actions of God. Instead the nineteenth-century revivalist movements increasingly appealed to God's love and mercy toward all persons.[33]

Mathews dates the final period of American Christianity from the second half of the nineteenth century to the twentieth century. This period is characterized by the growth of democracy and the increased dominance of the democratic-scientific social mind. Consequently the conception of God in terms of political sovereignty becomes further weakened and questioned. The social behavior and political institutions of democratic America no longer supply the pattern in which traditional theistic thought has been formed. The rise of the natural sciences, moreover, has led to such a domination of the scientific mentality that it became necessary to provide an understanding of God in terms of this scientific pattern of thought.[34] This challenge to traditional theism was that which Dean Mathews and the Chicago School sought to respond to by formulating a modernistic understanding of Christianity that would correlate to the political and social patterns of America and its ideals. Just what these ideals are and how Mathews understands the present situation of America can be illustrated by an analysis of his notion of Americanism.

Americanism and the Democratic Faith. Shailer Mathews states that any serious study of the significance of Americanism must raise "the fundamental question as to what Americanism really is. Have we as a people any distinguishing characteristics?"[35] He insists that Americanism does not consist in those characteristics often attributed to Americans that fall short of being ideals. Initiative, efficiency, pragmatism, and an orientation to financial success are not the characteristics of Americanism.[36] Instead Mathews suggests that individual freedom, a democratic way of life, a written constitution, and a cooperative sovereignty are the four basic ideals of the nation.[37] These ideals are not abstract, a priori constructions, but concrete tendencies that are manifest in America from its origin and enduring until the present. What is obvious is that they correspond to the democratic and individual spirit that reaches its culmination in the modern democratic social mind-set. Moreover, Mathews reveals how closely he sees the interrelationship between religion and culture insofar as he constantly points out how these ideals of American culture also have either a religious origin or a religious expression. The ideal of individual freedom is a part of the very foundation and origin of

America. Although economic motives were undoubtedly present, the Pilgrims and Puritans should not be perceived primarily as economic adventurers or pioneer exploiters of virgin resources, but rather, as individual groups seeking freedom from national state churches. The exploiters or adventurers are those who remained at home and waited for the ships to return. The search for religious and political freedom went hand in hand. Any attempt to distinguish them would do injustice to their interrelationship. The origin and emergence of America took place during the nationalistic social period. In America, however, this emergence had the distinctive feature of a search for religious as well as political freedom.[38]

The democratic ideal of equal participation in government also indicates the interrelation between the religious and political dimensions. The congregational churches maintained voting rights and lay participation in church administration. The democratic spirit evident in the town meeting reflects the social mind that was also operative in the congregational churches, giving a religious justification to equality and democracy. The rights of the colonists were looked upon as rights granted by God.[39] Moreover, Mathews not only maintains this early interrelationship between religious and political democracy, but asserts that the full blossoming of democracy in America was to no small extent influenced by religious movements. Although democracy was the ideal of our founding fathers, they were themselves aristocratic. The signers of the Declaration of Independence as well as the members of the Constitutional Convention appear as a sort of American peerage. In Mathews's opinion democracy was achieved not with Jefferson, but rather, on the frontier and during the Jacksonian era. The Quaker preachers, the Methodist itinerants, and the Baptist evangelists preached the gospel to all. They had neither the elitist congregations or doctrines of the East, but impressed upon all the value of the human soul, the possibility of immediate access to God, and insignificance of social distinction in the eyes of God.[40] In America, as elsewhere, political and religious ideals are intertwined.[41]

The foregoing descriptions of Shailer Mathews's seven social mind-sets as well as his interpretation of American Christianity indicate the extent to which the political dimension is the overriding factor in his analysis of any cultural/theological tradition. Sovereignty, freedom, and democracy are the key notions in his development of successive social mind-sets as well as in his characterization of Americanism. In this sense Shailer Mathews's understanding of all cultures and of American culture in particular is a prime example of what is today known as American civil religion. The "civil virtues" of America are placed at the apex of cultural development and are given a theological justification. Mathews therefore provides a provocative challenge for any theological assessment of the relationship between theology and culture.

MATHEWS'S MODERNISTIC UNDERSTANDING OF AMERICAN CULTURE AS A THEOLOGICAL PROBLEM

Does Shailer Mathews's modernistic and functional approach to American Christianity and American culture contribute significantly toward understanding the relationship between religion and culture as a systematic and theological problem? This question can be approached by first inquiring into the distinctiveness of his methodology and subsequent interpretation of American Christianity, then by analyzing the weaknesses of his position, and finally by outlining some possible contributions that his method can make for a better understanding of American culture and civil religion.

The Distinctiveness of Mathews's Method and Interpretation. In his functional correlation between theological doctrines and social mind-sets, Mathews does not argue for a distinct structure of political influences nor for a distinct structure of religious influences. Instead economic, political, and religious changes all take place within the same social framework. Whereas H. Richard Niebuhr first argued in *The Social Sources of Denominationalism* for the social factors influencing religion, and then in *The Kingdom of God in America* stressed the independence of faith and its molding power upon culture,[42] Mathews underscores their inextricable interrelationship. Political, religious, and social factors are not independent of one another but are knit together so that it becomes very difficult to speak of a priority of one over the other.[43] Mathews spells out this interrelationship very clearly:

> Such a social approach to the idea of God does not necessarily imply that a religion is passive in a social order or that it may not itself be efficient in furnishing patterns for other aspects of social life such as politics. One has only to remember the origin of the contract theory in government and of declarations of rights to see the influence on politics. Changes in religious conceptions may be both causes and effects of changes in other aspects of social life.[44]

This specific character of Mathew's understanding of America and American Christianity can be clearly illustrated by a brief contrast with H. Richard Niebuhr's interpretation. As we have discussed above, Mathews places America precisely within the context of a modified political sovereignty and sees America as standing in the vanguard of democracy. Therefore he sees a gradual weakening and limiting of God's sovereignty within American theology. In this respect he and Niebuhr offer fundamentally divergent interpretations. Whereas Niebuhr interprets Puritanism and early American religious thought as a radical affirmation of the divine sovereignty,[45] Mathews sees this period as representative of a limited affirmation of that authority. America is seen not as an example of the Protestant affirmation of God's ineluctable power, but as a modification of that power, a modification manifest in covenant theology. This limitation of sovereignty increases in the liberal Enlightenment of the seventeenth and eighteenth centuries, and reaches its high point in the American democratic experience.

Whereas Niebuhr sees the development of American religious thought as the continued affirmation of God's sovereignty, Mathews sees America as the place where democracy becomes the dominant social mind with the consequent weakening of the traditional notion of God's sovereignty. The tension between the traditional doctrine and the present democratic experience presents a challenge for modern theology to rethink its concept of God according to a more highly developed pattern.[46]

Niebuhr, on the other hand, can interpret liberalism only as a secularization of Christianity, which he ridicules as conceiving a God without wrath, human persons without sin, and Christ without a cross.[47] Such an interpretation is directly contrary to that of Mathews.

The Vulnerability of Mathews's Position. If Niebuhr's view can be faulted for not granting Liberalism and Modernism a proper place within the development of American Christianity, the contrary criticism can be and has been raised against Mathews: that he overvalues and absolutizes the liberal understanding of Christianity. This criticism does point to several weaknesses in Mathews's position. First of all, his interpretation tends to identify American culture and American politics. Insofar as it does so, Mathews's attempt to interrelate theology and culture not only involves a positive evaluation of American culture, but also gives a theological and religious legitimization for a specific political system. Mathews thereby sanctions the American form of government in its opposition to the political systems of other countries, especially socialistic systems.[48] Thus Mathews's idea of American civil religion is the exaltation of the democratic faith with the historical ideals of freedom and equality. His position borders on religious nationalism, especially in his *Patriotism and Religion.* Fortunately, his dedication to internationalism and international morality acts as a corrective upon his idealization of democratic patriotism and American cultural values.

The second trend present in Mathews's work is the de facto assimilation of the American ideal into the American reality. Although he insists that America as a social reality does not correspond to America as an ideal and that these ideals will always be in a process of realization, he does in fact overlook many aspects of American history that would speak against these ideals. Moreover, insofar as his method is empirical and seeks to determine American cultural values not abstractly but from the trends of American history, he has implied that these values have to a large extent already been realized in America.[49]

Finally, Mathews tends to place American history at the apex of world history. Although Mathews does not imply that a later stage in history is better than a previous stage and is merely content to correlate the needs of a particular age with the doctrines of that age, he does seem to apply an evolutionary model to cultural history. History appears to be moving toward more freedom and democracy for the individual. Since America is the paradigm of this freedom and democracy, it is radically affirmed and idolized as the present culminating point of history, even if this idolization is only implicitly asserted. Mathews's identification of American culture and American politics indicates the extent to which much of the neo-orthodox criticism of Liberalism and Modernism was justified. Yet despite this negative evaluation, Mathews's position can provide a perspective for viewing the problem of American civil religion.

The Contribution of Shailer Mathews. The perspective that Mathews offers counteracts much of the facileness within the present discussion of American civil religion. Both the defenders and the critics of civil religion presuppose a clear distinction between civil religion and church or denominational religion. Robert Bellah speaks of civil religion as existing "alongside of and rather clearly differentiated" from the religion of the church. Richey and Jones follow Luckmann in distinguishing general religion and church or denominational religion in reference to civil religion.[50] What Mathews contributes through his use of social mind-sets to interpreting the history of Christianity is that the social mind-set is expressed and reflected in the traditional teachings, practices, and institutions of Christianity as well as in the political development of the society in question.[51]

From this viewpoint the problem of the American civil religion is much more complex than critics such as Jürgen Moltmann and Richardson assume. It is not enough for them to argue that Christianity preaches the gospel of the crucified Christ and has an ecclesial model rather than a political or civil model for its normative judgments. However, as Mathews has sought to demonstrate, Christianity's gospel of the crucified Christ and its preaching of God exhibit the changing social mind-sets just as much as political ideas and organizations do. The history of Christianity, and of American Christianity in particular, reveals that there is not a clear-cut and definite expression of an eternal Christian gospel that stands outside the flow of history and the dynamics of culture. Any interpretation of the Christian message itself undergoes the very same changes that the culture is undergoing. It is precisely because the ecclesial model undergoes the same cultural influences in its organization and self-understanding that it has, in the case of the American civil religion, failed to criticize the misuse of democracy, the exploitation of minorities, and the waging of war against opposing governmental systems. This does not mean that the church cannot exercise a prophetic stance toward its own culture, but it means that the challenge is much more difficult than many assume.

If Mathews's provocative insight was that the Christian faith, as well as Christian theology, exists and expresses itself only within particular cultures and specific historical situations, then it should be seen that this insight does not necessarily involve a tendency to absolutize culture or to idolize the present sociopolitical situation, but precisely the opposite. His distinction between pattern and analogy is crucial here. When an analogy becomes literally accepted, affirmed, and presupposed as true fact, then it becomes a pattern. Although Mathews brought this distinction to bear on the past history of Christianity and its teachings, he failed to employ it in analyzing the American cultural situation and in presenting a constructive interpretation of American Christianity. This failure of Mathews lies not so much in the conceptual framework of his Modernism as within his de facto reading of American history and culture. If he had appropriated his own distinction between pattern and analogy, he would have seen the relativity of the democractic experience and would not have used it to criticize other forms of government. He would also have been more perceptive toward the enormous deviations of America from its ideals. The modernistic principle of the interrelation between theology and social mind-sets is a principle not of absolutization and idolization, but rather, a critical principle that points out the revelativity of *all* social, cultural, and political patterns. If Mathews had realized this consequence of Modernism, then Modernism could have exercised not only a critical judgment upon the past but also a prophetic challenge to the present. It would have done so at a time when America entering the twentieth century would have most needed it.

NOTES

1. Sydney E. Ahlstrom, "Theology in America: A Historical Survey," in *The Shaping of American Religion*, ed. James Ward Smith and A. Leland Jamison (Princeton: Princeton University Press, 1961), pp. 232–35. For an illustration of how Ahlstrom has worked out the derivative character of America in relation to immigrant traditions, see his, *A Religious History of the American People* (New Haven: Yale University Press, 1972) and compare with Martin E. Marty, *Righteous Empire: The Protestant Experience in America* (New York: Dial Press, 1970) and Robert T. Handy, *A Christian America: Protestant Hopes and Historical Realities* (New York: Oxford University Press, 1971).

2. Robert Bellah, "Civil Religion in America," first appeared in *Daedalus* 96 (1967), pp. 1–21, and was then reprinted with modifications in *The Religious Situation 1968*, ed. Donald R. Cutler (Boston: Beacon Press, 1968), pp. 331–93. For a discussion of the issues, see the essays collected by Russell E. Richey and Donald G. Jones, *American Civil Religion* (New York: Harper & Row, 1974), especially the concluding essay by Bellah, "American Civil Religion in the 1970s," pp. 255–72. See also his full-length treatment in his most recent book, *The Broken Covenant: American Civil Religion in Time of Trial* (New York: Seabury Press, 1975).

3. Shailer Mathews, *The Faith of Modernism* (New York: Macmillan, 1924), pp. 54–83.

4. *The Epistle to the Romans*, trans. from 6th ed. by Edwyn C. Hoskyns (New York: Oxford University Press, 1933), pp. 1–15, for the introductions to the first (1918) and second (1921) editions. Cf. Francis Fiorenza, "Dialectical Theology and Hope, I," *Heythrop Journal* 9 (1968), pp. 143–63, for a historical contextualization and a contrast between Liberalism and neo-orthodoxy. For a more systematic elucidation of the issue, see my article, "The Security and Insecurity of Faith," *Proceedings of the Twenty-Eighth Annual Convention of the Catholic Theological Society of America*, ed. Luke Salm (New York: Manhattan College, 1973), pp. 181–97.

5. *An Interpretation of Christian Ethics* (New York: Charles Scribner's Sons, 1935), p. 15.

6. *The Church against the World*, co-authored with Wilhelm Pauck and Francis P. Miller (Chicago: Willet & Clark, 1935), p. 124.

7. For the distinction between evangelical Liberalism and modernistic

Liberalism as well as for the location and development of Mathews's thought within this framework, see Kenneth Cauthen, *The Impact of American Religious Liberalism* (New York: Harper & Row, 1962), chaps. 2 and 8 respectively.

8. Winthrop S. Hudson, *Religion in America* (New York: Charles Scribner's Sons, 1965), p. 276. For the founding and history of the University of Chicago, cf. Thomas W. Goodspeed, *A History of the University of Chicago, Founded by John D. Rockefeller: The First Quarter Century (1891–1916)* (Chicago: University of Chicago Press, 1916), as well as his larger history, *The Story of the University of Chicago* (Chicago: University of Chicago Press, 1925).

9. Cf. Daniel Day Williams, "Tradition and Experience in American Theology," in *The Shaping, op. cit.,* pp. 464–68. Charles Harvey Arnold, *Near the Edge of Battle: A Short History of the Divinity School and the "Chicago School of Theology," 1866–1966* (Chicago: University of Chicago Press, 1966) divides the Chicago School into three phases: era of sociohistorical method, 1906–26; philosophical-theological method, 1926–46, and constructive theology, 1946–66. Mathews is seen as the leading representative of the sociohistorical method. Cf. also Bernard Meland, "The Chicago School of Theology," in *Twentieth Century Encyclopedia of Religious Knowledge* (Grand Rapids: Baker Book House, 1955).

10. *Op cit.,* p. 42.

11. Cf. Mathews, "Theology as Group Belief," in *Contemporary American Theology,* ed. Vergilius Ferm (Manhasset, N.Y.: Round Table Press, 1933), vol. 2, pp. 161–93, and "Theology and the Social Mind," *The Biblical World* 46 (October 1915), pp. 201–48, as well as his autobiographical statement, *New Faith for Old, An Autobiography* (New York: Macmillan, 1936).

12. For the difference between social mind and group mind, cf. Edwin E. Aubrey, "Theology and the Social Process," in *The Process of Religion,* ed. Miles Krumbine (New York: Macmillan, 1930), pp. 15–52, especially pp. 34 ff.

13. Mathews, *The Atonement and the Social Process* (New York: Macmillan, 1930), p. 30.

14. *The Growth of the Idea of God* (New York: Macmillan, 1931), p. 9.

15. For shorter treatments of the material covered in the two books mentioned in notes 13 and 14, see "The Functional Value of Doctrines of the Atonement," *The Journal of Religion* (1921), pp. 146–59, and "Social Patterns and the Idea of God," *The Journal of Religion* 11 (1931), pp. 159–78.

16. "The Historical Study of Religion," in G. B. Smith, ed., *A Guide to the Study of the Christian Religion* (Chicago: University of Chicago Press, 1916), p. 54. Cf. also Kenneth Cauthen's excellent introduction to Shailer Mathews, *Jesus on Social Institutions* (Philadelphia: Fortress Press, 1971; originally published in New York by Macmillan in 1928), pp. xiii–lxxiii, and Leander E. Keck, "On the Ethos of Early Christians," *Journal of the American Academy of Religion* 42 (1974), pp. 435–53.

17. "Theology and the Social Mind," *op. cit.*, pp. 206–13.

18. "The Historical Study of Religion," *op. cit.*, pp. 59–64. Mathews distinguishes a social mind that is "dominant" and "creative" and one which is not. The latter is called a "counter-social mind." New doctrines appear at tension points of cultural and social progress. Whereas the creative social mind is productive and contributes to the cultural and social development, the countermind expresses the social experience that remains unproductive and ineffective for immediate future development. He suggests that one doctrine might triumph over another because it has better served the needs of the continuing social experience. CF. "The Deity of Christ and Social Reconstruction," *Constructive Quarterly* 8 (1920), pp. 39–54.

19. *Atonement, op. cit.*, pp. 89–98.

20. *Ibid.*, pp. 99–114.

21. "Theology and the Social Mind," *op. cit.*, pp. 231–36.

22. *Growth, op. cit.*, pp. 172f.

23. *Ibid.*, pp. 174–76.

24. "Theology and the Social Mind," *op. cit.*, p. 240.

25. *Ibid.*, pp. 241–42.

26. Mathews, *Christianity and Social Process* (New York: Harper & Brothers, 1934), pp. 98–178.

27. In "Theology and the Social Mind," *op. cit.*, p. 243, Mathews refers to democracy as the countermovement to capitalism and as a creative conception from which religious and political influences are beginning to flow. In *Growth, op. cit.*, p. 183, he points out that science has replaced politics as the dominant interest. Hence science rather than politics will provide the patterns. He makes his constructive proposals with heavy indebtedness to philosophers of science, especially Alfred North Whitehead.

28. *Atonement, op. cit.*, pp. 140–42.

29. *Ibid.*, pp. 153–63.

30. *Growth, op. cit.*, p. 176.

31. *Atonement, op. cit.*, pp. 144–48.

32. *Growth, op. cit.,* p. 177.

33. *Ibid.,* pp. 177–79.

34. *Ibid.,* pp. 179–242. See also his further development in: *Is God Emeritus?* (New York: Macmillan, 1940).

35. *The Validity of American Ideals* (Nashville: Abingdon Press, 1922), p. 180.

36. *Ibid.,* pp. 179–86.

37. *Ibid.,* pp. 42–175.

38. *Ibid.,* pp. 42–92.

39. Cf. Mathews, *Patriotism and Religion* (New York: Macmillan, 1918), pp. 1–76.

40. *Validity, op. cit.,* p. 108.

41. *Ibid.,* pp. 123–75.

42. Respectively: New York: World Publishing, 1957; originally published by Henry Holt and Company, New York, in 1929, and New York: Harper & Row, 1937. For an analysis of Niebuhr's development, see James W. Fowler, *To See the Kingdom: The Theological Vision of H. Richard Niebuhr* (Nashville: Abingdon Press, 1974).

43. *Atonement, op. cit.,* pp. 134 f.

44. "Social Patterns and the Idea of God," *The Journal of Religion* 11 (1931), pp. 159–78: quotation from p. 177. At times he describes theology as an effect and neglects to spell out how it is a cause of social life, for example, "Theology from the Point of View of Social Psychology," *The Journal of Religion* 3 (1923), pp. 337–51, and *Faith, op. cit.,* p. 72.

45. *Kingdom, op. cit.,* pp. 45–87.

46. "Social Patterns," *op. cit.,* pp. 159–78.

47. *Kingdom, op. cit.,* p. 193. See his evaluation in *Christ and Culture* (New York: Harper & Row, 1951).

48. *Patriotism, op. cit.,* pp. 34–71.

49. *Validity, op. cit.,* pp. 13–41. Since the origin and practice of the ideals testify to their validity, Mathews's interpretation presupposes that they have in practice shown their validity. His optimism is especially evident in his early book *The Spiritual Interpretation of History* (Cambridge: Harvard University Press, 1916). Yet he is not without criticism of the present cultural situation; see his *The Making of To-morrow: Interpretations of the World To-day* (New York: Eaton & Mains, 1913).

50. See *American Civil Religion, op. cit.,* for Bellah, p. 21, for Richey and Jones, p. 3.

51. It would have been helpful if Bellah had placed his interpretation

of American civil religion in the context of his ideas on religious development; see his article "Religious Evolution" in *Beyond Belief. Essays on Religion in a Post-Traditional World* (New York: Harper & Row, 1970).

III.

Prospects for
the Future

DAVID M. THOMAS

american technocracy
and the religious spirit:
an unholy alliance?

Salesmen and sages of all eras often remind the thoughtful that to be successful in any endeavor you must know the territory. With that wisdom in mind, I contend that America in the last quarter of the twentieth century will become more and more entrenched in the thought patterns demanded by its technological operations. Granted that the roots of a technological mentality extend to the dawn of human existence, the pervasity of technological reasoning today seems practically coextensive with the boundaries of American cultural life. Although many definitions of this mentality are available, Robert Nisbet, eminent American sociologist, provides a useful focus in stating: "What is central to technology is the application of rational principles to the control or reordering of space, matter and human beings." [1] The key to the American spirit, I suggest then, is the desire to *control* the total domain of human life, and equipped with today's know-how and tools of technological ingenuity, the hope for successful control is enhanced. Contemporary humanity is geared for manipulation of self and others wherever and whenever the opportunity comes. Cultural frustration is most felt when the desire for control fails. This orientation, of course, is not limited to the United States; it is a general trait of postindustrial life. Rudolf Bultmann recounts Martin Heidegger's comment that the twentieth century is the epoch of subjectivity, meaning "the era in which the world conceived as object is subjected to the planning which is controlled by the values which man himself establishes." [2]

Setting up the control orientation as central to grasping American life brings forth the issue of whether this mentality is compatible with what we term the "religious spirit." Certainly times are changing with the acceleration of technological change, which in turn ensures even greater deliberate control of the change process. Emmanuel Mesthene, well-known investigator of the impact of technology on American culture, sees humanity each day deciding in greater degree *which* possibilities will be created" and therefore exerting strong "influence over the rate and direction of change." [3]

Much discussion of the relationship between religion and technology deals with either the extent to which religion has facilitated technological development or the impact of religion on particular activities or products of technology, especially in areas relating to ethical considerations. This study, however, reverses the question to consider the effect of technology on religion; more precisely, the effect on religious thinking of mental patterns demanded by a society which gives prime value to its technology. In more theological language, the issue is the effect of technological culture on the life of faith.

Not long after research is begun into this topic one discovers that the weight of opinion falls on the side of those who see an *incompatibility* between the technological mentality and traditional religious thinking. Usually decried is the loss of a sense of transcendent involvement in human affairs. Sociologist Gerhard Lenski observed that "a transcendental faith is gradually being transformed into a cultural faith." [4] Sociologist Daniel Bell discerns that particular qualities of technology prevent one from thinking in a religious manner. "Technology is not simply a "machine,' but a systematic disciplined approach to objectives, using a calculus of precision and measurement and a concept of system that are quite at variance with traditional and customary religious, aesthetic, and intuitive modes." [5] These comments imply that technological reasoning demands a reduction of reality to a manageable size. Sam Keen calls it an eclipse of wonder in that the real is only what is subject to human control and manipulation.[6] A sense of totality is lost. Philosophically, a feeling for being dissolves. Thomas O'Dea, a leading American sociologist of religion, catches the human dilemma which results: "Without an orientation to being, modern man cannot put himself together into a whole. Having lost transcendence, he finds himself without practical leverage in effectively changing his world." [7]

One manner of conceiving the religious scene today is to perceive a shrinking of the imagined domain of God's power while human power increases its range of actualization. This brings to mind the ancient task of where to draw the line—bracketing out the possibility of whether a sharp line need be drawn at all—between the realm of the sacred and the profane. A technologized person looks into the heavens as a place for launching satellites or space vehicles, not as a locus for the transcendent.

Although the issue of relating technology and religion obviously overlaps the spread of secularism arising from modern science, the technological orientation emphasizes human *activity* and what one must do to survive, to grow and develop as a human being. The technological mentality is a dynamic orientation to action, change, and control. It has been admitted that technology is always part of human life. As far as the religious question goes, Daniel Callahan is right in stating that the debate concerning the *pro* or *con* of technology is not the real issue. The significant question before us is "how much, and when and in what circumstances" is technological activity appropriate? [8] But to deal with this latter question one must see clearly the contours of our contemporary technological culture and the effect which the technological mentality first causes in human sensitivity and experience.

IS THAT ALL THERE IS?

Just as there can occur a methodological approach to an investigation which reduces the dimensions of the object under scrutiny, so also can there occur an approach to life which effectively reduces all that might be felt, known, or appreciated. When life is lived so as to gain control over its totality, when it is reduced to an organized system, life is technologized. Mesthene states that in its broader dimension technology is simply "the organization of knowledge for practical purposes." [9] The French theologian Jacques Ellul argues that the operational model of technique, with its abiding demand for efficiency, is now extended to every field of human activity.[10] Samuel Miller lists the wide-reaching application of technique: "There are techniques of research, techniques of prayer, techniques of sex, techniques of counseling and of communication, techniques of skiing, hairstyling, embalming, gardening, cattle raising and gaining friends —everything thinkable has been reduced to a technique, a 'how-to-do-it' pattern guaranteed to work." [11] Note the inclusion of religion in the technique framework. Of course, if one translates technique into method, one will recognize a rather common component in traditional religion extending from methods of mystical prayer to "guaranteed" prayers which seek personal favors from God. The point of this study is to suggest that the technique or control mentality today will assume a more central role in religion, if not becoming the *essential* pattern of religion in a technological culture.

The intentional focus of the technological mentality is on means of enactment rather than on the end or goal of activity. One attempts to direct the means of achievement in the *most effective manner* to gain a goal. Commenting on this, Samuel Miller suggests a significant effect of this kind of reasoning: "We are obsessed with the means, fascinated by the cleverness, the rapid application, the quick results of the means, until we become so immersed in them that we no longer ask ourselves what we are trying to attain." [12]

The reduction of concern to means also has the effect of reducing all reality to inanimate objects because things are more easily manipulated than persons or living entities. Theodore Roszak argues that modern America has effectively lost a sense of life by creating "a commitment to a single vision" which encompasses "an effort to turn what is alive into a mere thing." [13]

Certainly, if thing-consciousness replaces life-consciousness or person-consciousness, a religious spirit oriented to a living, personal transcendence disappears.

Paul Tillich has also sensed the disharmony between authentic religion and the technical mentality. He writes of a certain *style* of encountering reality which characterizes each age. The style of our era is one which confuses ends and means. "The production of means becomes an end in itself. Such distortion may affect a whole culture in which the production of means becomes an end beyond which there is no end. This problem, intrinsic in technical culture, does not deny the significance of technology, but shows its ambiguity." [14]

Allow me to offer two telling examples of how experience is reduced when the interests of technology gain dominance. The experience of natural wonders often creates a sense of awe and respect capable of bearing a transcendent meaning. But natural marvels can be sensed in different ways. Technological products can come between the viewer and the viewed. Roszak describes a humorous (and tragic) portrait of a typical American family viewing the magnificence of Old Faithful in Yellowstone National Park. Their interests involve capturing on film the geyser at its zenith. The central issue is when to snap the picture. Peering through their viewfinders, they wait to be overwhelmed as they capture forever that magic moment of excitement. Of course, it doesn't happen. They complain that their expectations were not realized and conclude in agreement that "Disneyland is better." [15] Roszak is accordingly depressed.

Joseph Fletcher, on the contrary, rejoices in the way we can gain more control over fundamental human experiences with our technology. This control is extended to the experience of life itself: life as it begins, develops, and concludes. In the past, these experiences have been central elements contributing to a religious sense, but for Fletcher it is more human to control life processes. His reflection on procreation (notice he terms it "reproduction") illustrates his approach: "Laboratory reproduction is radically human compared to conception by ordinary heterosexual inter-course. It is willed, chosen, purposed, and controlled, and surely these are among the traits that distinguish *Homo sapiens* from others in the animal genus . . . ." [16] Is *Brave New World* imminent?

What happens, therefore, in a technological culture is that an organizational principle develops which effectively subjugates experience to the proportions required for expedient control. The direct experiences of person, of life, of nature are brought into the control system. Samuel Miller comments that the most telling effect of the technological organizational principle on experience is that it robs experience of its "intrinsic power of impact." [17] The conclusion appears that where the technological mentality assumes such universal dominance over experience, the experience of transcendence is not so much denied as not even given an opportunity to occur.

A WORLD MADE (ONLY) BY HUMAN HANDS

With the transcendent out of the picture the affairs of the world assume only the meaning which humans provide. Whatever the action, whatever the experience, its significance is based on how well it fits human purpose: no less, no more. Langdon Gilkey admits that we do not live in an age of meaninglessness, but in an age where human meaning is all there is. "If modern man believes anything—and he does—it is that meaning is created by the passage of process into the future, and that this meaning is in part, if not as a whole, the result of his own decisions, his own intelligence, and his own moral decisions." [18]

All explanation and causation, all planning and prediction will remain on the level of finite causation. Gilkey adds: "All that is real and effective are the contingent and relative factors succeeding one another on a finite level." [19]

Consistent with our focus on technological culture, the issue is not that God does not exist, but rather, that God is not necessary to take into account when human planning or decision-making occur. The transcendent becomes irrelevant in the midst of life's tasks. It appears that Hannah Arendt's prediction that future humans will reject all notions that life is freely given in favor of grasping existence as "something he has made for himself" is being realized today.[20] Human life is all that humans make it to be: it becomes the era of self-made humanity. Rightly, Sam Keen argues that "the image of *homo faber* is the key to contemporary identity." [21] Erich Fromm further develops the meaning of *Homo faber*: "If man faces the truth without panic he will recognize that there is no meaning in life except the meaning man gives his life by unfolding of his powers, by living productively." [22] The emphasis on productivity arises from the essence of technological culture. The biblical axiom "By their fruits you will know them" is translated into "By their products you will value them." The foundation of evaluation arises not from being, but from doing, making, producing.

Greater technological might enhances the sense of autonomy. We often think of freedom as the result of political conditions, but freedom is just as much a matter of the self feeling that, once equipped with power and influence in a technological sense, one can even gain "mastery over the biological conditions of existence." [23] Being master of all is the goal of the technological mentality.

Of course, when a vital sense of transcendence fades from the human consciousness, acceptance of authority over human projects also departs. In fact, part of the attraction of technological progress is the increase of freedom it supplies. One might suspect that if God is no longer accepted as an authority who directs and oversees human activity, humanity would rush to take the position formerly occupied by the transcendent. However, I agree with Peter Homans that in technological society this doesn't happen.[24] The world is all finite; in effect, there is no empty throne. Perhaps this is the most telling theological criticism of the impact of technology on the religious spirit. When the question of the religious spirit of humanity is raised in a culture totally enamored by its technological orientation, the response might very well be: What religious spirit?

A loss of transcendent authority has other effects. With a departure of authority *over* human life goes transcendent authority in human life. Samuel Miller concludes that "an enhancement of meaning, the factor which heightens the value and significance of events or relationship" which formerly arose from giving transcendent meaning to human acts, is lost.[25] Stating this predicament more boldly, biologist-philosopher René Dubos writes: "If present trends were to continue for a few more decades, mankind would indeed be doomed—not to extinction but to a biologically and emotionally impoverished life." [26] So, in a sense, *Homo faber* appears willing to fall back on resources of human fabrication alone—facing the future with whatever challenges it presents.

THE ELIMINATION OF LIMITATION

But the challenges of human life are many. Traditionally, humanity did what it could to survive, and where its effective power fell short, it sought assistance from the transcendent. Of course, the desires of humanity are far more than simple survival: imagined possibilities for humanity know no clear-cut limitation. The passion for total fulfillment might appear as an abiding curse were it not for the fact that humanity can also possess a hope for realization. Kierkegaard termed religious hope a passion for the possible. The author and giver of the possible was ordinarily conceived of as transcendent. Today, however, to quote Kenneth Vaux, "Technology is the power by which man claims and actualizes hope." [27] And if religious hope is transformed into technological hope, what becomes of any recognition or need for a source of power outside unassisted human accomplishment?

The basic thrust of technology is to create a reality which satisfies human needs and desires. The goal of technology is fundamentally different from that of modern science. Science endeavors to discover what is; technology concerns itself with what can be.[28] And as technological desires become more influential in specifying the content of scientific research, technological developments usually come at a more rapid rate.

Our contemporary period is often described as unique. Although its specific uniqueness is pictured in various ways, the degree of present technological muscle is frequently central to the discussion. Mesthene mentions two characteristics which are both new and influential in today's culture: "First, we dispose, in absolute terms, of a staggering amount of physical power; second, most importantly, we are beginning to think and act in a conscious realization of that fact. We are therefore the first age that can aspire to be free of the tyranny of physical nature that has plagued man since his beginnings." [29]

Confidence in technology is buttressed by a rather steady growth in technological potential. Human interests gradually shift from what might be expected from God to what is anticipated from the laboratories, drawing-boards and factories. Thus Ian Barbour concludes that "confidence and trust in human capacities are expressed in technological power." [30]

Let us survey some examples of this new hope. Most bizarre, perhaps, is the growing interest in the technology of cryonics. By advanced freezing techniques with an effective freezer wrap, the hope is to put the terminally ill "on ice" until a cure for their malady is found. They are then defrosted and given the proper treatment. Aside from the "bugs" in the procedure, which as yet have not been worked out, the whole enterprise represents a technique of maintaining human hope for unending life. And whether cryonics ever reaches full effectiveness is a moot point, since cryonics is only the last facet of an already existing medical technology which also supports the same hope. The suggestion here is that persons living in the presence of a generally effective and continually developing medical technology live *as if* cryonics were totally effective.

Another interesting and more subtle form of technological hope is the contemporary sense of time.[31] in a pretechnological period people were accustomed to work on projects which saw their beginnings in earlier generations and gained their conclusions in the time of people not yet born. One sensed being a part of history because fulfillment both for the individual and for the group lay outside the person's lifetime. Now, however, with the advantage of greater technological energy at hand, projects are begun and finished in one's lifetime. One can experience projects reaching termination, unless, of course, the system breaks down. Technological citizens abhor waiting. If I may add a personal reflection, I feel great uneasiness—as I sense most others do—when waiting motionless for even minutes in an airplane for clearance to take off. It's the juxtaposition of contrary senses of time: the rapidity of air travel joined to the experience of standing still and going nowhere. One comes close to technological despair!

Another area of technological hope arises from a new sense of human evolution where humanity gears itself to alter and perfect its own nature. With the technique of cryonics, the issue was conquering death; with the new techniques created from experimentation in the life sciences, the goal is control of human life right from its beginning. The specter of a new human walking the earth, actively conceived *in toto* from the dreams of humanity, establishes the horizon of this new hope. Gilkey acknowledges this situation: "We are beginning to see that man can now create not only a new environment, but also literally a new man; and thus man can free himself from every aspect of his former bondage, from bondage both to the exterior and to the interior forces that have worked against his will." [32] Blind or passive processes of change give way to purposeful evolution where human intentionality is allowed its fullest actualization. Perhaps the goal is not about to happen tomorrow, but be confident—the eye has not seen what human ingenuity and know-how will eventually create.

Although it is as purposeful and manipulative as any of the previous examples, a final example of technological hope comes from a more subtle form of technique. Following the investigations of psychologist Philip Rieff, mention should be made of what he calls "psychological man." He points out that if "religious man was born to be saved, pscyhological man is born to be pleased." [33] The tool for gaining control over the inner processes of human life is the "analytic attitude" which "expresses a trained capacity for entertaining tentative opinions about the inner dictates of conscience, reserving the right even to disobey the law insofar as it originates outside the individual, in the name of a gospel of freer impulse." [34] Rieff's view that even conscience can be subjugated as one's inner techniques of self-control are developed serves as another example of a technology replacing a realm that religion once occupied. Again, the issue is not whether in fact the analytic attitude is proved effective, but whether a hope exists for believing in eventual effectiveness.

In all the examples just mentioned—cryonics, a new temporal sense, auto-creation, control over inner feelings—technology provides a new hope which aims at overcoming certain aspects of human finitude. Trust and reliance are placed in advancing technology. Ian Barbour describes the passage from religious hope to technological hope: "Technology is . . . the source of salvation, the agent of secularized redemption; technological advance is . . . secularized eschatology. Infinite progress through technology replaces the religious infinite." [35]

Barbour's comment is bold. Are we to conclude that with the arrival of technological culture all religion with a transcendent dimension is eradicated? If the technological mentality as it has been presented totally dominates cognitive and intentional life, then the answer will of course be affirmative. But the determination of whether this happens is most difficult. And the purpose of this study is not to examine the extent of its presence. I am more interested in describing a type, a way of thinking which, I suspect, is gaining greater influence in American cultural life. The present and potential effect of the technological mentality on the religious spirit is as significant a question to raise as I can imagine for religion in America today.

A THEOLOGICAL REFLECTION WITHOUT RESOLUTION

If we could retrace our cultural history and choose to return to an era where the dominance and presence of technology seemed less, we might overcome the apparent conflict between technology and religion. Aside from the obvious fact that we cannot go back, Emmanuel Mesthene warns that a rejection of scientific and technological progress implies a "surrender of the very qualities of intelligence, courage, vision and aspiration that make us human. 'Stop,' in the end is the last desperate cry of the man who abandons man because he is defeated by the responsibility of being human." [36] In equally strong terms Martin Marty rejects any nostalgic return to an Emersonian culture which antedates the present technological, pluralistic America: "Should [Americans] wish to regress to the metaphysical, pre-industrial, homogeneous religious and community life of their forefathers . . . they would have to move mentally and spiritually from a kind of maturity to adolescence. If they borrow only a memory of the old piety without becoming aware of its detail, they are in danger of using it ideologically to the impoverishment of the spirit." [37]

Behind the comments of both Mesthene and Marty is the contention that science and technology have participated positively in the total development of humanity up to now. Whether their roles are productive into the future should be our clear concern. A basic point of tension between technological culture and religion arises when the methods and interests of technology become the total content of human life. My conclusion accepts the role of technology as essential, but not central to human affairs. Huston Smith argues not for a lessening of technology but for more of other things: ". . . more checks on concentration of power in politics, more attention to the personal dimensions of life within society, more confidence in glimpses of reality sponsored by objectives other than those of science." [38]

Technology will extend its scope to the degree that people believe and put their confidence in its promises. If medical technology promises the eventual conquering of death—and people buy that claim—then whatever "solution" to death is offered by religion will not be sought. In considering, therefore, the promises of technology, an absolutely honest and open inquiry must take place to determine their credibility. Past accomplishments, present benefits, and future possibilities must be tested against something like Freud's reality principle.

Daniel Callahan suggests that technology ought to be expected to do the possible. But does it promise more? He offers a test case by asking whether modern technology has delivered a significantly greater degree of happiness. With some regret (I suspect) he concludes that clear evidence of happier, more satisfied people in advanced technological societies is not to be found: "However much life 'improves' it has not been enough to make happiness still seem any more than a vague and distant dream, an illusion." [39] Samuel Miller calls forth a similar need for reflection on the actual accomplishments of technology. If confidence in technology results, let it be. "The strain between the measure of our hearts and the measure of our technical know-how represents our severe uneasiness and not altogether hidden fear that our very success at one level may be our undoing at another." [40] Certainly, the environmental crisis should remind us of the mixed blessings of technology.[41]

Technology becomes what we sense of so many other major facets of life: it is neither destructive in itself nor beneficial without qualification. Modern technology is a complex phenomenon and those who make critical evaluations of its role had better be well informed. Mesthene feels that this is particularly important for a religious judgment of technology: ". . . the churches must above all know whereof they speak. They must know the society's knowledge, appreciate its power and understand its aspirations. They must show God to man as he is, not as they would have him be, for that would be blasphemy." [42] Modern technology has developed from humanity's God-given desire to establish a human habitat which serves the best interests of human life. Of itself, however, technology is humanly ambivalent. It functions beneficially or destructively in accord with the intentions of its makers. It serves its creators all too faithfully.

Advancing technology can be appreciated as a continuing expression of the relentless spirit of humanity seeking greater and greater actualization as it unites itself with the latent forces of the total created environment. It can be seen as a forceful manifestation of the terrestrial human condition persuing the greater, the higher. Thomas O'Dea expresses this dynamism well: "To be relevant, religion must support those human aspirations that cry for fulfillment in terms of modern technological capacity. It must become relevant to the effort toward a more abundant life for man." [43]

In pointing to a religious dimension of technological development, the obvious is not displayed because it is characteristic of a scientific and technolgical culture to appreciate the world as encompassing only finite reality. So a reminder, a proclamation of the underlying framework of human aspiration is necessary. Gilkey points out that without a broader sense of direction, scientific and technological endeavors tend to turn back destructively upon their creators: "A scientific culture can become demonic if science is not used by men whose self-understanding and thus whose public action is guided by symbols that transcend the limits of scientific inquiry and illumine the spiritual, the personal and free dimensions of man's being." [44]

Religion then adopts a positive, yet critical stance vis-à-vis modern technology. It is cognizant of the direction of technology's orientation to greater control. This can be understood as the human spirit's attempt to be released from its condition of finitude. Religion judges the orientation as being fulfilled, however, only in a personal relationship with the transcendent.

Yet religion ought not to support an expectation that God will bring about this fulfillment while humanity passively or quietistically waits. Humanity bears a responsibility to respond actively to its transcendent orientation, with part of that response being an active participation in perfecting human life. Mesthene portrays God as drawing the best from humanity's creative impulses: "Symbolic formulation of God as ideal possibility and as infinite perfectibility can then accord with a conception of an active God, drawing us on and guiding us in the effect to harness our tools to our aspirations and make a world responsive to human potentiality." [45]

I began this essay with the advice of the anvil salesman from *The Music Man* that you have to know the territory. American culture, I have argued, is deeply entrenched in its technological pursuits and if religion is to remain a vital force, it must gain a clear understanding of that culture. Religion's role in this culture is as necessary now as it has ever been. Gilkey argues that the transitional symbols of religion—the spirit of humanity opening to the infinite, the persistent human tendency to identify the created self as a self-made godlet, and the forgiving judgment of God—are quite necessary for scientific and technological society: "Only on these terms can the mystery, the risk, and the destiny of a scientific culture be comprehended and borne." [46]

Religion can, therefore, support a vision of technological America endowed with a profound sense that it is going somewhere. The religious spirit can thrive in an advanced technological milieu being filled with a hope that *with God* the human powers of open intelligence and relentless pursuit of a more enriched life will experience eventual fulfillment.

NOTES

1. Robert Nisbet, "The Impact of Technology on Ethical Decision-Making," *The Technological Threat*, ed. Jack D. Douglas (Englewood Cliffs, N.J.: Prentice-Hall, 1971), p. 41.

2. Rudolf Bultmann, "The Idea of God in Modern Man," *Translating Theology into the Modern Age*, ed. Robert W. Funk (New York: Harper & Row, 1965), p. 86.

3. Emmanuel Mesthene, "Technological Change and Religious Unification," *Harvard Theological Review* 65 (1972), pp. 39 f. See also Mesthene, "Technology and Religion," *Theology Today* 23 (1967), pp. 381–95.

4. Gerhard Lenski, *The Religious Factor* (Garden City, N.Y.: Doubleday, 1966), p. 54.

5. Daniel Bell, "The Trajectory of an Idea: Toward the Year 2000," *Daedelus* 96 (1967), p. 643.

6. Sam Keen, *Apology for Wonder* (New York: Harper & Row, 1967), p. 26.

7. Thomas O'Dea, "The Crisis of the Contemporary Religious Consciousness," *Religion in America*, ed. William G. McLoughlin and Robert N. Bellah (Boston: Beacon Press, 1968), p. 198.

8. Daniel Callahan, *The Tyranny of Survival* (New York: Macmillan, 1973), p. 61.

9. Emmanuel Mesthene, "Symposium: The Role of Technology in Society," *Technology and Culture*, ed. Melvin Kranzberg and William Davenport (New York: Schocken, 1972), p. 492.

10. Jacques Ellul, *Technological Society*, trans. John Wilkinson (New York: Vintage Books, 1964), p. xxv.

11. Samuel Miller, *Religion in a Technical Age* (Cambridge: Harvard University Press, 1968), p. 3.

12. *Ibid.*, p. 10.

13. Theodore Roszak, *Where the Wasteland Ends* (Garden City, N.Y.: Doubleday, 1972), p. 228.

14. Paul Tillich, *Systematic Theology* III (Chicago: University of Chicago Press, 1963), p. 62.

15. Roszak, *op. cit.*, p. 25.

16. Joseph Fletcher, "Ethical Aspects of Genetic Controls," *New England Journal of Medicine*, September 30, 1971, p. 61.

17. Miller, *op. cit.*, p. 125.

18. Langdon Gilkey, "Biblical Symbols in a Scientific Culture," *Science*

and Human Values in the Twenty First Century, ed. Donald Brophy (Philadelphia: Westminster Press, 1971), p. 75.

19. Langdon Gilkey, *Religion and the Scientific Future* (New York: Harper & Row, 1970), p. 68.

20. Hannah Arendt, *The Human Condition* (Garden City, N.Y.: Doubleday, 1955), p. 3.

21. Keen, *op. cit.*, p. 117.

22. Erich Fromm, *Man for Himself* (Greenwich: Fawcett Premier Books, 1967), p. 53.

23. Christopher Lynch, "Birth, Death and Technology: The Limits of Cultural Laissez-Faire," *Hastings Center Report* 2 (June 1972), pp. 1–2.

24. Peter Homans, *Theology after Freud* (New York: Bobbs-Merrill, 1970), pp. 149–94.

25. Miller, *op. cit.*, p. 17.

26. René Dubos, *A God Within* (New York: Charles Scribner's Sons, 1972), p. 220.

27. Kenneth Vaux, "Religious Hope and Technological Planning," *To Create a Different Future*, ed. Kenneth Vaux (New York: Friendship Press, 1972), p. 111.

28. Henryk Skolimowski, "The Structure of Thinking in Technology," *Philosophy and Technology*, ed. C. Mitchem and R. Mackey (New York: Free Press, 1972), p. 44.

29. Emmanuel Mesthene, "Religious Values in the Age of Technology," *The Evolving World and Theology*, ed. Johannes Metz (New York: Paulist Press, 1967), p. 110.

30. Ian G. Barbour, *Science and Secularity* (New York: Harper & Row, 1970), p. 59.

31. Yves R. Simon, "Pursuit of Happiness and Lust for Power," in *Philosophy and Technology*, p. 176.

32. Gilkey, *Religion and the Scientific Future*, p. 79.

33. Philip Rieff, *The Triumph of the Therapeutic* (New York: Harper & Row, 1966), pp. 24 f.

34. *Ibid.*, p. 35.

35. Barbour, *op. cit.*, p. 70.

36. Mesthene, "Religious Values in an Age of Technology," pp. 119 f.

37. Martin Marty, "The Spirit's Holy Errand: The Search for a Spiritual Style in Secular America," *Religion in America*, p. 180.

38. Huston Smith, "Technology and Human Values: The American Moment," *Human Values and Advancing Technology*, ed. Cameron P. Hall (New York: Friendship Press, 1967), p. 28.

39. Calahan, *op. cit.*, p. 8.

40. Miller, *op. cit.*, p. 4.

41. Barry Commoner, *The Closing Circle* (New York: Alfred A. Knopf, 1971). Commoner's basic argument throughout this work is in support of the major role which technology plays in present ecological destruction.

42. Mesthene, "Religious Values in an Age of Technology," p. 124.

43. O'Dea, *op. cit.*, p. 202.

44. Gilkey, *Religion and the Scientific Future*, p. 89.

45. Mesthene, "Technological Change and Religious Unification," p. 50.

46. Gilkey, "Biblical Symbols in a Scientific Culture," p. 90.

LEONARD J. BIALLAS

america:
the myth of the hunter

The Bicentennial has precipitated much discussion about
national identity and, in some quarters, a search for a single
symbol that would express the quintessential meaning of the American experience. Some critics consider the pursuit of the elusive
American dream of economic prosperity for all or the struggle for
freedom through continuing revolution as that which is peculiarly
American. Others nostalgically take refuge in catch phrases such
as the New Frontier or America the Innocent and the Invincible.
Still others find solace in the image of a hero who rises from
obscurity to success through sheer courage or who brings law and
order to the uncivilized frontier. Such images all portray a portion
of the American reality, but not its entirety. Goals are often no
more than futile pursuits, slogans are often chauvinistic and
materialistic, and some heroes are motivated by ambition and
profit. Perhaps it is just not possible to capture the essence of
America in one symbol. The reality is multifaceted and includes
guilt as well as innocence, greed as well as humanitarian gestures,
failures as well as achievements.[1]

In spite of the apparent impossibility in finding an all-encom-
passing symbol, I would like to suggest the myth of America the
Hunter for drawing together many threads of America's collective
history. It has both a universal and a cultural value. On the
universal level, the myth of the hunter expresses every person's
spiritual quest for meaning and value in life, the struggle to

achieve the erotic goals of love and pleasure and the aggressive goals of power and success. Culturally, it provides insight into the psychological value of the wilderness and frontier experiences in American history and expresses the fictive justification for the process by which the wilderness was expropriated and exploited.

Before describing the meaning of the myth of the hunter, it is imperative to clarify the use of the terms "myth" and "hunter." First, "myth" is used here in a technical sense to describe the stories, narratives, and symbols that a culture tells itself in order to give significance to its values and actions.[2] A myth is the expression of the entire American community, drawing on its historical experiences, world-view, and self-concept as well as on the sources of feeling, fear, and aspiration which are buried deep in the unconscious. To many, myth connotes what is unreal or fictitious. Here, however, it refers to the very foundation of the structure of reality as well as a kind of human behavior. It goes beyond distinct rational formulas to clarify man's encounter with the spiritual world. Not a fantasy or a legend, it is a veiled explanation of the truth, concentrating the whole history of a people into one experience.

Second, the term "hunter" in our context does not necessarily refer to one who goes out to kill game for food or sport. Rather, it is a generic term that combines and correlates the attributes of several other hero types of the American tradition—whether explorers, cowboys, or military heroes. The hunter is at once a pioneer and a settler, a wanderer and a cultivator. He personifies America's passion for both society and solitude, stability and movement. Unlike the heroes of the wilderness and the frontier, who represented an exciting part of the American past, the hunter changes his image along with the culture, and reflects the culture in its different forms. For example, Daniel Boone and Buffalo Bill would certainly remind us of a wide-open land of unlimited opportunity, but they make us forget the consequences of the industrial revolution and the problems of social welfare occasioned by the move to the cities. The American hunter-hero is variously the one who tames the wilderness, the one who leads the nation overland to the riches of the West, and finally, with no more terrestrial frontiers or boundaries to cross, the one who rockets into space, in search of new adventure. The hunter, suggests Teddy Roosevelt, is the archetype of freedom. And yet, looking over the scenario of national progress, we find that the American hunter has gone after prey out of necessity rather than diversion. He is a man of movement, ever alert to thrill and excitement. Spontaneous and resourceful, he always seeks out new possibilities and new fortunes. In whatever guise, the hunter embodies the physical and moral effort that has always been expended to bring out the best in every person, until he is liable to collapse from sheer exertion, success, or triumph.[3]

Whether such a characterization is valid, or whether it is due to the fanciful imagination of motion pictures and TV programs, the hunter continues to exert a power over our civilization. The hunter appears, for example, in the person who sets out ambitiously to attain economic prosperity or a high niche in politics (the more money or the higher the office, the bigger the prey he stalks). He is the astronaut who shows how man uses technological progress to struggle against his essential limitations in space and time. The hunter calls our attention to the trophies on his bar and the stuffed heads which adorn the walls of his den. He is found on TV today, not so much as the western cowboy, but as the problem-solving doctor and lawyer, and especially as the intellectual investigator and detective who chases his prey in the cities, the wilderness of the 1970s.

With this preliminary understanding of the two terms, we are now in a position to describe the myth of the hunter. Basically it follows the archetypal mythology of the heroic quest that Joseph Campbell has outlined under the rubric of *monomyth*. Following a universal pattern, the hero "ventures forth from the world of common day into a region of supernatural wonder: fabulous forces are there encountered and a decisive victory is won: the hero comes back from this mysterious adventure with the power to bestow boons on his fellow man." [4] This, then, is the monomyth: a separation from the world, a penetration to some source of power, and a life-enhancing return. Though the variations are limitless, the monomyth describes the anxiety and excitement each person experiences in the various phases of life. It does this through the form of a bigger-than-life hero, in this case the hunter. To outline the myth of the hunter in more detail, and thus summarize the direction that this essay will take, the monomyth can be divided into four stages: initiation, maturity, death and resurrection, and finally apotheosis or ascension.

The first part of the monomyth (and the myth of the hunter) is the initiation, the period of preparation and growth. Born often in mysterious circumstances, the hero is raised in a state of innocence, unaware of his latent powers. This is a culture's way of expressing its hopes for a fresh beginning, its longing for a second chance. Early in the hero's life, often concomitant with adolescence, he goes into the wilderness, or the forest, or the desert, where he must struggle with diabolical forces that he cannot understand, often symbolized by wild animals. These monsters represent the challenge of the dark and the unknown. They punctuate the fact that there is no such thing as total protection from the permanent reality of evil. The hero's withdrawal into the wilderness is essential for his growth in self-understanding, and only through his internal struggle with unknown forces is he able to return to society with a conviction of his own importance.

This brings the hero to the second stage, the period of maturity and the prime of life. Now his previous trials are intensified, for he has to make a name for himself by his contribution to society. His mode of operation is to triumph over, control, and kill the quarry in order to confirm his new character and give him full possession of the powers in the wilderness. No easy task, this demands many labors, often violent. The achievement of maturity depends on his ability to assume the power and knowledge of the prey in the forest and to differentiate himself from them. Moving into the external forum, he must now exercise his adult responsibility by sharing his insights with others. One insight leads to another, however, and he quickly realizes that he can bring the boon, a spiritual gift, to mankind not by dominating the forces of the wilderness but only through union with them. This realization prepares the hunter-hero for the third stage, namely death and resurrection.

In the third stage, the hero bears the brunt of the guilt and fears of the culture and dies, often through some violent means such as hanging from a tree or dismemberment. His sacrificial death has positive value, however, for he promises to bring positive benefits and a new life of the spirit. He undertakes still another voyage, now on the cosmological level, into the realm of the underworld. Here, after an allotted period of time and usually with the help of a woman (for example, Isis, Aphrodite, or Cybele), he is able to return to earth as an agent of restoration and renewal by showing that death has been defeated. He emerges not in his masculinity, but totally integrated, having incorporated the feminine powers that are essential for his new life.

After briefly teaching the lesson of his new life, the hero is ready for the fourth and final stage, where he will be taken out of the cycle of life forever. This stage is the moment of apotheosis or ascension. By a gift of the gods, the historical hero now becomes a divine hero, free from the human condition. He now enjoys a liberation from all time: there is a "realization that the distinction between eternity and time is only apparent—made, perforce, by the rational mind, but dissolved in the perfect knowledge of the mind that has transcended the pairs of opposites." [5] The hero is now beyond the reach of change, free of all fear. The divine element within him has become active in his relation to all persons and events. Indeed, "he who loses his life shall find it."

Having glanced at an overview of the universal myth of the hunter, we are now able to apply it on the cultural level to America. We shall treat each of the four stages at some length, but in outline we may say that America went through its phase of initiation in the wilderness experiences from the time of the first settlers until the early part of the nineteenth century. As an adolescent hunter, America wore a coonskin cap, struggled alone with its self-identity, and discovered the beauty of the wilderness only as it disappeared. The last 150 years have been the period of America's adulthood, the second stage. The hunter wore variously a cowboy's hat, a policeman's cap, and a space-helmet. America was on the move continuously, crossing frontiers and overcoming barriers. But unfortunately America felt compelled to prove its adulthood was masculine and this involved the use of violence. At the present time, America is in the third period, that of death and resurrection. A sobering feeling of failure due to Vietnam and Watergate, a desire to repudiate the negativities of the past, and a shrunken view of future prospects all point to the necessity of finding the feminine element that will act as agent in the process of regeneration. The stage of apotheosis, which involves getting out of the hunter myth altogether, has not yet arrived and will come only as a gift from the transcendent.

THE HUNTER AND THE WILDERNESS

The first settlers to America came hoping for a fresh beginning. The poor dreamed of becoming rich, the energetic were eager to work, and the weak felt they would have a chance to become strong. All came hoping for a freedom, not only from and for various religious convictions but also in order to appropriate their own existence. They came, as did the immigrants in later centuries, because they felt they could become a new race, a new nation, by penetrating to the wilderness of the continent. Through the mythical voyage over a large body of water they crossed the threshold of adventure and became engaged in seeking a new identity. This constituted their hope for initiation into a higher form of life, no longer in the inherited world of their European parents, but a new world carved out of the wilderness. They saw themselves as shapers of their own destiny.

America's stage of initiation and adolescence is intimately connected with the wilderness. The wilderness was the source of that constant struggle and frustration which are necessary for growth. Here it was that America the Hunter went to achieve a communion with the forces that rule the universe, where he could acquire a new moral character, a new set of powers. At first the wilderness represented a formidable adversary, and living in the wilds produced a bias against them mainly because they symbolized the constant struggle for survival and success. The relationship to the wilderness was utilitarian: it had to be conquered and cultivated, because safety and comfort, and even the necessities of life, depended on it. Domesticating the wilderness, from Maine to California, became a national goal: early Americans wanted to convert it into a desirable residence for man. In doing so, they were symbolically conquering the wild savages and beasts, ordering chaos, and changing evil into good. This demanded sacrifices and exacted its toll, but it did result in breaking free from the European heritage, and enabled young America to break down various stereotypes of class structures and to bolster its ego by pointing to its achievements, and justifying its struggle for independence by its success.

Once he had made the decision to withdraw into the wilderness to take on its powers so as to master it, the hunter became immersed in it, seeing it as the solution to all his problems and as the balm for failing fortunes. The terrors in the woods were embraced as the signs of nature's power. To take on these powers was to take on vitality, heroism, and toughness on one hand, and a certain delicacy, sensitivity, and moral growth on the other hand. Gradually he came to realize that the wilderness had attractive rather than repulsive qualities. Benjamin Franklin summed up the positive value of the wilderness in commenting on the country: "The people of the trading towns may be rich and luxurious, while the country possesses all the virtues, that tend to produce happiness and public prosperity." [6] There was a certain capacity for meeting fundamental human needs that life in the towns left unsatisfied. On the level of physical health, the wilderness demanded self-sufficiency, a certain amount of stamina, and a reliance on one's own resources. Psychologically, it represented relief from the drabness of society and civilization: it called the hunter to challenge, to adventure, and especially to freedom. Where he had previously found monsters and the mysterious, now he could find peace, solitude, and silence.[7]

The wilderness drew the hunter from the safe world of parental nurture into a realm of independent responsibility. Here he had to carry on a struggle through which he could learn to take upon himself the power of give-and-take with his environment, and carry on that constant dialog so necessary for self-knowledge. This was a gradual affair, for the woods represented symbolically the center of the universe, and the hunter, in penetrating deeper, was coming into contact with his deepest self. As he became accustomed to the wilderness, he took on heroic stature in the eyes of other Americans, while to the Europeans he was considered a degenerate. The wildness of the land, with its harshness and its potential fertility, evoked the presence of the mysterious native Americans who lived there. Gradually, as the hunter discovered himself, he derived strength from the Indians with their special wisdom and strength of character. He did not go so far, however, as to take on Indian ways. The Indian was a "wild savage," admired yet feared. The early settlers saw him as one who tried to achieve an acceptable relationship with the unknown power that affected his life, and they admired this. They admired the Indian ability to empathize with other humans and with nonhuman living creatures who seemed to share the same life-force. The early whites thought that all the Indian needed for salvation was conversion to a Puritan Christianity.

THE HUNTER AND THE FRONTIER

The second part of the monomyth—America coming of age— reflects a shift in the image of the hunter. Previously the hunter was solitary and alone, a figure of innocence, a new Adam, forced to go into the woods to begin a new history. He hunted for game as a necessity for survival, he fought the Indians when misunder- standings arose, but mainly he was on the quest for self-identity. Now, at the threshold of adulthood, the hunter takes on the westward trek in earnest, adopting many guises but mainly that of the pioneer and the cowboy. Adulthood does not come overnight, of course, and the slow transition is reflected in the struggle between the adolescent's desire to be an adult and his fear and hesitation about the nature of adulthood. He has to resolve the dilemma between individual freedom from restraint and aggres- siveness, on one side, and social responsibility and community, on the other. This necessary life-giving agony was worked out as the hunter made his way westward across the frontier. Here his restless energy, his self-reliance, and his voluntary cooperation with others could develop to maturity.

The hunter is characterized by his movement. To continue to live the high adventure, he has to extend himself, to continue to expand. Only in this way will he find the gift that he is to bring to others. That is why the hunter as pioneer and cowboy is perhaps the most potent expression of the wandering spirit. He lived on the outer edge of civilization and expanded to find new opportunities. Movement meant adventure and openness. It meant not only farther away in space, but also farther away from the past. It meant seeking out ever new frontiers, which put a premium on expedient action, on bravery and resourcefulness. Movement expressed fitness and toughness, the essence of masculinity. With the closing of the last frontier, America continued its movement, expanding to other countries and taking over world leadership, even so far as to race into exploration in space.

The movement was always just beyond the frontier and back. Unlike the wilderness hunter who was basically a solitary figure, the frontier hunter was a mediator between civilization and the unknown. But just what was the frontier? Frederick Jackson Turner, the famous American historian who advanced the thesis that the true point of view of the history of America was not its European ancestry or the Atlantic coast, but the West, defined the frontier in several different ways. It was variously the area of free and open land, or the line of population density; it was the recurrent transition from primitive to complex society, or that spirit of opinion which differed from the East.[8] For the hunter, the frontier was whatever stimulated movement and progress and welded together a strong nation by encouraging aggressive nationalism. The frontier was that vague, ever changing territory where he could grow rapidly and expand into lands that were his own, all with the approval of the Federal government, which parceled out the public domain, then later protected it by army outposts, subsidies to the railroads, and the general promotion of economic development.

Though the hunter's continual movement along the changing frontier was necessary for his growth into adulthood, it caused mixed reactions among those who remained embedded in civilization. To some he was a courageous woodsman, to others a shiftless farmer. He was the bearer of civilization to undisciplined pagans, or the refugee from corrupt civilization. He destroyed old ways of life, or he made the frontier safe for others. Perhaps it would be more correct to say that the hunter was all of these, not just one or the other. It was precisely this blend of contradictory qualities that constituted the American contribution to civilization. As Aldo Leopold expressed it: ". . . if we have such a thing as an

American culture, its distinguishing marks are a certain vigorous individualism combined with ability to organize, a certain intellectual curiosity bent to practical ends, a lack of subservience to stiff social forms, and an intolerance of drones, all of which are distinctive characteristics of successful pioneers." [9] If, indeed, it was the pioneer who was so characteristically American, then how strange it is that in the American myth the frontier has always been considered the domain of the cowboy.

In the cowboy, the messianic age came to the frontier. On the most archetypal level, here was the triumph of good over evil, the establishment of a law and order higher than man. Tough, fun-loving, dirty, and hell-raising, the cowboy who went on the long cattle drives from Texas to the railheads in Kansas became the symbol of everything the American wanted to be. He was the hero of every person who had to start at the bottom and work up. He was the leader with the six-shooter, the one who was contemptuous of others, proud and easygoing, full of confidence, even bordering on arrogance. The cowboy was America the Hunter as an adult. He epitomized America's mastery over the immense continent, its smug consciousness of power, and its certainty that nothing could stand in the way.

At least this is the way Americans prefer to picture the cowboy. This is how Americans have chosen to narrate the myth of their own desires and goals. It seems, however, that in the process of mythologizing, the West was exempted from history. This matters little, however, for the truth of the myth is not whether it is historically accurate, but whether people use it to justify and give significance to their values, actions, and judgments. The foregoing characterization of the cowboy seems to be, actually, the work of eastern businessmen and the entertainment industry.[10] In reality, the cowboy was one who moved in to take advantage of the superabundance of the West, who exploited the rich lands, forests, and oil fields for profit. He fought the progress of the pioneers who straggled onto the prairies with their barbed wire and plows. Rather than living in an atmosphere of freedom where "seldom was heard a discouraging word," he was embroiled in social conflict, racial ugliness, and lynchings. His work was dull and lonely: he had to endure demands and discomforts, and could not gamble, drink, or even gallop his horse while on the trail. He was caught in the web of petty capitalists who were struggling for a stronger position in the market. Yet no matter how fabricated the image, how harsh the reality, the cowboy continues to symbolize the masculine adult hero for most Americans.

Nor is violence foreign to the cowboy symbol. The cowboy loved his individuality, but he demanded it at the end of a gun. The nineteenth century saw violence manifested in many ways, for example, in the brutality of groups like the Texas Rangers, the lynchings of the vigilantes, the struggles against the Chinese in building the transcontinental railroad, and in the battles of Federal troops and the labor unions. But violence is one thing, its meaning another. As the myth worked itself out, the American hero was undoubtedly masculine, and the hunter came into his adulthood with the six-shooter.[11] The gun became the ready answer both for those who wanted to rebel against authoritarian controls and for those who held positions of authority. The American soul had become, as D. H. Lawrence phrased it, hard, isolate, stoic, and a killer.

One of the most tragic expressions of this misguided masculinity was the violent treatment of the native American Indians. The Indians became *the* prey of the hunter. During the earlier wilderness period there had been a secret admiration for the Indian ways. Now, however, the Indians were a source of embarrassment for the white man, for they stood in the way of his progress westward. The Indians possessed and fought for their lands, and the white man, perhaps out of guilt, perhaps out of anger, felt he had to conquer them once and for all—if not exterminate them by mass genocide, at least slaughter their buffalo and force them onto reservations. The story of white/ Indian relations during this part of America's history is a sad one. We should not forget the Removal Act passed by Congress in 1830 where the Cherokee and other Indian nations were forced to march more than a thousand miles westward across the Mississippi to make room for cotton planters and gold miners, the ruthless massacres of the friendly Cheyenne at their winter base at Sandy Creek in 1864, the relentless pursuit of the last bands of Chief Joseph's Nez Percé right up to the Canadian borders in

1877, and the final inglorious burst of violence in the slaying of defenseless Sioux women and children at Wounded Knee in 1890. That the American hero felt he could assert his adulthood through violence was tragic but also ironic. For the archetypal hunter went too far and, rather than trying to identify with his prey, annihilated it, and in so doing, could no longer be a hunter since he had nothing to hunt. It is a kind of poetic justice that the Indian is often evoked today to symbolize the very qualities (such as manly vigor and defense of good against evil) that the pioneer and the cowboy were struggling to achieve.[12]

THE HUNTER AND THE PREY

In denying the Indian his own culture, America the Hunter ultimately destroyed his raison d'être. The hunt went on, of course. America became involved in two world wars, Korea, and Vietnam: "body count" was still important. Internal struggles, the rebellions of the blacks and other minority groups, the campus disturbances—all helped bring about the death of the hunter, though the explorations into space gave him one last frontier and delayed the inevitable process for a while. Now, however, the third phase of the monomyth—death and resurrection—is fully here. The death is symbolic, of course, and involves a descent to the underworld to struggle with hidden forces. These forces will actually help the hunter attain a new being, not by being conquered but by being assimilated. Appropriating these powers, the hunter will find his boon, and so increase his own personal strength, religious faith, and self-knowledge. His masculinity, till now so pronounced, will not help the assimilation, for the promised new life will come only through a sacrifice of the old. His aggressiveness must die so that the process of self-renewal (resurrection) can begin.

The hunter needs self-renewal because he no longer has any prey to hunt. The wilderness and the frontier have all but disappeared, and space is a challenge only for a distinct few. In the monomyth, a woman is often the instrument that brings the hero back to a new higher life. In terms of Jungian psychoanalysis, the hero needs the help of the anima for his resurrection. In our myth of America the Hunter, the "animal" that has been hunted till now is the anima, the lost part that the hunter needs to become an integrated new being. The anima is his undeveloped feminine side that subordinated intellect to feeling, that has been neglected in his quest for masculinity.[13] Only through assimilation of this other half, only through the union of the hunter and his prey, will the hunter achieve his own salvation and be able to bring salvation to his people. What had been the enemy now becomes the source of the new energy needed for triumph and transcendence. Formerly the hunt meant the death of the prey, now the prey means the life of the hunter. This mysterious transformation of the hunter cannot be hurried, otherwise he will not be so much a hunter as a plunderer. Recognizing and retrieving the anima is a work of patience, devotion, and ultimate self-sacrifice.[14]

It would be difficult to single out any one prey or anima in the myth of the hunter. To some degree all groups or nations which threaten America are the archetypal enemy. Rebellious urban blacks, various liberation groups, and the drug culture are prominent examples today. Here I would suggest that the native American Indian, chosen in the 1970s by the media and young people in rebellion as a symbol of the exploited poor and a symbol of the Golden Age of man's solidarity with God and creation, would certainly be one aspect of the anima. By stages a captor, a mystery, an embarrassment, a captive, the Indian now represents the possibility of fullness for the hunter. The Indian is part of the anima, that element the hunter needs to become a new creation, a new hero, which will no longer be individualistic, male, or aggressive.

The Indian till now has been the foil of the hunter, a savage in the dark forest or a stumbling block in the way of advancement of civilization. The hunter has foisted on him all the evil characteristics that he refused to acknowledge in himself, and has regarded the Indian merely as an object of exploitation. Lewis Mumford states this well: ". . . for the better part of four centuries the cultural riches of the entire world lay at the feet of western man; and to his shame, and likewise to his gross self-deprivation and impoverishment, his main concern was to appropriate only the gold and silver and diamonds, the lumber and pelts, and such new foods (maize and potatoes) as would enable him to feed larger populations." [15] By the time that the anthropologists and ethnologists could begin to study the Indian in depth and popular opinion began to see them as natural uncultivated heroes, the tribes had been decimated or dispersed, and the bulk were living on reservations.

Even though history is written by the conquerors, and the influence of the prey has seldom been the subject for dispassionate consideration, the Indian has influenced American culture to a great extent, and this will be even more evident as the hunter moves from death to resurrection.[16] Thus it is legitimate to ask, since the hunter must assimilate the anima, what traits of the Indian will the hunter have to take on in order to be resurrected to new life? To counterbalance his masculine powers, he will have to utilize the techniques of the shaman, appreciate the realm of visions and dreams, and learn the community value of ritual.

First the shaman. Akin to the medicine man and the priest, the shaman performs a curative, healing function in Indian cultures, and has a special role in the hunt.[17] The shaman is a mystic and a visionary. His way of hunting is the way of passivity and suffering. He puts himself at the mercy of the forces that govern man and the universe. In contrast to the hunter's code of killing, the shaman's morality is the way of self-abnegation, kindness, and peace. Rather than brute courage, his virtue is kinship with nature. The shaman constitutes a balance with the more masculine warrior-hunters: rather than dominating through exploitation and slaughter, he masters through a power to attract and sympathize with animals. In the hunting tribes the shaman had a symbolic role, for by his union with the animal spirits, with the beasts of the forest, with the trees, he showed that all creatures share the same universe. What this meant to the Indian hunters was that they were able to kill the animal, as they must, but with dignity, as if they were assisting at the death of a close relative rather than at a slaughter. Consider, for example, the Iroquois myth wherein the Stone Giant poignantly speaks to the hunter who, lost in the woods, has discovered the Giant's hiding place: "Be wise and learn my secrets, how disease is healed, how man and beast and plant may talk together and learn one another's missions. Go and live with the trees and birds and beasts, and fish, and learn to honor them as your own brothers." [18] Such a union with the prey changes the nature of the hunt, since the importance rests in identification with the prey, not merely in its death.

If the hunter can learn kinship with the prey through the shaman, he can also benefit from the Indian understanding of dreams. The Indians believed there was a whole environment of power that was only slightly removed from human sight and touch. They came into contact with this realm of psychic power through vigils, fasts, vision quests, and especially through their dreams. Dreams were thought to be instruments of the divine, to which they had to render their submission and follow with utmost exactness. Indians encouraged each other to remember their dreams and report them to the community where they could be acted out communally so that the god's demands or desires might be better understood. It was not enough to analyze the dream, interpret it, or take prompt individual action: the dream was acted out, sometimes literally, but usually through symbolic ritual. Otherwise some disaster might befall the whole society. Early testimony in the reports of the Jesuits working in the Seneca nation shows how they regarded their dreams:

> Most of the Hurons are very careful to note their dreams, and to provide the soul with what it has pictured to them during their sleep. If, for instance, they have seen a javelin in a dream, they try to get it; if they have dreamed that they gave a feast, they will give one on awakening, if they have the wherewithal; and so on with other things. And they call this Ondinnonk—a secret desire of the soul manifested by a dream. . . . [The Hurons] have, properly speaking, only a single divinity—the dream. To it they render their submission and follow all its orders with the utmost exactness.[19]

Taking the lead of the Indian, the hunter can learn to appreciate the importance of the realm of the psyche and to see its value in helping achieve that union with the anima which is indispensable for his resurrection as a new being.

The third element that the American hunter can appropriate from the native American Indians is their appreciation of rituals. Their dramatic prayers, their attitude toward the spirits and the universe, and their desire to maintain solidarity in community were all expressed in song and dance. Through rituals they were able to evoke unanimity of emotional reaction and religious sentiment. Also, they reenacted the history of the tribe, especially those moments of past contact between gods and men that had been so beneficial. The dances were a stimulus to unity with each other and with the spirits that were being propitiated. Rituals maintained the community in that right relationship with the universe by which they were more devoted to living than to getting. In the hunting rituals Indians danced to please the animals, such as buffalo or prairie chickens, and prayed for their increase, not so the hunters would have plenty of game, but rather so that killing the animals would not be so disastrous to their brothers. The Blackfoot Indians of Montana, for example, acted out the buffalo dance with slow and solemn song, ponderous and deliberate step. This was the magical means by which the buffalo that were killed by the people for their food should be restored to life. To be resurrected to a new life, the hunter does not have to learn the rituals so much as he has to learn their value. They served to reform and redirect the community to a sense of solidarity. The dance was performed in a sacred place, in what the Indians called the "center of the earth." By his participation, each person was centered in his own universe and found a common basis for spiritual and psychic integrity with the others who shared the dance.

THE HUNTER AND THE BOUNTY

America the Hunter is now in the stage of descent, waiting for the resurrection or rebirth that will come through reconciliation and identification with the prey. It is possible that the hunter can become a new being by taking on what the native American Indian has to offer, such as a feeling of kinship with the animal world, a sense of the reality of the whole realm of power in the psyche, and a ritual solidarity within the community. On a psychological level, the assimilation of the hunter and the anima may be achieved. Perhaps the Indian will yet succeed in conquering the white man, not by taking his land but by conquering him in spirit. But what about the fourth stage of the monomyth, the moment of apotheosis? Is it possible for America the Hunter to shun the illusion of a localized self? Will he be able to attain freedom from limitations of time? Will he achieve that breakthrough to be taken out of the cycle of life, death, and rebirth once and for all?

According to the monomyth, the hunter can achieve his ultimate transformation only through the help of the divine, only through "divine bounty." Symbolic death and resurrection are possible on a human level, but not the ascension. At best, the hunter can aim at the proper target. He is able only to glimpse at the final reality, to have what theologians call an eschatological anticipation of the End. Till now this has hardly been the case. As a wilderness-hero, as a pioneer-cowboy, the hunter has always considered the death of the animal (and the anima) as the goal of the chase. The cost of civilization, he felt, was the extinction of the Indian, the prey. Consequently he could not moderate his hunt so as not to destroy himself as well as his prey. America the Hunter tried to subdue nature, to command space and time. He thought the proper method was to hasten growth, quicken the pace, and break down distances by mechanical and technological means. He conquered by going faster and farther, attaining bigger and more. Has this made the resolution of the myth impossible?

Divine bounty can never be merited. However, the hunter is not entirely hopeless. Once the union between hunter and prey has been achieved, it is possible to anticipate overcoming the illusion of a localized self by changing the very aim of hunting. As Faulkner's Ike McCaslin expresses it in "The Bear" when he kills his first animal: "I slew you; my bearing must not shame your quitting life. My conduct forever onward must become your death." For his conduct to be suitable or becoming, he will have to change the aim of the hunt. No longer must the death of the prey be paramount, but rather, the chase itself. Henceforth the hunter must hunt for the sake of diversion, not for utilitarian motives. Hardship and risk will certainly be present still, for these are needed for diversion; however, they will no longer produce anxiety. By making the chase the goal, the hunter shows he is open to the process of ascension. He is open to what Lewis Mumford has called "organic plenitude." [20] There is a certain fullness of spirit, where the hunter is no longer concerned about the latest technological weapons, nor the greatest number killed. He now strives for an ecological system which allows him to leave a fresh imprint of meaning and value on every phase of the hunt. His goal becomes qualitative, not quantitative. Rather than continually chasing prey such as money, knowledge, and pleasure, he is immersed in the chase and rejoices in a certain amount of healthful exercise, spiritual distraction, and psychological diversion from his everyday life. In such a way he shows his ready anticipation for the divine gift.

In addition to realizing that the chase is more important than the death of the prey, the hunter can also participate in the process of apotheosis in a second way. The chase takes time, and the hunter will ultimately have to be free from his limitations in time. Once again, this is possible only as a divine gift, but the hunter is able to anticipate it, to have an eschatological glimpse of the End. The hunter is one who thrives on both certainty and uncertainty: on one hand, he wants the assurance that there is prey available and, on the other hand, he doesn't want it given to him even before he starts the chase. The eschatological moment of the chase occurs when this certainty and uncertainty coincide, namely at the moment he spots the prey. It is that moment, for example, in Melville's *Moby Dick* when the shout goes up: "There she blows! There! There!" This is the moment of ecstasy, the moment of transcendence, when the hunter is freed from his limitation in time. Joseph Campbell describes this moment as the release from bondage when

> the biological urges to enjoy and to master (with their opposites, to loathe and to fear), as well as the social urge to evaluate (as good or evil, true or false), simply drop away, and a rapture in sheer experience supervenes, in which self-loss and elevation are the same. Such an impact is "beyond words"; for it is not such as can be explained by a

reference to anything else. The mind is released—for a moment, for a day, or perhaps forever—from those anxieties to enjoy, to win, or to be correct, which spring from the net of nerves in which men are entangled. Ego dissolved, there is nothing in the net but life—which is everywhere and forever.[21]

At that moment, the hunter stands before the mystery of the wilderness. Filled with awe and wonder, he has anticipated, if only for a fleeting second, that glorification that will ultimately come as a boon from the gods.

The awareness that man can anticipate organic plenitude and the release from bondage is the hunter's ultimate boon for mankind. It is a gift that frees, for the realization that man can share in the deification process is a liberating experience. It means that no human goals or Utopias (and conversely no human failures) are ever final. In fact, such Utopias are dangerous precisely because they might succeed: the hunter would then be stuck in the cycle forever. For America the Hunter, this means specifically that the goals of life, liberty, and the pursuit of happiness can never be fully achieved. Further, those moments of peace and freedom that do come are to be enjoyed, not as the goal, but as anticipations of the End. In terms of Christian theology it means that a human freedom where economic and social justice are possible is not the divine liberation promised in the Gospels: rather, such a freedom is only the scent or trail of the prey that draws the hunter onward.

In fact, the myth of America the Hunter has many points in common with the Christian myth of liberation, the Good News. Becoming aware of an intimate union with his Father, Jesus spends a period of time meditating in the wilderness where he has a struggle with the evil forces that tempt him to be content with merely human pleasures and goals. Entering adulthood in his public ministry, he points to a new frontier—the Kingdom where loving, caring, and forgiving reign. He is forced to undergo violence due to the malice, stupidity, and spiritual blindness of his opponents and finally suffers and dies. His death is necessary, but not the end. After his descent to the underworld he is resurrected

and manifests the union between himself and the Father: Jesus is
the hunter and God is the prey. By his ascension, Jesus is taken
out of the cycle of life and death forever and bestows the bounty,
the divine gift on man. The gift is a liberating gift, for it proclaims
that the wholeness of every person comes not in killing God, but
in achieving union with him. In Jesus, the archetypal hunter, each
person sees that he can transcend space and time and can achieve
that organic plenitude that can fill the universe. He is no longer a
captive, but is released from bondage. St. Paul hints at these
similarities between the myth of the hunter and the Good News in
his letter to the Ephesians (4:7–10):

> Each of us has been given his gift, his due portion of Christ's
> bounty. Therefore Scripture says: "he ascended into the
> heights with captives in his train; he gave gifts to men."
> Now the word "ascended" implies that he also descended to
> the lowest level, down to the very earth. He who descended
> is no other than he who ascended far above all heavens, so
> that he might fill the universe.

NOTES

1. America, it seems, looks for a "saviour" who will bring freedom after
conquering the enemy, who will ride over the horizon to save the day just
as all is lost, or who will somehow or other preserve American innocence.
See John Kirvan, "Waking Up from the American Dream," *New Catholic
World* 216 (1973), pp. 148–52. He criticizes the myth of freedom and
liberation. Also see Michael Novak, *The Experience of Nothingness* (New
York: Harper & Row, 1971), who challenges America's attempts to be
religious, its need to be a booster or volunteer, its chauvinism in foreign
policy, and its prejudices in domestic affairs.

2. This particular understanding of myth comes out of the Jungian
tradition. See the formulations by Morton Kelsey, *Myth, History and
Faith: The Remythologizing of Christianity* (New York: Paulist Press,
1974) and Joseph Campbell, *The Hero with a Thousand Faces* (Princeton:
Princeton University Press, 1968). I am especially indebted to Richard

Slotkin, *Regeneration through Violence: The Mythology of the American Frontier, 1600–1860* (Middletown: Wesleyan University Press, 1973). Slotkin sees myths such as the captivity myth and the hunter myth as variations on the central myth of initiation into a new world and a new life.

3. This push toward success is most especially true of the athlete. C. G. Jung in *Collected Works* (New York: Pantheon Books, 1964), vol. 10 ("Civilization in Transition"), p. 512, sees the almost cruel and inhuman training of athletes as one of the characteristics peculiar to Americans.

4. Cf. Joseph Campbell, *op. cit.*, pp. 30, 36–37, for the various stages of the monomyth. David Adams Leeming, *Mythology: The Voyage of the Hero* (Philadelphia: J. B. Lippincott, 1973), divides the monomyth into eight segments and gives numerous examples of each.

5. Campbell, *op. cit.*, p. 152.

6. Benjamin Franklin, *Works of Benjamin Franklin* II, ed. Jared Sparks (Chicago, 1882), p. 450, quoted in Walker D. Wyman and Clifton B. Kroeber, eds., *The Frontier in Perspective* (Madison: University of Wisconsin Press, 1957), p. xviii.

7. In subsequent history, Americans have returned to the wilderness as a break from organized society. James Fenimore Cooper sought to integrate all the individual freedom of the savage state with all the order and social harmony of the highest degree of civilization. Henry Thoreau, Orestes Brownson, Francis Parkman, and others attempted to combine the hardiness of the Indians with the intellectualism of civilized man. Only at the turn of the twentieth century, however, did the American come to appreciate the wilderness as a symbol of a simpler, quieter past, especially with the writings of the conservationist John Muir. Now the preservation of the wilderness is threatened as much by a plethora of campers and hikers as by economic exploitation. One excellent work on the importance of the wilderness is Roderick Nash, *Wilderness and the American Mind* (New Haven: Yale University Press, 1967). His chapters on the efforts of Aldo Leopold and John Muir are classic. Charles Sanford, *The Quest for Paradise: Europe and the American Moral Imagination* (Urbana: University of Illinois Press, 1961), and Leo Marx, *The Machine in the Garden: Technology and the Pastoral Ideal in America* (New York: Oxford University Press, 1964), both comment on the American endeavor to find a compromise between wilderness and civilization. Henry Nash Smith, *Virgin Land: The American West as Symbol and Myth* (Cambridge: Harvard University Press, 1950), and Philip Slotkin, *op. cit.*, both discuss the mythical symbolism of the wilderness in American literature.

8. Cf. Frederick Jackson Turner, *The Frontier in American History*

(New York: Henry Holt, 1920). The best critiques of his position are by Richard Hofstadter, *The Progressive Historians* (New York: Alfred A. Knopf, 1968), especially chap. 4, "The Frontier as an Explanation," and Benjamin F. Wright, Jr., "Political Institutions of the Frontier," in Dixon Ryan Fox, ed., *Sources of Culture in the Middle West* (New York: Appleton-Century Co., 1934), pp. 14–38.

9. Aldo Leopold, quoted in Roderick Nash, *op. cit.*, p. 188.

10. Richard Hofstadter, *op. cit.*, p. 160, claims that the cowboy, rather than going west to be self-sufficient in the land of the free, went to "recreate for himself the American standard of living as he had seen it in the East, and not to forge a utopian egalitarian society but to re-enact the social differences of the older world—with himself now closer to the top." For similar pictures of the lifestyle of the cowboy, cf. Joe B. Frantz and Julian Ernest Choate, Jr., *The American Cowboy, The Myth and the Reality* (Norman: University of Oklahoma Press, 1955). This contains a superb bibliography. Also Marshall W. Fishwick, "The Cowboy: America's Contribution to the World's Mythology," *Western Folklore* XI, no. 2 (April 1952), pp. 77–92, and Ramon F. Adams, ed., *The Best of the American Cowboy* (Norman: University of Oklahoma Press, 1957). Robert V. Hine, *The American West: An Interpretive History* (Boston: Little, Brown, 1973), has fine chapters on the cowboy, the cult of masculinity, and the frontier experience.

11. Gun collecting and target shooting today are the latest reenactments of the myth of the cowboy and his six-shooter. Fifteen years ago, eight of the top ten television programs were westerns. Today these have been replaced by detective and mystery stories, but the violence has remained. For more on the gun culture and cowboy mentality, cf. W. Eugene Hollon, *Frontier Violence: Another Look* (New York: Oxford University Press, 1974), and Thomas Clark, *Frontier America: The Story of the Westward Movement* (New York: Charles Scribner's Sons, 1959).

12. It is ironic too that children play cowboys and Indians rather than pioneers and Indians. The heyday of the cowboy was after the Civil War, when there were few Indians left who had not already been herded onto reservations. The myth continues to be embellished.

13. Cf. C. G. Jung, *Collected Works* (New York: Pantheon Books), especially vol. 9, I ("Aion") and vol. 14 ("Mysterium Coniunctionis"). It is not by coincidence that there is such a strong movement for women's liberation in America today. A myth narrates what is most true about a culture, and in the American myth the hunter-hero, both in the wilderness and on the frontier, has been unmistakably masculine.

14. The union of hunter and prey is a common theme in classical

American literature. Daniel Boone marries the deer-woman; Melville's Ahab hunts the whale on a leg made of whalebone; Faulkner stresses the kinship between Ike McCaslin and The Bear. In the famous Sioux myth, the beautiful woman who gives the tribe the pipe is identified with the buffalo.

15. Cf. Lewis Mumford, *The Pentagon of Power: The Myth of the Machine* II (New York; Harcourt Brace Jovanovitch, 1970), pp. 10–11.

16. For example, Indian influence can be found in the names of twenty-six states, eighteen of our major cities, and several plants such as maize, pumpkin, squash, and tobacco. A. Irving Hallowell, "The Backwash of the Frontier: the Impact of the Indian on American Culture," in Walker D. Wyman and Clifton B. Kroeber, eds., *The Frontier in Perspective* (Madison: University of Wisconsin Press, 1957), finds a deep influence on our speech, economic life, clothing, sports and recreation, curative practices, folk and concert music, and several other areas. Peter Farb, *Man's Rise to Civilization* (New York: E. P. Dutton, 1968), pp. 260–66, also discusses the debt to the Indian. For the Indian's view of his contributions, cf. Harold E. Fey and D'Arcy McNickle, *Indians and Other Americans: Two Ways of Life Meet* (New York: Harper & Row, 1959).

17. Commentaries on the shaman are quite abundant. Cf. Mircea Eliade, *Shamanism: Archaic Techniques of Ecstasy* (Princeton: Princeton University Press, 1964), and also the pertinent chapters in *Myths, Dreams, and Mysteries* (New York: Harper & Row, 1967), pp. 73–112. Other Classics are W. Z. Park, *Shamanism in Western North America* (Evanston: Northwestern University Press, 1938), and Joseph Campbell, *The Masks of God: Primitive Mythology* (New York: Viking Press, 1972), pp. 229–81.

18. Quoted in Edmund Wilson, *Apologies to the Iroquois* (New York: Farrar, Straus, & Cudahy, 1959), p. 217.

19. *Ibid.*, pp. 228–29. Cf. also Anthony F. C. Wallace, *The Death and Rebirth of The Seneca* (New York: Alfred A. Knopf, 1969), pp. 59–75; William Brandon, *The Last Americans: The Indian in American Culture* (New York: McGraw-Hill Book Co., 1974), p. 370; and Benjamin A. Reist, *Theology in Red, White, and Black* (Philadelphia: Westminster Press, 1975), pp. 114–20.

20. Cf. Lewis Mumford, *op. cit.*, p. 402. "Under a regime of organic plenitude, abundance is permissive, not compulsive: it allows for extravagant expenditures to satisfy man's higher needs for knowledge, beauty, or love. . . . The life-negating ideals and methods of the power system [are] renounced, and a conscious effort made, at every level and in

every kind of community, to live not for the sake of exalting power but for reclaiming this planet for life through mutual aid, loving association, and biotechnic cultivation."

21. Joseph Campbell, *The Masks of God* (New York: Viking Press, 1972), p. 469.

RUSSELL L. JABERG

search for a center

In the record of man's efforts to make a rational and comprehensive statement, three major themes have appeared regularly: the world, God, and man. The Greeks began with assumptions primarily concerning the cosmos. The continuing life of Western culture resulted in concepts of man and the world which were derived from persuasions concerning the Deity. The Renaissance marked the beginning of a development out of the perspective of man, with a resultant emphasis on human culture.

But culture, because of its obviously dynamic, complex, and problematic nature, resists simplification. Therefore let us begin with the modest assertion that there is change abroad in our modern world. It will be our purpose to try to identify one aspect of our changing culture. Here we suggest that the Renaissance concept and perspective of man has now run its course. We shall try to establish the present direction of a search for a cultural principle, and offer a few implications of this principle for religion.

ABANDONMENT OF THE PERSPECTIVE OF MAN

We understand the perspective of man to involve three quintessential characteristics: a persuasion concerning human potential and a commitment to the expansion of knowledge; the acceptance of an increasing control over all things by man as an unbounded good; and the freedom and dignity of man as values which are, or should be, supreme within society. But several disciplines in the modern world militate against the continuing maintenance of this principle of man.

1. The words "to have dominion" have been in the record for centuries, but the mastery of external nature as we know it can be traced to several sources. The following are noteworthy: Machiavelli's conception of the mastery of fortune; the pantheistic speculations of Giordano Bruno in the sixteenth century; and Francis Bacon's confident hope that nature could be made to serve the business and conveniences of man. Bacon saw the goal ". . . to stretch the deplorably narrow limits of man's dominion over the universe to their promised bounds." [1]

We may well take for granted the pattern of movement from scientific discovery, to technological innovation, to industrial production. By this program, admittedly, the life and lot of Western man has been changed. A contemporary view of Shakespeare's Prospero would picture him as a modern man possessing the knowledge and tools which science and technology have provided. Freud described man as a prosthetic god—in that man has acquired the powers once ascribed to mythological divinities.

From the fiction of Dickens, to the Bauhaus, to the contract negotiations of the United Auto Workers, to the distress of nations, there is the pressing question whether or not we have been deluding ourselves in pursuit of man's control over the external world. There is a kind of cultural trauma induced by the disillusionment over what man has wrought. Several items appear to be relevant: (a) There is the devastation, the dirt, the ugliness attendant to an industrial community. A dump worker said to Loren Eiseley: "We get it all. Just give it time to travel. We get it all." [2] (b) There is the dehumanization of the producers and the products in the system with which man has burdened himself. (c) There is the awareness that the domination of nature brings inescapably the domination of man. (d) We stand in fearful awe at the application of science/technology to the material of war.

2. We turn now to the role of man discoverable in art. With the Renaissance there was the beginning of new status for the artist. The dynamic of individualism may be illustrated by Cellini, who was not content to let his art speak for him, so he wrote a blustery

autobiography. We recall, as well, the development of linear and atmospheric perspective, by reason of which a two-dimensional medium acquired a three-dimensional naturalism because the perspective of man, the viewer, was introduced. The works of Leonardo da Vinci and Michelangelo bear testimony to the concept and role of man in Renaissance art.

Western art turned a corner with Impressionism; the perspective of man then became the perspective and/or the expression of an individual. Nature could be reconstructed according to the personal vision of the individual artist.[3]

In 1972 in Kassel, West Germany, *Documenta 5*, an international art exhibit, was organized in an attempt to present a genuine spectrum of art as it is being created at the moment. As the largest and most complete survey of advanced art up to that time, the exhibition was organized thematically as it carried through its investigation. With a catalog which reportedly weighed nine pounds and cost ten, the reviewer in *Connoisseur* said that "it seemed a genuine reflection on the present confusion." [4] Another concluded that the most significant feature of *Documenta 5* was: "Art is directionless: it evokes no past . . . and points to no future." [5]

Les Levine wrote in the *Saturday Review of the Arts* of February 1973: "The problem we are facing at the moment is this: is art a suitable vehicle for assessing or understanding our culture? The answer for the moment is no. The public is no longer willing to consider seriously an art that is constantly talking about itself and to itself." [6] We suggest that a period of art which was launched on the basis of the perspective and role of man has now thinned out. Indeed, French artist Ben Vautier created a huge banner which was hung over the access of the larger of two buildings which housed *Documenta 5*. It read: KUNST IST ÜBERFLÜSSIG (Art Is Unnecessary).

Lewis Mumford has alleged that art has served only to acclimate modern man to all the ugliness of the habitat which "megatecnics" is bringing into existence.[7]

3. Philosopher Suzanne Langer has described the function of art as the creation of forms which are symbolic of human feeling. This

would pertain to musical patterns and practices of the Renaissance. St. Francis of Assisi knew the music of troubadors. He set the people singing with his lauds, and these caught up the word of religion in popular airs which the people could sing and feel. Luther's encouragement of the use of popular hymns is well known.

We should find the human character of music in the Renaissance to be particularly exemplified in the motet that the composer Guillaume Dufay wrote for the dedication of the Florentine Church of Santa Maria del Fiore—which was brought to completion with Filippo Brunelleschi's dome. The inner structure of this music was intended to be expressive of the harmonies of the universe. Dufay combined melody, harmony, and rhythmic forms to make the motet pleasing to the ear. Music critic Charles Warren[8] has demonstrated that the size and proportions of the nave and presbytery of Santa Maria del Fiore are summarized by Brunelleschi in his dome. Warren has also shown that the exact mathematical proportions of the dome are the proportions of Dufay's motet. The dome is pleasing to the eye and the sound of the motet a delight to man's ear; these sounds are established in proportions which are comprehended and formulated by the human mind.

In our contemporary world we are aware of the concept of, and we have as well confronted, the mystique of the actual in aesthetics. In music, for example, there is the acknowledged modern intent simply to create sounds. These sounds need not have, and probably do not have, any significant relationship with man. They need not be symbolic in the Langer sense. John Cage has written: "The sounds of music should simply be themselves rather than expressions of human sentiments." [9]

We suggest an indifference to man in electronic music. A student of ours wrote the score for a campus production. After hearing it, we observed that it was played so loudly as to render impossible any appreciation or critique. He recognized that the total corpus of sound was too loud for discernment by the human ear, but he explained that the volume was determined by a necessary accommodation to the synthesizer. Just recently, a friend of ours attended a program of electronic music. He was quite dizzy for several days after, and learned from his physician that the sounds had created a disturbance in his middle ear.

A modern objective is primarily a thereness of sound; sounds may simply have an existence of their own. Consideration of man, meaningful symbols of and for man, acceptability to human senses—all may be set aside by reason of what theologian Nathan Scott has termed the "anthropocentric fallacy."

4. We may think of the age of man as one which pictures Western man moving along a path of great achievement. We generally tend to measure achievement by the fulfillment of a potential which is envisioned for man. We may understand this vision in terms of growth of knowledge, enlargement of freedom, fulfillment of responsibility, realization of value—and in particular, the worth of the individual man. However, if we should speak of man as unique, free-willed, an individual personality, then man so understood "has been constructed from our ignorance, and as our understanding increases, the very stuff of which he is composed vanishes." [10]

The issue, we are told, is survival. The response here is that we shall survive only if we scientize man. This means the abandonment of prescientific ideas such as choice, initiative, thinking and feeling self, and free will. As we are aware, the scientizing of man would look to the establishment of a type of environmental determinism in which behavior is determined by forces that impinge upon man. There would be the intent of setting aside the narcissistic anthropomorphism, and building a culture in which a humbler but wiser creature might be able to survive.[11] In the projected environmental world, conscious life would be doomed and real persons would effectively be abolished.

The point for us here is the abandonment of the perspective of man. We do not wish to burden B. F. Skinner beyond his willingness to run out scientific speculation to its end. Such scientizing has been with us in some fashion for a long while. This point of view comes to the fore now perhaps because Skinner just says it better, or says it more honestly, or by reason of modern predilection for psychology. In addition, we should not leave Skinner with a total responsibility. We might remind ourselves that the development of this prospect for man was aided by grants from the National Institute for Mental Health in the amount of $283,603. One commentator has observed: "All the same there is something truly Orwellian about the notion that society should pay for research which generates theories and techniques for the manipulation and control of human beings and popularizes the assumed need for such control." [12]

We suggest that the perspective of man for Western culture is hardly reinforced when the voice of one of the modern scientific disciplines asserts: "To man *qua* man we readily say good riddance." [13] In support of our contention, we point to what we regard as indicators. We may pursue this study at greater length in these areas, and we may look to other aspects of culture as well: philosophy, literature, drama, and religion.

Summary

The perspective and/or role of man has been the determinative principle of our culture for several centuries. The goal of man's domination of the external world has succeeded, only to threaten man with extinction. The arts have ceased to possess a meaningful role. Man's growth of knowledge has resulted in the rejection of "man" out of consideration for his own survival.

There is change in our culture. We submit that one aspect of this change is the abandonment of the perspective of our culture which has existed for the last three hundred years. We venture to be more specific. We should simply assert that man has died; certainly not the two-legged vertebrate, but man as a being once credited with powers of mind, creative spirit, and the capability for love. Man with language, a sense of his own worth, a commitment to truth and values. Man with a restlessness in bondage. Man as the *imago Dei*. Or, if you like, Skinner's "autonomous man." Man has died. And our culture wavers from the loss of a center which no longer holds.

A POSSIBLE PERSPECTIVE

If man as the principle of our culture has died, the question might be raised: Where is our society turning for some ordering of life

f236   AMERICA IN THEOLOGICAL PERSPECTIVE

and mind? Religion does not seem to be supplying the answer; nor is philosophy, which has been content with secondary issues.

Yet there is basic need for a frame of reference, a background, by which and within which humans seek to live. We want to propose such a perspective which is now operative in our society, even though it is not yet elaborated into a developed cultural pattern. We borrow a term from the American philosopher Alburey Castell to describe this: planetology.[14] By this we mean that the earth—our planet—has become the locus, the perspective within which we seem disposed at present to make a statement about the meaning of existence.

1. We offer some considerations by way of support for planetology, since it responds to certain problems which have surfaced within the last five to ten years: man's interference with the biosphere; the threat of genetical calamity through increased radiation and chemical damage; increased danger of epidemics and mass starvation; the threat to human survival arising from the growth of more resistant pests and microbes in response to more powerful drugs; and political and social threats which arise out of growing urban areas that exist only by maximizing technological economies. Walter Jeffko, who as a philosopher is committed to a personalist concept of human reason, has described the issue: ". . . the quality of the environment is one of the few major issues today upon which people of different persuasion seem to agree." [15]

We do not have a cosmology here. There is no philosophical issue. It is not a matter of economics or sectarianism. Planetology is the blunt derivative from the persuasion that this is the only planet we have, and so far as we know this is the only place where the life of man can be sustained on any long-term basis. The environment of this planet which is supportive of life must be maintained, or life itself will cease. That is the either/or of planetology. Since we have what economist Barbara Ward calls *Only One Earth*,[16] there is the pressured demand that modern man must establish—or reestablish—a significant unity with *this* planet. Our existing human situation provides background for the punch line of the television commercial which says: "It's not nice to fool Mother Nature." Indeed, it can be fatal. Howard T. Odum, an environmental engineer and energy expert at the University of Florida, has written:

> Man will survive as he reprograms readily to that which the ecosystem needs of him so long as he does not forget who is serving whom. What is done well for the ecosystem is done well for man. However, the cultures that say only what is good for man is good for nature will pass and be forgotten like the rest.[17]

Odum adds that natural systems have been protecting man for millions of years, but that as man becomes more and more influential in the ecosystem, the natural systems become less and less capable of offering protection against man's wastes. Odum symbolizes a new reverence for nature by his prescription of Ten Commandments governing man and his relationship with the earth.[18]

2. In any hard evaluation of the present state of civilization, a key word is "finite." And this word "finite" can now be described in specific terms of limitations by this planet.

a. There are statistics on resources all over the place.[19] A Massachusetts Institute of Technology study was published under the title, *The Limits of Growth*. *Fortune* ran a two-part study using the word "finite" in the title. Surveys like these disclose that if current trends continue, all known reserves of silver, gold, platinum, and tin will be used up in twenty years. E. J. Mishan asserts:

> The earth and its resources are finite, all too finite, and our continued absorption of them on an even larger scale must eventually exhaust them. The only question would be *when*. And the answers (in the absence of technology) would all seem to fall within the next half-century.[20]

Using such information, some doomsday predictions foresee the total collapse of the world industrial economy within the next century.

b. Energy, however, is the key to all resources. We refer to Odum's *Environment, Power and Society*. He suggests that energy rather than money might well be used as the single common denominator of man-made economies and the natural systems. We simply cannot continue to use finite resources at exponential rates. The M.I.T. study says that for the first time it is possible to foresee the eventual limits on the amount of energy that will be available at any price. And beyond this, no energy source imaginable can be used on an unlimited scale; at some point the sheer volume of heat associated with energy usage will threaten to alter the earth's climate.

c. We can apply "finite" again, this time in relation to the need of foodstuffs. Using 1965 production as the base, a United Nations conference on population and food needs estimated that the total food output would have to be increased by 261 percent by the year 2000. All of this must come from arable lands, the fruitfulness of seeds, and the life of the oceans. "Extended indefinitely, currently expanding rates of population and consumption will finally collide disastrously against the fixed amount of the earth's resources. That's axiomatic." [21]

We suggest that our culture is turned again and again inescapably to the earth, which places finite limits upon resources, energy, and food.

3. This is a cultural review and we shall use that as justification for mentioning the fad which Time[22] declared has grown into a phenomenon of our time. In a special report, Time asserted: "It is one of the stranger facts about the contemporary U.S. that Babylon's mystic conceptions of the universe are being taken up seriously and semi-seriously by the most scientifically sophisticated generation of young adults in history." [23]

Obviously, we refer to astrology, which was born in a geocentric world. It was Ptolemy who codified astrological tradition in his Tetra biblos, the source-book for all modern astrologers. Astrology is an "in" thing of our culture. By a recent count there were more than ten thousand full-time practicing astrologists and more than 175,000 part-time astrologists in our society. Time Pattern Research Institute, Inc. has programmed a computer which can turn out a 10,000-word horoscope reading in two minutes—to accommodate the demand. Most newspapers carry a daily astrology feature.

There are modern counterparts to the chairs of astrology which

could be found in the fourteenth century at the universities of
Padua, Florence, Paris, and Bologna. Responsible institutions are
offering courses in astrology, and inviting special lecturers to their
campuses. A major west coast university has included an astrolo-
ger as a staff member of its counseling center. Presumably, if man
needs hope in our day, show business reminds us that we are at
the dawning of the Age of Aquarius. Whereas some of us have
been accustomed to ask the question, "What is man?" there is
presently another and popular question posed, namely, "What
sign are you?" Reasons for the recrudescence of astrology in our
time might include our deep longing for some order in the world,
an order which science, philosophy, and religion in an age of
unbelief do not provide.

4. We do well to note a broad dedication to nature as an
example and a source of purity and health. The urban and
suburban sprawl form a familiar pattern. In the midst of this,
however, there is another spirit. From the flowerbox in an
apartment window, to planters for trees in center city, to the
development of state and national park systems, there is the
expressed desire for a closer contact with nature. If we are to find
recreation, it must be in something living.

In mass numbers we are akin to the family of Robert Louis
Stevenson, about whom he observed: "I come of a gloomy family
always ready to be frightened about their precious health." In
pursuit of health, we can find broad acceptance of the proposition
that we have homogenized, refined, and processed away most of
the health-giving properties of our foods. There is something
patent about the recommendation for a product which is "nature's own." There is a still greater and deeper commitment to
nature as a source of mental and moral purity. Of course, this is
not new, but it is present in our culture. Nature stands in sharp
contrast to the artificiality of man's civilization. Thus Wordsworth
in "The World Is Too Much with Us" could write:

> This Sea that bares her bosom to the moon;
> The winds that will be howling at all hours,
> And are up-gathered now like sleeping flowers;
> For this, for everything, we are out of tune;

It moves us not.—Great God! I'd rather be
A Pagan suckled in a creed outworn:
So might I, standing on this pleasant lea,
Have glimpses that would make me less forlorn. . . .

Romanticism that may be, but it is also one of the primary thrusts
of modern counterculture.[24]

There is a mystique in our at-onement with nature. Here one
may find beauty, strength, health, purity, and a union with the
vital springs of our life.

Summary

We submit that a dominant cultural perspective of our times is of
the earth, earthy. This primary consideration of the earth—and
man's essential relationship to it—is what we mean by planetology. Certainly a sense of man's involvement with the external
world is not new, but our present attention to the earth has its
own character by reason of its urgency. This earth-mindedness has
been bulldozed into our consciousness, and we have hardly had
time yet to work out a position on it. Indeed, it may well be that
some of the forces which constrain us at this time may yet fail to
be legitimate or lasting.

So far as we can see this now, we may make several
observations. Man is presently without that cultural center which
has obtained for several centuries. From the perspective of
planetology, man need no longer feel himself isolated, for he can
find himself in a definable way to be a part of an ecosystem which
is given. This is a perspective which neither rejects nor swallows
whole the technological capability of man, but this perspective
acknowledges the superiority of the earth system. The pursuit of
knowledge has the goal of enabling man to achieve the best
adaptation for a continuing life within the system. The perspective of planetology is not now enlarged in the sense of a
cosmology; hence there is no offense to the antimetaphysical bias
with which we have all been nurtured. It is a perspective by
which we may see life sustained, limited, and dominated by the
planet on which human life is set.

SOME POSSIBILITIES FOR RELIGION

1. If religion chooses to ignore it, some of the implications of planetology are not too difficult to anticipate. If, for example, this perspective should prevail, religious institutions might be expected to continue for a time on the basis of inertia and sentimentalism. From an earth perspective, reverence in the cathedral of nature would seem more appropriate than religious rites in temples made with hands. Organizations of religious studies might properly look forward to becoming a subdivision of a historical association. There may be something prophetic for all institutions associated with religion in an item in the London press about a congregation of Auguste Comte's Religion of Humanity. The newspaper recorded that the congregation arrived for its annual meeting in one taxi, and at the end of the meeting left in two taxis.

Then too, the role of the priest in Greek antiquity might be suggestive. Religion could well become a kind of ceremonial icing to decorate occasions in individual and community life. We already have some indication of this ceremonial role with the appearance of a religionist as a part of the pregame show in a stadium or coliseum. Appropriate here is our recollection of a Britisher telling us that the average British man went into a sanctuary three times during his life, once vertical and twice horizontal.

2. By way of response, religion should exercise its responsibility to give its measure of this cultural thrust. Several possibilities appear. Religion knows idolatry. In biblical terms, the exaltation of the external world—in part or in whole—would be idolatrous. Religion can draw upon an abundance of historical examples to delineate the consequences of idolatry for man, his society, his morality.

Religion knows—or ought to know—that the only long-term satisfaction for man is to be found in some effort to grasp the universal game that is going on about us, of which we are a tiny part. We may and probably should make serious effort to put the external world into some kind of context. This may mean new and renewed looks at the Hebrew vision of creation; a glance at this has already commenced. We may try to explore the many evidences of man's awareness of his creatureliness. We may make another effort at such terms as being, or reality. As a starter, we recall Emil Brunner's effort to understand reality:

> It [i.e., concept of reality] is determined by the thought that God is the creator and the world His creation. God therefore is the primary reality. Whatever else we call real is secondary, dependent reality.[25]

We may gulp at the biblical cosmology and cosmogony, but for religion to ignore the earth-commitment of our culture would be to miss the mood entirely.

Again, religion may find the modern creation of myth to be useful. The struggle for the maintenance of the environment and what at times seems the lemming-like character of human society, may be put into a cosmic background. The space fiction of C. S. Lewis suggests that our world may be viewed as the present arena of a cosmic struggle—a struggle which Dr. Ransom, Lewis's planetary traveler in *Out of the Silent Planet*, says is projected to go from world to world.[26]

3. If there is at this time a turn to this planet as a principle of our culture, then perhaps a religious reaction should be, "Very well then, let us also turn to this world of ours." Here we suggest that Thoreau qualifies as a guide for us to learn what nature might have to say. He did posit the natural world as a deity in the fashion in which it presented itself to his senses. I am indebted at this point to Stephen Railton's comparative study of Thoreau's *Journal* and *Walden*.[27]

At the beginning of his career, Thoreau never doubted the sanctity of this visible deity.

> I would be as clean as you, O woods. I shall not rest till I be as innocent as you.

> We need pray for no higher heaven than the pure senses can furnish, a purely sensuous life. The divine world of nature is pure.

In such spirit Thoreau began, in 1849, spending at least three hours every day visiting the Concord countryside; he made notes which he then transcribed in his *Journal*. In following the record of the *Journal*, there is a first suggestion of impurity in nature when he found the lower jaw of a hog. Thoreau, however, was especially interested in the plant kingdom. In June 1852 he noted that flowers are at once the most beautiful and the ugliest objects. And then he came upon the water lily. He wrote:

A superb flower, our lotus, queen of the waters. . . . How sweet, innocent, wholesome its fragrance! How pure its white petals, though its root is in the mud.

In August 1853 comes a note that perhaps nature herself is unchaste. He described fungi as follows:

They impress me like humors or pimples on the face of the earth . . . a sort of excrement they are.

About this time, Railton notes that the word "transmute" begins to appear in Thoreau's vocabulary.

On June 16, 1854 Thoreau wrote of the water lily:

It is the emblem of purity, and its scent suggests it. Growing in stagnant and muddy water, it bursts up so pure and fair to the eye and so sweet to the scent, as if to show us what purity and sweetness reside in and can be extracted from, the slime and muck of earth.

This was a paradigm, writes Railton, on which Thoreau could pattern his life. The conflict of purity and impurity is apparently resolved to Thoreau's complete satisfaction.

Perhaps religion, too, may find here a parable to commend to a culture turned earthward. We may follow Thoreau from purity, down to muck and slime, and back to the water lily. We may mark Thoreau's discovery of nature's ability to transmute baser elements into purity and sweetness. In the water lily is a pattern. It is not unlike the dying and rising god. We may suggest that it is not unlike the passage from freedom into captivity and exile, with return and restoration through the provision of God. Christian faith may note the Incarnation, Crucifixion, and Resurrection.[28]

Christian faith may assert that the water lily is an earthy illustration of what the New Testament discloses to be the nature and grace of the eternal God. St. Paul wrote concerning Jesus Christ: "Him who knew no sin he made to be sin on our behalf; that we might become the righteousness of God in him" (2 Corinthians 5:21).

What shall we say then about the demise of man in our culture? We suggest that this is only a step. If you will, we are at the beginning of the Waste Land.[29] We are now at the point where we like to think of happier days, ". . . mixing memory and desire . . . ," as T. S. Eliot would have it. We are a troubled civilization, so we read much of the night and go south in the winter. We have not yet come to the Waste Land of rocks and no water, of hallucination produced by human despair. So far as I know, there is as yet no cultural cry, "My God, why hast Thou forsaken me?" It is at such occasion—the muck and slime of our earth paradigm—that there is the possibility of the transformation of man and his culture through divine grace.

Meanwhile, Christian faith knows the groaning and travailing of the whole creation which is waiting for the manifestation of the sons of God. Christian faith may help men to shore up what fragments they possess, in order that they may fight a good fight against the ruins of culture. It may counsel self-sacrifice, compassion, and self-discipline, and so speak the word of peace to those engaged in the struggle. Christian faith would do well to sustain its knowledge of God as One who can and will make all things new—including man himself.[30]

This paradigm of nature which can be learned from Thoreau may remind Christian protagonists of their obligations and opportunities in a culture turned earthward.

NOTES

1. Francis Bacon, *The Masculine Birth of Time*, as translated and cited by Benjamin Farrington, *The Philosophy of Francis Bacon* (Chicago: University of Chicago Press, 1966), p. 62.

2. Loren Eiseley, *The Unexpected Universe* (New York: Harcourt, Brace & World, 1969), p. 28.

3. Cf. Morton Feldman, "After Modernism," *Art in America* 59 (1971), pp. 68–77.

4. Marina Vaizey, "Documenta 5," *Connoisseur* (October 1972), pp. 148, 149.

5. Harold Rosenberg, "Inquiry '72: On the Edge," *New Yorker*, September 9, 1972, pp. 72–82.

6. Les Levine, "It's Realistic, but Is It Art?" *Saturday Review of the Arts*, February 1973, p. 18.

7. Lewis Mumford, "The Cult of the Anti-Life," *The Virginia Quarterly Review* 46 (1970), pp. 198–206.

8. Charles Warren, "Brunelleschi's Dome and Dufay's Motet," *The Musical Quarterly*, January 1973, pp. 92–105.

9. John Cage, *Silence* (Cambridge: M.I.T. Press, 1967), p. 2.

10. B. F. Skinner, *Beyond Freedom and Dignity* (New York: Bantam/Vintage, 1972), p. 191.

11. Cf. James E. Loder, "Secularized Calvinism," *New Catholic World* 215 (1972), pp. 11, 36–37.

12. Cf. "Grant K6-MH-21775," *Nation* (January 10, 1972), p. 37.

13. B. F. Skinner, *op. cit.*

14. In a personal conversation with this writer.

15. Walter G. Jeffko, "Ecology and Dualism," *Religion in Life* 42 (1973), pp. 117–27.

16. Cf. Barbara Ward and René Dubos, *Only One Earth* (New York: Norton, 1972).

17. Howard T. Odum, "Energy, Ecology, and Economics," *AMBIO* 2 (1973), pp. 220–27.

18. Howard T. Odum, *Environment, Power and Society* (New York: Wiley/Interscience, 1971), p. 244.

19. Cf., for example, Edmund Faltermayer, "Our Finite Riches I," *Fortune*, September 1972, pp. 101, 178–92. Also, "Our Finite Riches II," *Fortune*, October 1972, pp. 109–12, 164 ff.

20. E. J. Mishan, "To Grow or Not to Grow," *Encounter*, May 1973, pp. 9–29.

21. Peter Steinfels, "The End of the World?" *Commonweal* (May 12, 1972), p. 232.

22. Douglas Auchinloss, "Astrology: Fad and Phenomenon," *Time*, March 21, 1969, pp. 47–56.

23. *Ibid.*, p. 47.

24. Cf., for example, Robert Pirsig, *Zen and the Art of Motorcycle Maintenance* (New York: Morrow, 1974).

25. Emil Brunner, *Christianity and Civilization* (New York: Charles Scribner's Sons, 1948), p. 18.

26. C. S. Lewis, *Out of the Silent Planet* (New York: Macmillan, 1965): Ransom: "I think he would destroy all your people to make room for our people; and then he would do the same with other worlds again. He wants our race to last for always, I think, and he hopes they will leap from world to world . . . always going to a new sun when an old one dies . . . or something like that" (pp. 132 f.).

27. Stephen Railton, "Thoreau's Resurrection of Virtue!" *American Quarterly*, May 1972, pp. 210–27. The Thoreau quotations are from this article.

28. I shall opt for pursuing this theme in Christian terms.

29. The references to T. S. Eliot, *The Waste Land*, in these lines are obvious.

30. For example: Revelation 21:5; 2 Corinthians 5:17; Galatians 6:15; Romans 6:4; John 3:3.

List of Contributors

Leonard J. Biallas has worked extensively on Jungian archetypes and theology. He teaches at Quincy College in Illinois.

Francis S. Fiorenza teaches theology at the University of Notre Dame. He was recently elected to the Board of Directors of the Catholic Theological Society of America.

Joseph F. Gower teaches courses on American religious thought at St. Joseph's College in Philadelphia. His dissertation on Isaac Hecker is being completed at the University of Notre Dame.

Thomas O'Brien Hanley, S.J., is a resident Jesuit scholar and lecturer at Loyola College, Baltimore. He is editor of *The John Carroll Papers* (3 volumes).

James Hennesey, S.J., is President of the Jesuit School of Theology in Chicago. He has lectured widely on American Catholic religious history.

Russell L. Jaberg is an Associate Professor within the Humanities Division at the University of Florida.

Franklin H. Littell is a noted scholar in the theology of the Radical Reformation, and teaches at Temple University. His *From State Church to Pluralism: A Protestant Interpretation in American History* is a significant work in the area of American religious history.

Thomas M. McFadden (editor) is chairman of the College Theology Society's Publication Committee. He teaches at St. Joseph's College in Philadelphia, and was the area editor in religion and theology for the *New Catholic Encyclopedia* (1967–74 Supplement).

Elizabeth K. McKeown is an Assistant Professor in the Theology Department at Georgetown University.

Daniel C. Maguire has written extensively on ethics from within the American Catholic tradition. His most recent book is *Death by Choice*.

John J. Mawhinney, S.J., is a member of the Jesuit Center for Social Study at Georgetown University.

Marie Augusta Neal, S.N.D., is a Professor of the Sociology of Religion at the Divinity School, Harvard University.

Mary L. Schneider teaches at Michigan State University in East Lansing, as a member of the Religious Studies Department.

David M. Thomas teaches at the St. Meinrad School of Theology in St. Meinrad, Indiana. He has specialized in the relationship between technocracy and religion.

Date Due

APR 3 0 1982			

Demco 38-297